THE 360° LEADER

25 WAYS TO WIN WITH PEOPLE

JOHN C. MAXWELL

THOMAS NELSON
Since 1798

NASHVILLE DALLAS MEXICO CITY RIO DE JANEIRO

Published in Nashville, Tennessee, by Thomas Nelson. Thomas Nelson is a registered trademark of Thomas Nelson, Inc.

Published in association with Yates & Yates, www.yates2.com.

Thomas Nelson, Inc., titles may be purchased in bulk for educational, business, fund-raising, or sales promotional use. For information, please e-mail SpecialMarkets@ThomasNelson.com.

ISBN: 978-1-4002-8098-8

Library of Congress Cataloguing-in-Publication Data Available

Printed in the United States of America
10 11 12 13 14 WC 6 5 4 3 2 1

THE 360° LEADER

DEVELOPING YOUR INFLUENCE FROM ANYWHERE IN THE ORGANIZATION

This book is dedicated to Dan Reiland—

a friend

a student

a teacher

a partner

—a 360-Degree Leader

Contents

Section IV: The Principles 360-Degree Leaders Practice to Lead Across

Section V: The Principles 360-Degree Leaders Practice to Lead Down

Section VI: The Value of 360-Degee Leaders

Acknowledgments

I'd like to say thank you to

Charlie Wetzel, my writer;

Stephanie Wetzel, who reviewed the early drafts of the manuscript;

Dan Reiland, who helped us think through and land the concepts for this book;

David Branker, Doug Carter, Chris Hodges, Billy Hornsby, Brad Lomenick, Rod Loy, David McKinley, Todd Mullins, Tom Mullins, and Douglas Randlett, each of whom have spent time leading as 360-Degree Leaders in the middle of organizations, for their valuable feedback on the outline of the book; and

Linda Eggers, my assistant.

SECTION 1

The Myths of Leading from the Middle of an Organization

These are classic pictures of leadership: William Wallace leading the charge of his warriors against the army that would oppress his people and him. Winston Churchill defying the Nazi threat as much of Europe collapsed. Mahatma Gandhi leading the two-hundred-mile march to the sea to protest the Salt Act. Mary Kay Ash going off on her own to create a world-class organization. Martin Luther King Jr. standing before the Lincoln Memorial challenging the nation with his dream of reconciliation.

Ninety-nine percent of all leadership occurs not from the top but from the middle of an organization.

Each of these people was a great leader and impacted hundreds of thousands, if not millions, of people. Yet these pictures can also be misleading. The reality is that 99 percent of all leadership occurs not from the top but from the middle of an organization. Usually, an organization has only one person who is *the* leader. So what do you do if you are not that one person?

I've taught leadership for nearly thirty years. And in just about every conference I've taught, someone has come up to me and said something such as, "I like what you teach about leadership, but I can't apply it. I'm not the main leader. And the person I work under is, *at best,* average."

Is that where you live? Are you working somewhere in the middle of your organization? You may not be a follower at the lowest level of the organization, but you're not the top dog either—yet you still want to lead, to make things happen, to make a contribution.

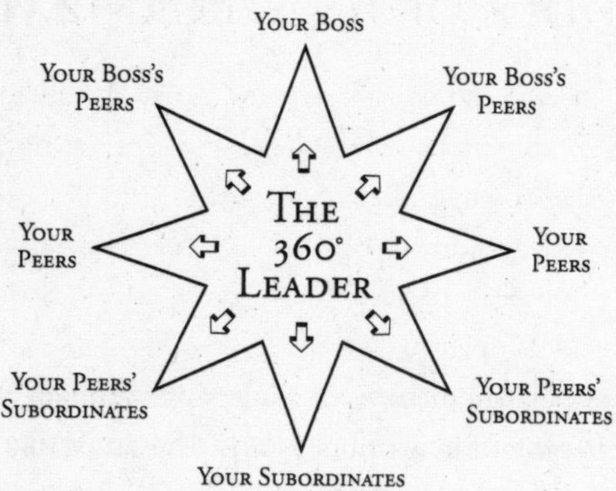

You do not have to be held hostage to your circumstances or position. You do not have to be the CEO to lead effectively. And you can learn to make an impact through your leadership even if you report to someone who is not a good leader. What's the secret? You learn to develop your influence from wherever you are in the organization by becoming a 360-Degree Leader. You learn to lead up, lead across, and lead down.

Not everyone understands what it means to influence others in every direction—those you work for, the people who are on the same level with you, and those who work for you. Some people are good at leading the members of their own team, but they seem to alienate the leaders in other departments of the organization. Other individuals excel at building a great relationship with their boss, but they have no influence with anyone below them in the organization. A few people can get along with just about anybody, but they never seem to get any work done. On the other hand, some people are productive, but they can't get along with anybody. But 360-Degree Leaders are different. Only 360-Degree Leaders influence people at every level of the organization. By helping others, they help themselves.

At this point, you may be saying, "Leading in every direction—that's easier said than done!" That's true, but it's not impossible. In fact, becoming a 360-Degree Leader is within the reach of anyone who possesses average or better leadership skills and is willing to work at it. So even if you would rate yourself as only a five or six on a scale of one to ten, you can improve your leadership and develop influence with the people all around you in an organization—and you can do it from anywhere in the organization.

Leading in all directions will require you to learn three different sets of leadership skills. You may already possess an intuitive sense of how well you lead up, across, and down. I want to help you make a more accurate assessment of those skills because it will help you to know how to direct your personal leadership growth. For that reason, I have arranged for purchasers of this book to be able to go to www.360DegreeLeader.com and take a free assessment of their 360-Degree Leadership skills. What's offered is a simple, straightforward on-line questionnaire that will ask you to rate yourself on issues related to leadership in each of the three areas. The assessment will take only about fifteen minutes, and when you're done, you will be able to download a lengthy report with your results.

If you look on the reverse side of the dust jacket of this book, you will find a personal identification code that can be used to access the assessment. If you are reading a paperback, international version of this book, you'll find your code on the sticker inside the cover. Go to http://www.360DegreeLeader.com. Once there, follow the instructions and, when prompted, type in your personal identification code to take the test free of charge.

I recommend that you complete the assessment before reading the rest of the book. That way, you'll know where your strengths and weaknesses are as you learn about each skill set. However, before we get into those, we need to address other issues, starting with seven myths believed by many people who lead from the middle of organizations. That is the subject of this first section of the book.

Myth #1

The Position Myth:

"I can't lead if I am not at the top."

If I had to identify the number one misconception people have about leadership, it would be the belief that leadership comes simply from having a position or title. But nothing could be further from the truth. You don't need to possess a position at the top of your group, department, division, or organization in order to lead. If you think you do, then you have bought into the position myth.

A place at the top will not automatically make anyone a leader. The Law of Influence in *The 21 Irrefutable Laws of Leadership* states it clearly: "The true measure of leadership is influence—nothing more, nothing less."

Because I have led volunteer organizations most of my life, I have watched many people become tied up by the position myth. When people who buy into this myth are identified as potential leaders and put on a team, they are very uncomfortable if they have not been given some kind of title or position that labels them as leaders in the eyes of other team members. Instead of working to build relationships with others on the team and to gain influence naturally, they wait for the positional leader to invest them with authority and give them a title. After a while, they become more and more unhappy, until they finally decide to try another team, another leader, or another organization.

People who follow this pattern don't understand how effective leadership develops. If you've read some of my other leadership books, you might be aware of a leadership identification tool I call "The Five Levels of Leadership," which I introduce in *Developing the Leader Within You*. It captures the dynamics of leadership development as well as anything I know. Just in case you're not familiar with it, I'll explain it briefly here.

5. PERSONHOOD

Respect
People follow because of who you are and what you represent.
NOTE: This step is reserved for leaders who have spent years growing people and organizations. Few make it. Those who do are bigger than life.

4. PEOPLE DEVELOPMENT

Reproduction
People follow because of what you have done for them.
NOTE: This is where long-range growth occurs. Your commitment to developing leaders will ensure ongoing growth to the organization and to people. Do whatever you can to achieve and stay on this level.

3. PRODUCTION

Results
People follow because of what you have done for the organization.
NOTE: This is where success is sensed by most people. They like you and what you are doing. Problems are fixed with very little effort because of momentum.

2. PERMISSION

Relationships
People follow because they want to.
NOTE: People will follow you beyond your stated authority. This level allows work to be fun. Caution: Staying too long on this level without rising will cause highly motivated people to become restless.

1. POSITION

Rights
People follow because they have to.
NOTE: Your influence will not extend beyond the lines of your job description. The longer you stay here, the higher the turnover and the lower the morale.

Leadership is dynamic, and the right to lead must be earned individually with each person you meet. Where you are on the "staircase of leadership" depends on your history with that person. And with everyone, we start at the bottom of the five steps or levels.

That bottom (or first) level is position. You can only start from the position you have been given, whatever it is: production-line worker, administrative assistant, salesperson, foreman, pastor, assistant manager, and so forth. Your position is whatever it is. From that place, you have certain rights that come with your title. But if you lead people using only your position, and you do nothing else to try to increase your influence, then people will follow you only because they have to. They will follow only within the boundaries of your job description. The lower your stated position, the less positional authority you possess. The good news is that you can increase your influence beyond your title and position. You can "move up" the staircase of leadership to higher levels.

If you move to level two, you begin to lead beyond your position because you have built relationships with the people you desire to lead. You treat them with dignity and respect. You value them as human beings. You care about them, not just the job they can do for you or the organization. Because you care about them, they begin to trust you more. As a result, they give you permission to lead them. In other words, they begin to follow you because they want to.

The third level is the production level. You move to this phase of leadership with others because of the results you achieve on the job. If the people you lead succeed in getting the job done because of your contribution to the team, then they will look to you more and more to lead the way. They follow you because of what you've done for the organization.

To reach the fourth level of leadership, you must focus on developing others. Accordingly, this is called the people-development level of leadership. Your agenda is to pour yourself into the individuals you lead—mentor them, help them develop their skills, and sharpen their leadership ability. What you are doing, in essence, is leadership reproduction. You value them, add value to them, and make them more valuable. At this level, they follow you because of what you've done for them.

The fifth and final level is the personhood level, but it is not a level one can strive to reach, because reaching it is outside of your control. Only others can put you there, and they do so because you have excelled in leading them from the first four levels for a long period of time. You have earned the reputation of a level-five leader.

Disposition More than Position

When potential leaders understand the dynamics of gaining influence with people using the Five Levels of Leadership, they come to realize that position has little to do with genuine leadership. Do individuals have to be at the top of the organizational chart to develop relationships with others and get them to like working with them? Do they need to possess the top title to achieve results and help others become productive? Do they have to be president or CEO to teach the people who report to them to see, think, and work like leaders? Of course not. Influencing others is a matter of disposition, not position.

> *Leadership is a choice you make, not a place you sit.*

You can lead others from anywhere in an organization. And when you do, you make the organization better. David Branker, a leader who has influenced others from the middle of organizations for years and who currently serves as an executive director in a large church, said, "To do nothing in the middle is to create more weight for the top leader to move. For some leaders—it might even feel like dead weight. Leaders in the middle can have a profound effect on an organization."

Every level of an organization depends on leadership from someone. The bottom line is this: Leadership is a choice you make, not a place you sit. Anyone can choose to become a leader wherever he is. You can make a difference no matter where you are.

Myth #2

The Destination Myth:

"When I get to the top, then I'll learn to lead."

In 2003, Charlie Wetzel, my writer, decided he wanted to tackle a goal he had held for more than a decade. He was determined to run a marathon. If you were to meet Charlie, you'd never guess that he is a runner. The articles in running magazines say that at five feet ten inches tall, a distance runner should weigh 165 pounds or less. Charlie weighs more like 205. But he was a regular runner who averaged twelve to twenty miles a week and ran two or three 10K races every year, so he picked the Chicago marathon and decided to go for it.

Do you think Charlie just showed up at the starting line in downtown Chicago on race day and said, "Okay, I guess it's time to figure out how to run a marathon"? Of course not. He started doing his homework a year in advance. He read reviews of marathons held around the United States and learned that the Chicago marathon—held in October—enjoys great weather most years. It utilizes a fast, flat race course. It has a reputation for having the best fan support of any marathon in the nation. It was the perfect place for a first-time marathoner.

He also started learning how to train for a marathon. He read articles. He searched Web sites. He talked to marathon runners. He even recruited a friend who had run two marathons to race with him in

Chicago on October 12. And, of course, he trained. He started the process in mid-April, increasing his mileage every week and eventually working his way up to two training runs of twenty miles each in addition to his other sessions. When race day came around, he was ready—and he completed the race.

Leadership is very similar. If you want to succeed, you need to learn as much as you can about leadership before you have a leadership position. When I meet people in social settings and they ask me what I do for a living, some of them are intrigued when I say I write books and speak. And they often ask what I write about. When I say leadership, the response that makes me chuckle most goes something like this: "Oh. Well, when I become a leader, I'll read some of your books!" What I don't say (but want to) is: "If you'd read some of my books, maybe you'd become a leader."

Good leadership is learned in the trenches. Leading as well as they can wherever they are is what prepares leaders for more and greater responsibility. Becoming a good leader is a lifelong learning process. If you don't try out your leadership skills and decision-making process when the stakes are small and the risks are low, you're likely to get into trouble at higher levels when the cost of mistakes is high, the impact is far reaching, and the exposure is greater. Mistakes made on a small scale can be easily overcome. Mistakes made when you're at the top cost the organization greatly, and they damage a leader's credibility.

How do you become the person you desire to be? You start now to adopt the thinking, learn the skills, and develop the habits of the person you wish to be. It's a mistake to daydream about "one day when you'll be on top" instead of handling today so that it prepares you for tomorrow. As Hall of Fame basketball coach John Wooden said, "When opportunity comes, it's too late to prepare." If you want to be a successful leader, learn to lead before you have a leadership position.

Myth #3

The Influence Myth:

"If I were on top, then people would follow me."

I once read that President Woodrow Wilson had a housekeeper who constantly lamented that she and her husband didn't possess more prestigious positions in life. One day the lady approached the president after she heard that the secretary of labor had resigned from the administration.

"President Wilson," she said, "my husband is perfect for his vacant position. He is a laboring man, knows what labor is, and understands laboring people. Please consider him when you appoint the new secretary of labor."

"I appreciate your recommendation," answered Wilson, "but you must remember, the secretary of labor is an important position. It requires an influential person."

"But," the housekeeper said, "if you made my husband the secretary of labor, he would be an influential person!"

People who have no leadership experience have a tendency to overestimate the importance of a leadership title. That was the case for President Wilson's housekeeper. She thought that leadership was a reward that someone of importance could grant. But influence doesn't work that way. You may be able to grant someone a position, but you cannot grant him real leadership. Influence must be earned.

A position gives you a chance. It gives you the opportunity to try out your leadership. It asks people to give you the benefit of the doubt for a while. But given some time, you will earn your level of influence—for better or worse. Good leaders will gain in influence beyond their stated position. Bad leaders will shrink their influence down so that it is actually less than what originally came with the position. Remember, a position doesn't make a leader, but a leader can make the position.

You may be able to grant someone a position, but you cannot grant him real leadership. Influence must be earned.

Myth #4

The Inexperience Myth:
"When I get to the top, I'll be in control."

Have you ever found yourself saying something like, "You know, if I were in charge, we wouldn't have done this, and we wouldn't have done that. Things sure would be different around here if I were the boss"? If so, let me tell you that there's good news and bad news. The good news is that the desire to improve an organization and the belief that you're capable of doing it are often the marks of a leader. Andy Stanley said, "If you're a leader and leaders work for you, they think they can do a better job than you. They just do (just like you do). And that's not wrong; that's just leadership."[1] The desires to innovate, to improve, to create, and to find a better way are all leadership characteristics.

Now here's the bad news. Without experience being the top person in an organization, you would likely overestimate the amount of control you have at the top. The higher you go—and the larger the organization—the more you realize that many factors control the organization. More than ever, when you are at the top, you need every bit of influence you can muster. Your position does not give you total control—or protect you.

As I write this, a story has broken in the business news that provides a good illustration of this fact. Perhaps you are familiar with the name Carly Fiorina. She is considered one of the top business executives in the nation, and in 1998, *Fortune* magazine named her the most powerful woman executive in the United States. At that time she was the president of Lucent Technologies' Global Service Provider Business, but soon afterward she became CEO of Hewlett-Packard, the eleventh largest company in the nation at the time.[2]

In 2002, Fiorina made a bold move that she hoped would pay off big for her organization. She orchestrated a merger of Hewlett-Packard and Compaq in an effort to become more competitive with chief rival Dell. Unfortunately, revenues and earnings didn't meet expectations during the two years after the merger, but even as late as December of 2004, Fiorina was upbeat about her future. When asked about the rumor that she might transition her career into politics, she responded, "I am the CEO of Hewlett-Packard. I love the company. I love the job—and I'm not finished."[3] Two months later she was finished. Hewlett-Packard's board of directors asked for her resignation.

To think that life "at the top" is easier is to think the grass is greener on the other side of the fence. Being at the top has its own set of problems and challenges. In leadership—no matter where you are in an organization—the bottom line is always influence.

Myth #5

The Freedom Myth:
"When I get to the top, I'll no longer be limited."

Sometimes I think people get the wrong idea about leadership. Many people hope that it's a ticket to freedom. It will provide a solution to their professional and career problems. But being at the top is not a cure-all.

Have you entertained the idea that being in charge will change your life? Have thoughts such as these come to mind from time to time?

When I get to the top, I'll have it made.
When I finally finish climbing the corporate ladder, I'll have time to rest.
When I own the company, I'll be able to do whatever I want.
When I'm in charge, the sky will be the limit.

Anybody who has owned a company or been the top leader in an organization knows that those ideas are little more than fantasies. Being the top leader doesn't mean you have no limits. It doesn't remove the lid from your potential. It doesn't matter what job you do or what position you obtain; you will have limits. That's just the way life is.

When you move up in an organization, the weight of your responsibility increases. In many organizations, as you move up the ladder, you may even find that the amount of responsibility you take on increases faster than the amount of authority you receive. When you go higher, more is expected of you, the pressure is greater, and the impact of your decisions weighs more heavily. You must take these things into account.

To see how this can play out, let's say, for example, that you have a position in sales, and you're really good at it. You make sales, work well with clients, and bring $5 million in revenue for your company every year. As a salesperson, you may have a lot of freedom. Maybe you can work your schedule however you want. As many salespeople do, you may work from home. It doesn't matter if you want to work at 5 a.m. or 10 p.m., as long as you serve your clients and company well. You can do things in your own style, and if you drop a ball, you can probably recover pretty easily.

In many organizations, as you move up the ladder, you may even find that the amount of responsibility you take on increases faster than the amount of authority you receive.

But let's say you become a sales manager over half a dozen people who do what you used to do. You are now more limited than you were before. You can't arrange your schedule however you want anymore because you have to work around the schedules of your six employees, who have to work with their clients. And if you're a good leader, you will encourage the members of your team to work using their own style to maximize their potential, making it that much more difficult for you. Add to that the increased financial pressures that the position brings since you would be responsible for maybe $25 million in revenue for your company.

If you move up again, let's say to the level of a division manager, then the demands on you increase yet again. And you may now have to work with a number of different departments, each with its own problems, skill sets, and cultures. Good leaders go to their people, connect, find common ground, and empower them to succeed. So in some ways, leaders have less freedom as they move up, not more.

When I teach leadership, I often use the following diagram to help potential leaders realize that as they rise up in the organization, their rights actually decrease instead of increase:

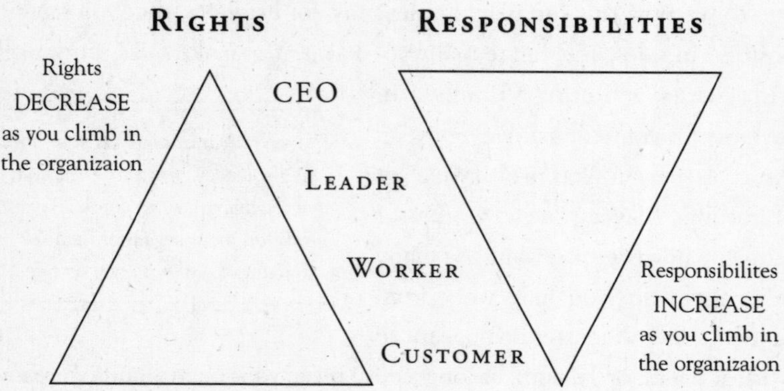

Customers have great freedom and can do almost anything they want. They have no real responsibility to the organization. Workers have more obligations. Leaders have even more, and because of that, they become more limited in terms of their freedom. It is a limitation they choose willingly, but they are limited just the same. If you want to push the limits of your effectiveness, there is a better solution. Learning to lead will blow the lid off of your potential.

Myth #6

The Potential Myth:

"I can't reach my potential if I'm not the top leader."

How many kids say, "Someday I want to grow up to be vice president of the United States"? Probably none. If a child has political aspirations, he wants to be president. If she has a bent toward business, she wants to be a company owner or CEO. Few people aspire to reach the middle. In fact, several years ago, Monster.com, an online job search service, poked fun at this idea by running a television ad showing children saying things such as, "When I grow up, I want to file all day long" and, "I want to claw my way up to middle management."

I believe that people should strive for the top of their game, not the top of the organization.

Yet the reality is that most people will never be the top leader in an organization. They will spend their careers somewhere in the middle. Is that okay? Or should everybody play career "king of the hill" and try to reach the top?

I believe that people should strive for the top of their game, not the top of the organization. Each of us should work to reach our potential, not necessarily the corner office. Sometimes you can make the greatest impact from somewhere other than first place. An excellent example of that is Vice President Dick Cheney. He has enjoyed a remarkable career in politics: White House chief of staff to President Gerald Ford, six-term congressman from Wyoming, secretary of defense to President George H. W. Bush, and vice president to the second President Bush. He possesses all the credentials one would need to run for president of the United States. Yet he knows that the top position is not his best role. An article in *Time* magazine described Cheney this way:

> When Richard Bruce Cheney was a student at Natrona County High School in Casper, Wyo., he was a solid football player, senior-class president and an above-average student. But he wasn't the star . . . Inconspicuous, off to the side, backing up a flashier partner, putting out fires when called upon—it's a role Dick Cheney has played his entire life. Throughout his remarkable career . . . Cheney's success has derived from his unparalleled skill at serving as the discreet, effective, loyal adviser to higher-profile leaders. He did once flirt with the idea of twirling the flaming baton himself, considering a 1996 run for president. But the idea of putting himself on that stage . . . would have required a rewiring of Cheney's political DNA. Instead he took an offer in business, figuring he would retire in the job and then do a lot of hunting and fishing. But George W. Bush had a different plan, one that returned Cheney to the role he plays best. As Lynne Cheney told *Time*, her husband "never thought that this would be his job. But if you look back over his whole career, it's been preparation for this."[1]

Cheney has reached his potential in the position of vice president, a position few would set as a lifetime career goal. He is highly effective, and he seems to be content. Mary Kay Hill, a longtime aide to former Wyoming senator Alan Simpson, who worked with Cheney on Capitol Hill, said, "You plug him in, and he works anywhere. He just has a real good way of fitting in and working his environment." Cheney appears to be an excellent example of a 360-Degree Leader, someone who knows how to influence others from whatever position he finds himself in.

Myth #7

The All-or-Nothing Myth:
"If I can't get to the top, then I won't try to lead."

What are the prospects for your getting to the top of your organization, of someday becoming *the* leader? The reality for most people is that they will never be the CEO. Does that mean they should just give up leading altogether?

That's what some people do. They look at an organization, recognize they will not be able to make it to the top, and give up. Their attitude is, "If I can't be the captain of the team, then I'll take my ball and go home."

Others enter the process of leadership but then become frustrated by their position in an organization. Why? Because they define *success* as being "on top." As a result, they believe that if they are not on top, they are not successful. If that frustration lasts long enough, they can become disillusioned, bitter, and cynical. If it gets to that point, instead of being a help to themselves and their organization, they become a hindrance.

But what good can people do if they sit on the sidelines?

Consider the case of six men who were featured in *Fortune* magazine in August of 2005. In the article, they are hailed as unsung heroes of the civil rights movement, yet there is no evidence that they ever marched or sat in at a lunch counter. Their contributions—and their battles—

occurred in corporate America. They led their way into the executive suite of companies such as Exxon, Phillip Morris, Marriott, and General Foods.

Clifton Wharton, who became the first black CEO of a large company (TIAA-CREF) says, "Gordon Parks has this great expression, 'choice of weapons.' In terms of fighting, you always have a choice of weapons. Some of us chose to do our fighting on the inside."[1]

When Wharton and fellow pioneers Darwin Davis, James Avery, Lee Archer, James "Bud" Ward, and George Lewis entered corporate America in the 1950s and '60s, what chance did they think they had to become CEO of their organizations: Equitable, Exxon, General Foods, Marriott, and Phillip Morris? Not much! When Avery started with Esso (now Exxon), he couldn't even use the same restroom or water fountain as other citizens. Yet it was his goal to lead. That desire was part of his first career choice: teaching. And it prompted him to change careers in 1956 when an Esso executive approached him.

"I loved being a teacher," Avery says. "But if I could wear a shirt and tie and work for a major corporation? Doing that was much more important."[2] Avery succeeded as a leader despite incredible obstacles and prejudice, and rose to the post of senior vice president. He retired in 1986.

Bud Ward, who retired as senior vice president at Marriott, has a similar story. When he was hired by Bill Marriott, Ward became the hotel industry's first black vice president. During his twenty years of leadership at Marriott, he opened 350 hotels, helped to develop the Courtyard by Marriott chain, and oversaw the company's infotech team.

Ward is aware of the impact he made. "It was a two-pronged thing," he says. "You do the marching and the raising hell and whatnot, but you've got to have somebody on the inside to interpret that to the individuals that you're trying to reach. I saw that as my role."[2]

What these men—and many others—did has made a lasting impact. In the same issue of *Fortune* was a special section called "The Diversity List." It profiled the most influential African Americans, Latinos, and Asian Americans in the country. Most people on the list are CEOs, presidents, chairmen, or founders of their organizations, positions that it would have been more difficult to attain had others not gone before them and led well.

You do not need to be the top dog to make a difference. Leadership is not meant to be an all-or-nothing proposition. If being someplace other than the top has caused you great frustration, please don't throw in the towel. Why? Because you can make an impact from wherever you are in an organization, even if you face additional obstacles, as these six men did.

Being a leader stuck in the middle brings many challenges. You can learn to navigate them. Becoming an effective 360-Degree Leader requires principles and skills to lead the people above, beside, and below you in the organization. You can learn them.

I believe that individuals can become better leaders wherever they are. Improve your leadership, and you can impact your organization. You can change people's lives. You can be someone who adds value. You can learn to influence people at every level of the organization—even if you never get to the top. By helping others, you can help yourself.

The first place to start is by learning to overcome the challenges that every 360-Degree Leader faces. So turn the page and let's get started.

Section I Review
The Myths of Leading from the Middle of an Organization

Here is a brief review of the 7 Myths every leader in the middle faces:

Myth #1	The Position Myth: "I can't lead if I am not at the top."
Myth #2	The Destination Myth: "When I get to the top, then I'll learn to lead."
Myth #3	The Influence Myth: "If I were on top, then people would follow me."
Myth #4	The Inexperience Myth: "When I get to the top, I'll be in control."
Myth #5	The Freedom Myth: "When I get to the top, I'll no longer be limited."
Myth #6	The Potential Myth: "I can't reach my potential if I'm not the top leader."
Myth #7	The All-or-Nothing Myth: "If I can't get to the top, then I won't try to lead."

How well are you doing overcoming these seven myths? If you're not sure, take the 360-Degree Leadership assessment offered free of charge to people who have purchased this book. Visit 360DegreeLeader.com for more information.

SECTION II

The Challenges 360-Degree Leaders Face

If you are a leader in the middle of an organization, you don't need me to tell you that you have a challenging job. Many of the middle leaders I meet are frustrated, tense, and sometimes tempted to quit. I hear them say things such as, "It's like banging my head against a brick wall." "No matter how hard I try, I never seem to get anywhere." "I really wonder if it's all worth it."

If you and I were to sit down and talk for a few minutes, I bet you could list at least half a dozen problems you face because you are trying to lead from the middle. Perhaps you even feel you have been struggling to succeed where you are. But did you know that the things that frustrate you also frustrate nearly every other middle leader? Everyone who attempts to lead from the middle of the organization faces common challenges. You are not alone.

As I've mentioned, the best opportunity for helping yourself—and your organization—is to become a 360-Degree Leader. However, before you dive into the principles that 360-Degree Leaders practice to lead up, across, and down, I think you ought to acquaint yourself with the seven most common challenges that leaders in the middle face. Defining and recognizing them will help you to navigate the world of the middle, where you are trying to be a good leader even though you are not *the* leader.

I believe the challenges will resonate with you, and you will find yourself saying, "Right on." And, of course, I've offered some suggestions to help you, since recognizing the challenges is of little value without solutions. Read on so that you can resolve some of these issues and get ready to lead 360 degrees.

Challenge #1

The Tension Challenge:

The Pressure of Being Caught in the Middle

The Key to Successfully Navigating
the Tension Challenge:
Learn to lead despite the restrictions others have placed on you.

One of the toughest things about being a leader in the middle of an organization is that you can't be sure of where you stand. As a leader, you have some power and authority. You can make some decisions. You have access to some resources. You can call the people in your area to action and direct them in their work. At the same time, you also lack power in other areas. And if you overstep your authority, you can get yourself into real trouble.

My friend and colleague Dan Reiland calls this "the pressure of feeling like you have all power and no power." If you are not the top leader, you are not running the show, but you may be responsible for it. Even if you think you possess the vision and skill to take the organization to a higher level, if it requires the organization to go in a different direction from its present course, you don't have the authority to make such changes on your own. And that can make you feel like you are caught in the middle.

As a leader in the middle of an organization, the authority you do possess is not your own. Unless you are the owner and CEO of the company, the power you have is on loan from someone with higher authority. And that person has the power to take that authority away from you by firing you, demoting you, or moving you to another area of the business. If that does not create tension, nothing will.

Factors That Impact the Tension

The effects of the Tension Challenge are not experienced equally by everyone trying to lead from the middle of an organization. A leader's temperament and ability certainly come into play. In addition, the way the tension impacts a leader is affected by the following five factors:

1. Empowerment—How much authority and responsibility does the person above you give you, and how clear are the lines?

In his book *It's Your Ship*, former navy Captain D. Michael Abrashoff recounted how he turned around the performance of the crew of the U.S.S. *Benfold* using empowerment.

> When I took command of *Benfold*, I realized that no one, including me, is capable of making every decision. I would have to train my people to think and make judgments on their own. Empowering means defining the parameters in which people are allowed to operate, and then setting them free.
>
> But how free was free? What were the limits?
>
> I chose my line in the sand. Whenever the consequences of a decision had the potential to kill or injure someone, waste taxpayers' money, or damage the ship, I had to be consulted. Short of those contingencies, the crew was authorized to make their own decisions. Even if the decisions were wrong, I would stand by my crew. Hopefully, they would learn from their mistakes. And the more responsibility they were given, the more they learned.[1]

Not everyone experiences the kind of freedom to succeed—and safely fail—that Abrashoff's crew did. How clearly the lines of authority and responsibility have been drawn greatly impacts how strongly we feel the Tension Challenge. The more vaguely the lines are drawn, the greater the potential for stress.

If you've led a volunteer organization, as I have, then you may have observed that high-powered leaders and entrepreneurs often experience the Tension Challenge when they step out of their business world and volunteer. As top leaders, they are used to their authority being equal to their responsibility. They are used to casting vision, setting direction, and making things happen. When they volunteer to serve in an organization, they no longer possess all the authority, and they find themselves in the gray area of the middle. Many are not sure how to navigate in that environment. (That's especially true when they are better at leading than is the person running the volunteer organization.) Many of these business leaders respond by either trying to take over or going off in their own direction. Others simply give up and return to the world they know best.

Good leaders rarely think in terms of boundaries; instead, they think in terms of opportunities.

2. INITIATIVE—HOW DO YOU BALANCE INITIATING AND NOT OVERSTEPPING YOUR BOUNDARIES?

Good leaders rarely think in terms of boundaries; instead, they think in terms of opportunities. They are initiators. After all, the number one characteristic of leaders is the ability to make things happen. Sometimes that desire to initiate leads to the expansion of their responsibilities—and their boundaries. Other times it leads to conflict with the people who lead them.

You need to realize that the stronger your natural desire to initiate, the greater the potential for tension. If you continually push the limits, it's likely you will rub others the wrong way. The good news is that if you work in an environment where leaders at all levels are empowered, people may tolerate your challenging the process of how things get done. If you challenge the vision or the authority of your leaders, however, you may go from being caught in the middle to being on the outside, looking for another job.

3. ENVIRONMENT—WHAT IS THE LEADERSHIP DNA OF THE ORGANIZATION AND LEADER?

Every organization has its own unique environment. If you have a military background, you can't walk into a corporate environment and expect it to function like the army or marines. If your experience is in large corporations, and you go to work in a mom-and-pop business, you will have problems if you don't adapt. That's just common sense.

Likewise, an organization takes on the personality of its leader. The leadership DNA of the *Benfold* changed during the course of Abrashoff's command. He wanted to create an environment of empowerment where initiative and ownership were valued. People who demonstrated those characteristics were rewarded. And as long as Abrashoff was in command, the ship's environment exhibited those characteristics.

If you are a leader in the middle of an organization, assess your environment. Is it one that increases or decreases the Tension Challenge? Can you thrive in the kind of environment you're in with the level of tension it presents? Do the positive aspects of the organization outweigh the negative effects of the environment on you? An environment may be fine for one leader but not for another. Only you can make the assessment for yourself.

4. JOB PARAMETERS—HOW WELL DO YOU KNOW YOUR JOB AND HOW TO DO IT?

Have you ever noticed the level of tension you experience when starting a new job? It's pretty high, isn't it? The less familiar the work, the greater the tension. If you don't know how to do the job, you're going to be stressed, even if you're a fast learner and have a teachable attitude. Even after you know how to do the work, if you have no idea what others' expectations are of you, you won't be on solid ground. Only when you really have a handle on your job and you are good at your work does it reduce the tension of being in the middle.

5. APPRECIATION—CAN YOU LIVE WITHOUT THE CREDIT?

Someone once said, "What's causing so much disharmony among the nations is the fact that some want to beat the big drum, few are willing to face the music, and none will play second fiddle." The reality of leading from the middle of an organization is that you are not going to get as much public recognition and appreciation as leaders at the top. That's just the way it is. The greater your desire to receive credit and recognition, the more frustrated you are likely to become working in the middle of an organization. You need to decide for yourself if you receive enough satisfaction to keep you going where you are.

HOW TO RELIEVE THE TENSION CHALLENGE

It's not enough to merely recognize that leading from somewhere in the middle of an organization can be stressful. It's not good enough to simply survive. You want to thrive, and to do that, you need to learn how to relieve the tension. Here are five suggestions:

1. BECOME COMFORTABLE WITH THE MIDDLE

We often think leadership is easier at the top. The reality is that it's actually easier to lead from the middle—if a really good leader is above you. Good leaders at the top break ground for their people. They create momentum for the entire organization. Haven't you seen average or even below-average leaders succeed because they were part of an organization that was led well overall? Haven't you seen colleagues overachieve because their leader made them better than they were on their own?

When you have excellent leaders, you don't need as much skill and energy to make things happen. You benefit from everything they do. So why not enjoy it—and learn from them too? I've long admired the following poem by Helen Laurie:

How often I've been put to the test
To make the best of second-best,
Only to wake one day and see
That second-best is best for me.

Being in the middle can be a great place—as long as you have bought into the vision and believe in the leader.

So how do you get comfortable with the middle? Comfort is really a function of expectations. The wider the gap between what you imagine to be and reality, the more disappointed you are likely to be. Talk things out with your boss. The more you know about what's expected of you, what's normal in the organization, and how much authority you have, the more comfortable you will be.

Comfort is really a function of expectations.

2. Know What to "Own" and What to Let Go

Nothing frees a person from tension like clear lines of responsibility. When I became the senior pastor at Skyline Church in California in 1981, even before my first day, I found out what I had to own personally. (Even leaders at the top can still be in the middle—the board was my boss.) I asked the members of the board to give me their short list of things I had to do that no one else could do for me. There were four things on that list:

- *Take final responsibility.* The buck stopped with me. I answered for whatever happened in the church.

- *Be the main communicator.* I needed to determine what was communicated during the services, and I needed to be in the pulpit most Sundays.
- *Be the main representative of the church.* I was to be the primary face and voice for the church, within the congregation and to the community.
- *Live a life of integrity.* Author and entrepreneur Byrd Baggett defines *integrity* as "doing what you said you would do, when you said you would do it, and how you said you would do it." Nothing is more important in the life of a leader who desires to represent God to others.

One of the best things you can do is ask what is expected of you, and then maintain a dialogue concerning expectations with the people to whom you answer. Todd Mullins, who works on staff for his father, Tom Mullins, at Christ Fellowship in West Palm Beach, Florida, often found that ongoing communication helped them to resolve this tension in their somewhat fluid environment. Tom does a lot of speaking around the country, and when he would come back to the church, he would want to step back into leadership in some areas where others had been leading. Todd learned to ask, "Is this mine or yours?" (And by the way, in cases like this, it is the responsibility of the staff to communicate with their leader.) That made it possible either for Todd to step back as Tom stepped in, or for Tom to be gracefully reminded not to make a mess in an area where he didn't really want to lead.

3. Find Quick Access to Answers When Caught in the Middle

I can think of few people who get caught in the middle more than executive assistants. They experience the Tension Challenge to a high degree every day. I know that's true for my own assistant, Linda Eggers. The people she interacts with on my behalf are very demanding. And for that matter, so am I. One of the best ways I can help Linda is to get information to her as quickly as possible. If she asks me a question, I try to give her an answer right then. When I am traveling and we haven't spoken in twenty-four hours, I call her. She always has a list of questions to ask and issues to discuss. If I don't keep her waiting, she can do her work much more effectively.

Everybody needs to find a way to get quick answers in order to succeed when caught in the middle. Sometimes that can be difficult, especially if the people you work for are not communicative. In such cases, you need to find others who can help you. That may take time. And it will require that you have good rapport with the people around you. As you develop the skill of 360-Degree Leadership, it will become that much easier for you.

4. Never Violate Your Position or the Trust of the Leader

If you want to know what will increase the Tension Challenge to the breaking point, it's violating the trust given to you with your authority or position. That can mean abusing the power of your position, intentionally undermining your leader, or using the organization's resources for personal gain. David Branker, executive director of a large organization in Jacksonville, Florida, said, "Trust is built one block at a time, but when it is violated, the entire wall comes crashing down. When you have been empowered with authority you exercise that on behalf of those you report to. It's never to serve your own interest. Over the course of your leadership journey your character and integrity will invariably be tested."

> *"Trust is built one block at a time, but when it is violated the entire wall comes crashing down."*
> —DAVID BRANKER

As someone leading from the middle of an organization, your ability to sustain the authority that has been invested in you is entirely dependent upon your faithfulness in serving the people who gave you that authority. Accordingly, you must guard against the temptation to try to advance at the expense of your leader. And it would be wise not to allow yourself to have an "if I were in charge" conversation with another staff member. If you have difficulties with your leaders, talk to them about it.

5. Find a Way to Relieve Stress

You will never completely eliminate the stress of the Tension Challenge, so you need to find a way to relieve it. Rod Loy, who leads a large organization in Little Rock, Arkansas, says that when he was a leader in the middle of an organization, he kept a file called "Things I will never do to my team when I become the top leader." As a leader in the middle, he knew that his natural temptation would be to let off steam with his coworkers. He short-circuited that tendency to vent his frustrations to others by simply writing down his observations and putting them in a file. It cleared the air for him, prevented him from violating his leader's trust, and ensured that he would remember the lesson of any mistakes made by his leader.

That kind of thing may work for you. If not, find something else: hit golf balls, jog, take up kickboxing, do aerobics, take a walk, get a massage—it doesn't matter what, as long as it is a good, healthy outlet for when the stress of the Tension Challenge gets to be too much for you.

Nobody said becoming a 360-Degree Leader would be easy. Leading from the middle of an organization is stressful, but so is being the top leader. And so is being a worker who has no say in how his job should be done. The key to succeeding is to learn to deal with the tension of whatever position you are in, overcome its obstacles, and make the most of its advantages and opportunities. If you do that, you can succeed from anywhere in the organization.

Challenge #2

The Frustration Challenge:

Following an Ineffective Leader

The Key to Successfully Navigating the Frustration Challenge:

Your job isn't to fix the leader; it's to add value. If the leader won't change, then change your attitude or your work address.

On February 6, 1865, the Congress of Confederate States of America, the government of states that had been battling to secede from the United States for nearly four years, did something that Robert E. Lee had hoped to prevent. It adopted a resolution making him general-in-chief—leader of all the nation's armies, not just the Army of Northern Virginia.

Why would the Southern leaders do such a thing? Because they could see that Lee, a great military leader, was following an ineffective leader—their president, Jefferson Davis—and they still hoped to win their independence from the United States in what they thought of as the second American Revolution.

Most people agree that Lee was the most talented military leader on either side during the American Civil War. In fact, as the Southern states seceded, President Lincoln offered Robert E. Lee command of all Union forces in the field. But Lee declined Lincoln's offer. His loyalty was to his home state of Virginia. He chose to fight for the Confederacy. Lee, a West Point graduate and experienced army officer, quickly distinguished himself on the battlefield and soon became commander of the Army of Northern Virginia.

As the war continued, leaders within the Confederate States of America became restless because of their lack of victory. Jefferson Davis, they found, did not have the leadership skills required to win the war, despite his credentials—a West Point education, respected military service, experience as a U.S. representative, senator, and secretary of defense. Many Confederate leaders wanted to make Lee commander-in-chief, a move that would have usurped Davis's authority and stripped him of power over the military. But Lee would not allow it. He was loyal to his state, his cause, and his leader. He worked within the hierarchy. So finally, in desperation, the Confederate congress did what they could—they made Lee general-in-chief, hoping it would change the South's fate.

It was obvious to many good leaders that Lee was being asked to follow someone who could not lead as well as he could. Even Lee's opponents, including General and later President Ulysses S. Grant, observed it. Grant remarked in his memoirs: "The Confederacy had gone a long way beyond the reach of President Davis, and there was nothing that could be done except what Lee could do to benefit the Southern people." Lee felt it was a point of honor not to overstep his bounds. That is one of the reasons the Confederates lost the war and the Union was preserved. Lee was faithful and respective, but there is no telling how differently things might have turned out if Lee had developed the ability to lead up!

LEADERS NO ONE WANTS TO FOLLOW

Few things can be more maddening to a good leader in the middle of an organization than working for an ineffective leader. I have not read anything indicating how Robert E. Lee felt about following Jefferson Davis. He was probably too much of a gentleman to express any negative feelings publicly. But I know it must have been frustrating.

There are many different kinds of ineffective leaders, all of whom are frustrating to follow. Here are a few particularly difficult examples:

The Insecure Leader

Insecure leaders think everything is about them, and as a result, every action, every piece of information, every decision is put through their filter of self-centeredness. When someone on their team performs exceptionally well, they fear being outshone, and they often try to keep him from rising up. When someone on their team does poorly, they react in anger because it makes them look bad.

Insecure leaders think everything is about them, and as a result, every action, every piece of information, every decision is put through their filter of self-centeredness.

More than anything else, insecure leaders desire the status quo—for everyone but themselves. They are like the company president who is reported to have sent a memo to the personnel manager with the following message: "Search the organization for alert, aggressive young leaders capable of stepping into my shoes. And when you find them—fire them!"

One friend I talked to while writing this book said that he once worked for a leader who had one basic leadership principle: keep everyone off balance. If someone working for him started feeling a little too secure, he would "shake him up."

In an organization, security flows downward. When leaders are insecure, they often project that insecurity down to the people below them. If you work for an insecure person, not only will you have to work to deflect that individual's insecurity from yourself, but you will also have to work harder to "break the chain" and create security for the people who work for you. If you don't, the people under your care will suffer.

The Visionless Leader

Leaders who lack vision create two immediate problems for the people who work for them. First, they fail to provide direction or incentive to move forward. The ancient Proverbs author wrote, "Where there is no vision, the people perish."[1] Why? Because they don't go anywhere or do anything. And that's no way to live. Second, people who lack vision almost always lack passion. They have no fire—and no fuel to keep themselves and their people going. That doesn't create the kind of positive environment that is exciting to work in.

The good news is that if you have vision when your leader does not, you can rely on your vision to create an environment of productivity and success for the people working within your area of responsibility. The bad news is that other people with a different vision—even a destructive one—may try to rush in and fill the void created by your leader. You must beware of the conflict that can create.

THE INCOMPETENT LEADER

Several years ago while traveling in Turkey, I listened as a tour guide talked about many of the sultans in Turkey's history and how they put their people under tremendous pressure. Often if someone didn't meet their expectations, the sultans would simply put the person to death.

The guide spoke about the sultan who had ordered the construction of the Blue Mosque in Istanbul. The sultan wanted the architect to make the building's minarets out of gold. The problem was that the architect knew there wasn't enough money to do that. The architect also knew that if he disagreed with the sultan, it might cost him his head. It was quite a dilemma, but the architect came up with a clever solution. The word for *six* was very similar to the word for *gold* in Arabic, *alti* versus *altin*. So the architect built six towers made of stone, and when the sultan questioned him, the architect feigned misunderstanding and explained that he thought the sultan had said *alti*, not *altin*.

> *"Advice is seldom welcome, and those who need it most like it the least."*
>
> —SAMUEL JOHNSON

Leaders who follow incompetent people often feel the pressure that the architect in the story did—though they usually don't face such potentially dire consequences. Incompetent leaders are ineffective, and they often stay that way. Poet and critic Samuel Johnson said, "Advice is seldom welcome, and those who need it most like it the least."

Incompetent leaders are trouble, not only for the people they lead, but also for their entire organization. They are "lids" on the parts of the organization they lead. The Law of the Lid states in *The 21 Irrefutable Laws of Leadership*, "Leadership ability determines a person's level of effectiveness."

The Selfish Leader

In *The Circle of Innovation*, author and business guru Tom Peters writes:

> The selfish leader will attempt to lead others for their own gain and for the detriment of others. These people believe that life is a point driven, zero-sum game, with winners and losers. They encourage others to be losers in the game of life so that they can collect all the spoils for themselves. This is the businesswoman who cheats suppliers in order to make her department look good in hopes of getting a raise. This is the father who selfishly motivates his son to excel in sports so that he might gain vicarious pleasure at his son's expense.[2]

A selfish leader advances at the expense of everyone around him or her. An executive I interviewed said that one of the leaders he worked for earlier in his career was someone who selfishly hoarded all the perks that came with his leadership position. As a result, now that the executive is a top leader himself, he makes it a point to share the perks of leadership with the people who work for him. That's good advice for anyone in a leadership position anywhere in an organization. Share whatever you have with

> *"The selfish leader will attempt to lead others for their own gain and for the detriment of others."*
>
> —Tom Peters

the people below you. Legendary basketball coach John Wooden said that to be successful "you must be interested in finding the best way, not in having your own way."

The Chameleon Leader

President Lyndon Baines Johnson used to tell the story of a young, unemployed schoolteacher who came to the Texas hill country during the Depression in search of a job. When the local school board asked him whether the world was round or flat, the would-be teacher panicked, fearing a trap, and blurted out, "I can teach it both ways!"

That's the chameleon leader's reaction when you try to pin him down. When people follow a chameleon leader, they never know how he will react. As a result, valuable time and energy that could be used getting work done is often wasted in trying to predict and anticipate the leader's next move.

The Political Leader

Similar to the chameleon leader are political leaders. They can be just as difficult to pin down, but where emotional issues often fuel the chameleon leader's problems, political leaders are motivated by the desire to get ahead. It's hard to follow people whose decisions are based on political ambitions rather than the mission or the good of the organization. They are like the mayor who was asked where he stood on a particular issue. He answered, "Well, some of my friends are for it. Some are against it. As for me, I'm for my friends."

The Controlling Leader

Have you ever worked for someone who wants to be in the middle of everything you do? Few things are more frustrating for a competent person. And few things are more irritating for a good leader. It's difficult to generate momentum when the person you work for is continually interrupting your progress by micromanaging you.

People who micromanage others are often driven by one of two things: the desire for perfection, which is unobtainable, or the belief that no one can do a job as well as they can, which really boils down to their thinking others' contributions aren't as valuable as their own. Neither makes for positive working conditions for the people answering to them.

The Solution to the Frustration Challenge: Adding Value

A normal reaction to the Frustration Challenge is to fix or replace the leader you're working for, but that is usually not an option for leaders in the middle of the pack. Besides, even if it were, it would be inappropriate. No matter what our circumstances, our greatest limitation isn't the leader above us—it's the spirit within us. Remember, your leadership is as much disposition as position. The role of leaders in the middle of an organization—in nearly every circumstance—is to add value to the organization and to the leader. The only time that is not true is when the leader above you is unethical or criminal.

No matter what our circumstances, our greatest limitation isn't the leader above us—it's the spirit within us.

What should you do when you find yourself following a leader who is ineffective? How do you add value in such circumstances? Most good leaders have had to ask themselves those questions at some time in their lives. In fact, the stronger you are as a leader, the more likely you are to face a situation where you can lead more effectively than the person to whom you report.

It may not be easy, but it is possible to survive—and even flourish—in a situation like this. Here is what I recommend:

1. Develop a Solid Relationship with Your Leader

The first reaction to working for an ineffective leader is often to withdraw from him or her and build relational barriers. Fight that urge.

If you make your leader your adversary, you will create a no-win situation. Instead, build a relational bridge. Try to get to know him, find common ground, and build a solid professional relationship. And in that process, reaffirm your commitment to the mission of the organization. Doing those things will put you on the same team.

2. Identify and Appreciate Your Leader's Strengths

Everybody has strengths—even an ineffective leader. Work to find them in the person you work for. Maybe it won't be easy. Maybe his strengths aren't qualities you value or admire. That doesn't matter. Find them, and then think about how they might be assets to the organization.

3. Commit Yourself to Adding Value to Your Leader's Strengths

The pathway to success in your career lies in maximizing your strengths. That is also true for your leader. Once you have discerned what your leader's strengths are and how those characteristics can be an asset to the organization, look for ways to help leverage those strengths.

4. Get Permission to Develop a Game Plan to Complement Your Leader's Weaknesses

Besides leveraging your strengths, one of the other secrets to job success is to staff your weaknesses. As a leader, you would be wise to empower some people who work for you to fill in your talent gaps. For example, if you are not good at details, then hire someone who is and have them work closely with you.

You can play that same gap-filling role with your leader. You must be very careful, however, in the way you approach this subject. Don't offer your opinion on her weaknesses unless she asks, and even then, be tactful. If she identifies one of her weaknesses to you, privately ask if she would be willing to let you carry the ball in that area. The idea is to do what she can't do so that she can do what she does best.

5. Expose Your Leader to Good Leadership Resources

If you are working to improve your leadership skills, then you've probably discovered many good leadership resources, such as books, CDs, or DVDs. Share those with your leader. Once again, the approach you take is very important. Rather than saying, "Boy, do you need this!" say something like, "I just got through with this book, and I thought you might enjoy it too." Or if you find some kind of a connection or hook that you think might appeal to him, say, "I was reading this wonderful book, and I thought of you; the author and you have a similar background. I think you might like it." And then give him a copy of his own. If that resource is well received, you might try following up with others.

6. Publicly Affirm Your Leader

Some people fear that if they say positive things about an ineffective leader they work for, they will be misleading others. Or they worry that others will think they have poor judgment. But other people are aware of an ineffective leader's limitations, and as long as your affirmation is truthful and focuses on your leader's strengths, it won't reflect badly on you. In fact, it will engender others' respect. Your affirmation for your leader will help him develop confidence, not only in himself but also in you.

It's hard to find a downside to adding value to your leader and organization, especially if you maintain a long view. In time, people will recognize your talent. Others will value your contribution. They will admire your ability to succeed and to help others—even those less talented than you—succeed. You just can't allow yourself to give in to the short-term frustration you feel. If you do find that the frustration is getting the better of you, it might be time to change jobs.

Challenge #3

The Multi-Hat Challenge:

One Head . . . Many Hats

The Key to Successfully Navigating the Multi-Hat Challenge:

Knowing what hat to put on and then enjoying the challenge.

I held my first leadership position in 1969, but it wasn't until 1974 that I hired my first employee, Stan Toler. I was delighted to have someone working with me, because I realized that I could not do my job alone. I hired Stan as my assistant pastor. That probably sounds simple enough, but if you were to talk to Stan, his side of the story would be a little different. I've heard him describe that job as choir director, youth pastor, senior-adult pastor, Sunday school director, Vacation Bible School director, bus-ministry pastor, custodian, and general gofer (including picking up my dry cleaning and gassing up my Ford Pinto). If ever there was a leader in the middle who had to deal with the Multi-Hat Challenge, it was Stan!

The Pressure of Wearing Many Hats

The predicament Stan faced isn't unusual for most leaders in the middle of an organization. While it's true that people at every level of an organization have strong demands placed on them, leaders in the middle who desire to practice 360-Degree Leadership experience pressures that others don't. Here's what I mean:

People at the Bottom of an Organization

When people are first starting out at the bottom of an organization, they usually perform a limited number of tasks that are assigned to them. Those tasks may be challenging. They may be physically or mentally demanding. They may require great skill. But most of the time, they require only one "hat." For example, thanks to Henry Ford, people on the production line were given one task to do, and they performed it over and over, though some companies now try to give workers some relief from endless repetition.

Cooks working on the line in a restaurant, such as the grill station, have a very narrow set of responsibilities: they get their stations ready before service, they grill food to order during service, and they clean their stations when they're done. Theirs are not jobs everyone can do—they require speed, skill, and stamina. But working a station on the line requires one set of skills. Likewise, representatives in a call center do one main thing—they talk to customers and either sell products, make appointments, or solve problems. Once again, it's not something everyone can excel at, but it is a responsibility that is very focused.

People who know their jobs and perform them well can become world-class practitioners of their craft. They can be content in their work and achieve success. But if they can do only one thing—or are willing to do only one thing—they will probably not "move up" as leaders. Leadership requires the ability to do many things well. To use a sports analogy, it's less like trying to win a single race and more like trying to compete in the decathlon.

People at the Top of an Organization

Leaders at the top of an organization have their own sets of challenges. For example, they feel the weight of success or failure for the entire organization—no doubt about it. But they also have a luxury that leaders in the middle don't—they can choose what to do. They can determine their priorities, focus on their strengths, and direct their time and energy to only those things that give the organization the greatest return. Anything else they can either delegate or dismiss.

It's ironic that to become leaders, people must be able to do many things well, but in order to become leaders at the top, they must do fewer things with great excellence. In fact, successful leaders figure this out as they move from the middle to the top of an organization. I've never met a successful CEO yet who isn't focused and who doesn't limit himself to the one, two, or three things he does best.

People in the Middle of the Organization

Leaders in the middle, on the other hand, usually experience the Multi-Hat Challenge on a daily basis. They must perform tasks and have knowledge beyond their personal experience. And they often are forced to deal with multiple shifting priorities, often with limited time and resources. My friend Douglas Randlett calls this the "handyman syndrome."

Leaders in the middle usually experience the Multi-Hat Challenge on a daily basis.

The following diagram illustrates the dynamic that most leaders in the middle of an organization have to deal with:

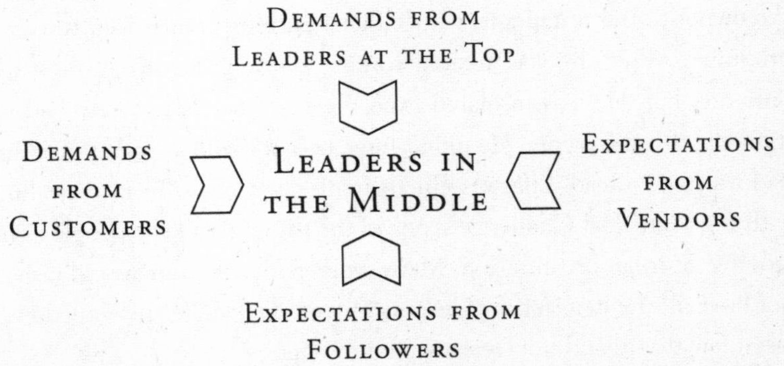

Take, for example, a grill cook who decides to move up and become a sous-chef (the person who usually runs the kitchen in a restaurant). When he was a cook, he had to please only one person, the sous-chef, and he took orders only from him or her. But when he becomes the sous-chef, his world changes because he is now the person who runs the kitchen day-to-day. As the sous-chef, there are specific things he must do during service. As each order comes into the kitchen, he must tell the cooks at every station what to cook. It's his job to coordinate all of the various cooks' efforts so that the food they are cooking on the different stations is ready at the same time for a table's order. He is also responsible for interacting with the waiters, helping them satisfy the customers, and solving their problems. When the waiters are under pressure and feeling the demands of the customers, the sous-chef feels it.

But those aren't the only pressures the sous-chef experiences. Every cook in the kitchen is looking to him for leadership. During service, he determines how the kitchen is run and sets the standard for how the food is prepared. He also schedules their work, makes sure they get paid, and mediates the disputes that always occur.

When he's not actually on the line during service, the sous-chef also has the responsibility of ordering food and supplies from vendors. His priorities are quality and price, but each vendor has expectations of him. They want his business and his time.

Of course, the sous-chef is also accountable to the chef de cuisine or the owner of the restaurant, who wants a business that is well run and profitable. When he was a cook working at the grill station, he wore only one hat. He was insulated from the customers. He rarely had to interact with the owner. He didn't have to work with vendors. And he had no staff to lead. Life was much simpler as a cook. In fact, dealing with the Multi-Hat Challenge is one of the things that keep people from moving up in an organization. Many workers decide they would rather not have all the headaches of leadership and stay where they are, doing just a few things and not wearing a lot of hats.

HOW TO HANDLE THE MULTI-HAT CHALLENGE

Billy Hornsby, cofounder of ARC and director for EQUIP's European leadership development initiative, said that being in the middle of an organization is like being the middle child in a family. These leaders have to learn to get along with everybody around them and survive the various "family" dynamics—following, leading, cajoling, appeasing, and partnering as needed. It's not an easy task.

> *"Being in the middle of an organization is like being the middle child in a family."*
> —BILLY HORNSBY

So what are leaders in the middle of an organization to do when they are required to wear many hats but have only one head? Here are my suggestions:

1. REMEMBER THAT THE HAT SETS THE CONTEXT WHEN INTERACTING WITH OTHERS

Every role or "hat" you are asked to wear has its own responsibilities and objectives. If you change hats, keep in mind that the context changes. You wouldn't interact in the same way with your spouse, your children, your boss, and your employees, would you? The goal often determines the role and the approach to take.

2. DON'T USE ONE HAT TO ACCOMPLISH A TASK REQUIRED FOR ANOTHER HAT

In her capacity as my assistant, Linda Eggers constantly attends meetings of my organization's top leaders when I am traveling. She does that so that she can keep me up to date on strategy and important changes that are occurring. When she is working in that capacity, Linda never abuses her "communication link" hat to get her own way, nor does she put on her "speaking for John" hat to preemptively stop leaders from taking action by saying something like, "John wouldn't want that." She is very cognizant that her words carry great weight.

Likewise, after Linda attends those types of meetings and she fills me in on what happened, she is also careful to represent the people in the meeting fairly and accurately. She will give her opinions, but she works not to "color" what has been said or done.

Linda, like many assistants, wears many hats. She has become an expert at knowing what hat to wear in any given situation, and she can change hats in an instant. She has a very powerful position, but she never uses one hat to accomplish tasks that may be required of her in another capacity. She takes the time to cultivate each working relationship on its own terms, and acts accordingly. It's often a balancing act, but it's one she does exceptionally well.

3. When You Change Hats, Don't Change Your Personality

I mentioned that you shouldn't treat your spouse the same way you treat your employees. That's just common sense. That doesn't mean, however, that you should change your personality according to who you're with. Your attitude and behavior should be consistent and predictable with everyone. Otherwise, you won't be trustworthy in the eyes of anyone you work with.

4. Don't Neglect Any Hat You Are Responsible to Wear

Before Rod Loy became a top leader, he served as an executive in a large organization. For six months during a leadership shortage, he also functioned as the interim leader of two different additional departments. To make sure he didn't drop any balls, he literally set up three offices. He would spend five hours a day in the executive office and work on only those responsibilities there. He would then go to one of the other department's office for two hours to do those duties, and finally to the third office for two hours to perform those duties.

Why did he do that? He discovered that if he neglected the duties of any hat for a day, he fell behind. The physical separation of the three offices helped him make the mental jump needed to keep all his responsibilities moving forward. You may not need or want to go to such lengths. However, if you are being asked to wear many hats by people in your organization, then you must be sure not to neglect any one of them.

5. Remain Flexible

The key to taking on the Multi-Hat Challenge is knowing what hat to put on at any time and enjoying the challenge it offers. How does one do that? The secret is to remain flexible. Because there are so many demands on leaders in the middle of an organization, they can't afford to be rigid; they need to be able to turn on a dime or change hats at a moment's notice.

Some people love a new challenge and thrive on the rapidly changing demands and nature of leadership in the middle of an organization. It energizes them. Others find it less appealing. But it's something all 360-Degree Leaders must learn to navigate if they want to be successful and influence others from wherever they are in the organization.

Challenge #4

The Ego Challenge:

You're Often Hidden in the Middle

The Key to Successfully Navigating the Ego Challenge:

Remember that consistently good leadership does get noticed.

Every now and then when I'm teaching a daylong leadership conference, an attendee will come up during the break, look at me, and say, "Wow, what a great job. I want to do what you do!"

My job is wonderful, and I'll admit that. But then I'll say to the person, "Yes, but do you want to do what I did to be able to do what I do?" People who meet me today see only the good stuff, the fruit of thirty years of work. They look at the well-lit platform, the large audiences, and the kind, warm reception I often get, and they see that other people do a lot of work to get things ready, while all I have to do is teach.

But it's naive for anyone to think it's always been this way. When I first started teaching leadership, I drove to engagements in my Pinto. I taught to groups of about a dozen people, and I didn't get paid to do it. I taught people just because I wanted to help them. As my reputation grew, so did people's requests for me to speak. Usually that meant finding a way to fit travel into an already packed schedule with long flights, unhealthy food, and long hours. In my early leadership conferences, for the price of admission, I taught about thirty hours of material over five days.

When I became "popular," my wife, Margaret, often had to travel with me, meaning that now two of us had to work to get the job done instead of one. (And we had to pay babysitters to take care of the kids.) We spent hours packing boxes of supplies, notebooks, and books, which we had to load into our trunk or lug onto planes. The few hours I spent on a stool teaching probably looked pretty glamorous to some people. The days spent preparing the lesson and dozens of hours of logistics and travel were not.

Successful leaders are like icebergs. When you look at an iceberg, you see only about 10 percent of it, and the rest of it is hidden under the water. When you look at successful leaders, you see only a fraction of their lives. You see the part that looks really good, but there's usually a lot that remains hidden that's neither exciting nor glamorous. Tennis star Arthur Ashe said, "True heroism is remarkably sober, very undramatic. It is not the urge to surpass all others at whatever cost, but the urge to serve others at whatever the cost." True leadership is the same.

> *"True heroism is remarkably sober, very undramatic. It is not the urge to surpass all others at whatever cost, but the urge to serve others at whatever the cost."*
>
> —ARTHUR ASHE

HOW TO HANDLE THE EGO CHALLENGE

It's normal for any person to want recognition, and leaders are the same. The fact that leaders in the middle of the pack are often hidden—and as a result they don't get the credit or recognition they desire and often deserve—can be a real ego buster. The challenge is to be a team player and remain content while contributing. Here's how to do that:

1. CONCENTRATE MORE ON YOUR DUTIES THAN YOUR DREAMS

Noted composer and conductor Leonard Bernstein was once asked which instrument he considered to be the most difficult to play. After a moment he responded, "Second fiddle. I can get plenty of first violinists, but to find one who can play second fiddle with enthusiasm—that's a problem." We can often become so focused on our dreams and goals that we lose sight of the responsibilities right in front of us.

> *We can often become so focused on our dreams and goals that we lose sight of the responsibilities right in front of us.*

Effective leaders pay more attention to production than to promotion. They get the job done. Poet Walt Whitman wrote:

> There is a man in the world who never gets turned down,
> wherever he chances to stray;
> He gets the glad hand in the populous town,
> or out where the farmers make hay;
> He is greeted with pleasure on deserts of sand,
> and deep in the aisles of the woods;
> Wherever he goes there is a welcoming hand—
> he's the man who delivers the goods.

If you consistently deliver the goods, you will be noticed. And more importantly, you will be content with the job you do even at those times when others don't recognize your efforts.

2. Appreciate the Value of Your Position

Not everyone will understand or appreciate the work you do. So it's important that you do. A cute anecdote from Nobel Prize–winner Charles H. Townes illustrates this well. Townes commented, "It's like the beaver told the rabbit as they stared up at the immense wall of Hoover Dam, 'No, I didn't actually build it myself. But it was based on an idea of mine.'"

Every position has value, but too often we don't value that position. You make it important by valuing it. If we despise the position we have, it may be because of what I call "destination disease," which can also be called the greener grass syndrome. If we focus on being some other place because we think it's better, then we will neither enjoy where we are nor do what we must to succeed.

3. Find Satisfaction in Knowing the Real Reason for the Success of a Project

In his book, *Good to Great* (Harper Business, 2001), Jim Collins writes about "level five" leaders. He says that these leaders, who led their organizations quietly and humbly, were much more effective than flashy, charismatic, high-profile leaders. One of the reasons I believe that's true is that good leaders understand they don't really deserve all the credit for the success of an organization. Success comes from the people who get the work done—especially the leaders in the middle of the organization.

If we focus on being some other place because we think it's better, then we will neither enjoy where we are nor do what we must to succeed.

When you do a job well, and you know the impact of the work you did, that should give you great satisfaction, and it should also motivate you. When you know you're making a significant contribution, you need less external motivation. The definition of high morale is: "I make a difference."

4. Embrace the Compliments of Others in the Middle of the Pack

There is no higher compliment than acknowledgment and appreciation from someone whose circumstances, position, or experience is similar to yours. Isn't that true? A musician may enjoy a compliment from a fan, but praise from another musician means more. When an entrepreneur says someone is good at spotting an opportunity, you believe her. Likewise, when someone else who is leading from the middle of the organization tells you, "Well done," take it to heart.

Novelist Mark Twain said, "One compliment can keep me going for a whole month." Based on his comment, I've come up with a scale that measures the power of a compliment and what I suspect is its lasting impact based on who says it.

Source of the Compliment	Duration
Those who've done your work	a year
Those who've seen your work	a month
Those who know of your work	a week
Those who think they know your work	a day
Those who don't know your work	an hour
Those who don't work	a minute

Everyone enjoys kind words from the boss, and many seek them out. But the praise of a colleague who's walked in your shoes really does mean more.

5. Understand the Difference Between Self-Promotion and Selfless Promotion

Sir Isaac Newton discovered the laws of gravity in the 1600s. When he introduced those laws to the scientific world, it revolutionized astronomical studies. But if it weren't for Edmund Halley, few people are likely to have learned about Newton's ideas.

Halley was a sounding board for Newton's ideas, he challenged Newton's assumptions, he corrected Newton's mathematical calculations when they were off, and he even drafted geometric diagrams to support Newton's work. When Newton was hesitant to publish his ideas, Halley first convinced him to write the manuscript, then edited it and supervised its publication. Halley even financed the printing of it, even though he had fewer financial resources than Newton. The final work, *Mathematical Principles of Natural Philosophy*, made Newton one of the most highly regarded thinkers in history.

Halley understood the difference between self-promotion and selfless promotion. It was more important to him to see Newton's ideas shared than to receive personal recognition for helping him. He knew how important those ideas were, and he wanted to get them out into the world.

That's what people do who understand selfless promotion. Take a look at the difference between the two kinds of promotion:

Self-Promotion	vs.	Selfless Promotion
Me first		Others first
Move up		Build up
Guard information		Share information
Take credit		Give credit
Hog the ball (star)		Pass the ball
Dodge the ball (blame)		Share the ball
Manipulate others		Motivate others

Self-promotion says, "If you don't toot your own horn, no one will toot it for you." Selfless promotion says, "I just want to help the team make beautiful music!"

Tim Sanders, author of *Love Is the Killer App* (Crown Business, 2002), talks about the abundance mind-set, an idea promoted by Stephen Covey a decade earlier. He says there are plenty of resources, credit, and opportunities to go around. In fact, he believes that a scarcity mind-set is at the root of most conflict. Leaders that excel in the middle of the pack have an abundance mind-set. And if you lead well from the middle of an organization, you won't stay there forever. Good leadership always gets noticed. Legendary Green Bay Packer football coach Vince Lombardi said, "Some of us will do our jobs well, and some will not. But we will all be judged by only one thing—the result." Good leaders get results—and they get noticed.

Challenge #5

The Fulfillment Challenge:

Leaders Like the Front More Than the Middle

The Key to Successfully Navigating the Fulfillment Challenge:

Leadership is more disposition than position—influence others from wherever you are.

Since you are reading this book, I assume that you either possess a natural leadership bent or have developed a desire to lead others. If that is true, then you probably want to be leading from "out front" or "on the top." Perhaps you've heard the old saying about the view from the middle of the pack. It's said that when you're the lead dog, your view always changes. If you're not the lead dog, your view always stays the same—and that view is not exactly what one would call "scenic." I enjoy that joke, and I've told it in conferences. But the truth of the matter is that the dog in front of the pack isn't the leader. The person driving the sled is—and that individual is actually in the back.

Wherever people find themselves in life, they usually possess the natural desire to move up. They want greater recognition. They want to make more money. They want to live in a better home. They want to advance and improve. Leaders are no different. They want to move up rather than stay put. They want to make a greater impact. They want to be at the front of a pack or the top of an organization, especially early in their lives and careers. But is being out front really all that it's cracked up to be? I think the answer is yes and no.

WHY LEADERS LIKE THE FRONT

There are advantages to being in front or on top of an organization. But the same things that can benefit leaders can also make leadership difficult. It is almost always a double-edged sword, and anyone who sees only the positives without recognizing the negatives is either naive or inexperienced. I think you will agree with my perspective as you read these observations about why leaders like to be out front.

1. THE FRONT IS THE MOST RECOGNIZED POSITION FOR A LEADER

Romanian essayist E. M. Cioran stated, "If each of us were to confess his most secret desire, the one that inspires all his plans, all his actions, he would say, 'I want to be praised.'" Isn't that true? Everyone enjoys praise and recognition. And since leaders, who are usually most visible, often receive the credit when a job is well done, many people desire to become leaders.

> *"If each of us were to confess his most secret desire, the one that inspires all his plans, all his actions, he would say, 'I want to be praised.'"*
> —E. M. CIORAN

Recognition is a double-edged sword. When things go wrong, the person recognized as responsible is also the leader. When the football team has a losing season, the quarterback gets the blame. When the baseball team keeps losing games, the manager gets fired. When the big account doesn't sign on with the company, the person who led the effort is held responsible. Yes, being in front can be good for your ego, but it can also cost you your job.

2. THE VIEW IS BETTER FROM THE FRONT

I once saw an interview that a newscaster conducted with an accomplished mountain climber. The journalist asked, "Why do you climb mountains? What is it that causes you to go through all the preparation, the training, the risk, and the pain?"

The mountain climber looked at the newsman and said, "It's obvious that you've never been to the top of a mountain." Isn't it true that the view from the top of a mountain is incredible? It's thrilling. The perspective is incredible. It must be even more exciting if it's a peak that can only be reached by climbing.

Tom Mullins, the former football coach I mentioned earlier who now leads a large organization in Palm Beach, Florida, said, "It's often hard to read the scoreboard from the middle of the pack. It's much easier to see it when you're at the top of the organization." There is a perspective one has from the front (or top) of an organization that cannot be had from anywhere else. But I believe responsibility comes with that perspective. If you see problems that threaten to derail the organization, harm employees, or cheat customers, you have a responsibility to try to resolve them—no matter how messy, costly, or difficult it is. Leaders at the front don't have the freedom to neglect what their position allows them to see.

Leaders at the front don't have the freedom to neglect what their position allows them to see.

3. Leaders in Front Get to Determine the Direction

When I first began leading, I thought that the leader in front could control many things in an organization. The longer I lead, the more I discover how little the leader controls. (The only people who have total control in their lives are those who don't lead anything. They are accountable only to themselves, not others.) Good leaders of organizations get to control mainly two things: direction and timing. Unfortunately, if they aren't leading well and people aren't following them, they can't even control those two things.

4. Leaders Can Set the Pace

Leaders love progress. It's one of their primary motivations. That's why explorer David Livingstone said, "I will go anywhere provided it is forward." As a leader, you probably love moving forward, and the faster the better. But that also can work against you. If you are running so far ahead that your people can't follow, then your organization won't succeed. Achievers often cross the finish line first, but leaders rarely do. A leader's success comes from bringing others across the finish line with them.

In *Winning with People*, the Patience Principle states that the journey with others is slower than the journey alone. That's true in every area of life where you are trying to lead. A trip to the grocery store is much faster alone than it is if you have to take your children. A business trip with a group of colleagues is never as fast as one by yourself. (Doesn't it take thirty minutes just to get everyone to agree on a place to eat?) A single golfer can play a course in nearly half the time it takes a foursome.

As a leader, you may be able to model the behavior you desire in others, but you will not be able to go as quickly as you want. Too many people seem to share the attitude of humorous poet Ogden Nash, who wrote, "Progress might have been all right once, but it's been going on entirely too long." The only people who will fight for progress the way you do, and move as quickly, will probably be other leaders.

5. Leaders Enjoy Being in on the Action

Because leaders like to make things happen, they always enjoy being where the action is. But many times that is not at the top or in front of an organization. Major decisions are made in those places, but often the action really occurs in the middle of an organization. That's where most of the exciting activity is. Doug Carter, who is vice president of EQUIP—the nonprofit organization I founded to teach leadership overseas—is a great example of a leader who loves the action. Doug could be the number one leader at dozens of first-rate organizations. In fact, he used to lead another outstanding nonprofit organization. But the vision and mission of EQUIP captivated him, and instead of being the top guy, he has chosen to be the number two person at EQUIP. Doug is making an impact internationally from that position. I cannot imagine the team without him.

How to Be Fulfilled in the Middle of the Pack: See the Big Picture

Education pioneer Henrietta Mears said, "The person who keeps busy helping the one who is below him won't have time to envy the person above him." The right attitude is absolutely essential to contentment in the middle of an organization. Truly, leadership is more disposition than position. With the right attitude and the right skills, you can influence others from wherever you are in an organization.

So how do you develop an attitude of contentment and fulfillment right where you are? Start by doing the following five things:

1. Develop Strong Relationships with Key People

A *Peanuts* cartoon by Charles Schulz shows Lucy telling Snoopy, "There are times when you really bug me, but I must admit there are also times when I feel like giving you a big hug." In reply, Snoopy thinks, *That's the way I am . . . huggable and buggable*. I think that's true of just about everybody—including myself. There are good and bad things about everybody. The key to fulfillment isn't making every interaction with others go smoothly; it comes from developing strong relationships with them.

> *"The person who keeps busy helping the one who is below him won't have time to envy the person above him."*
> —Henrietta Mears

It's more important to get along with people than to get ahead of them. If you make it your goal to reach out to others and build relationships with them, you will derive fulfillment wherever you are. And whatever you do, don't give up too easily on others if you at first don't like them or easily connect with them. You may be surprised by how, over time, a potential adversary can become an ally.

2. Define a Win in Terms of Teamwork

Legendary basketball coach John Wooden said, "The main ingredient of stardom is the rest of the team." In other words, teamwork is what creates success, and we shouldn't lose sight of that. One player may be crucial to a team, but one player cannot make a team. That is also true of leaders. One leader, no matter how good, does not make a team.

When I think of someone who created a win using teamwork and led others from the middle, I think of Bob Christian, former fullback for the Atlanta Falcons. Christian was called "the most complete fullback in football."[1] Dan Reeves, an NFL veteran coach with several Super Bowl rings said of Christian that he was the "best blocker I've ever seen."[2] More than once he was named player of the game strictly because of his blocking. Many people have never heard of Christian, even if they are football fans. His stats for runs, catches, and touchdowns may not have set any records, but he was fulfilled—and successful—as a ball player. Anyone who values teamwork and saw Christian play remembers him.

3. Engage in Continual Communication

One of the frustrations of leaders who aren't in front or on top is that they are several steps removed from the source of the organization's vision. And since the vision is constantly being shaped and formed, it's important to engage in continual communication. If you're "in" on the vision and continually keeping up-to-date, then you won't be blindsided by changes or demoralized by being out of the loop.

As a leader in the middle of an organization, being the recipient of communication is important, but equally or more important is communicating up. And that takes great effort because it doesn't occur naturally.

It takes effort and intentionality. As you interact with your leaders, let them know how you are advancing the vision. Get their feedback and ask questions to find out if there are other things you should know to more effectively pass on the vision to others. The more you effectively fulfill your role as a leader in the middle, the more fulfilled you will be.

4. Gain Experience and Maturity

In *The Autobiography of Harry Golden*, the author wrote, "The arrogance of the young is a direct result of not having known enough consequences. The turkey that every day greedily approaches the farmer who tosses him grain is not wrong. It is just that no one ever told him about Thanksgiving."

Maturity doesn't come automatically. My friend Ed Cole often said, "Maturity doesn't come with age. It begins with the acceptance of responsibility." When you begin looking at your life and work with more experience and a longer view, being in front doesn't seem as important. Focusing on the responsibilities with which you are entrusted wherever you are and completing them with excellence brings greater fulfillment than the position, title, or prestige one gets from being on top.

> *The more you effectively fulfill your role as a leader in the middle, the more fulfilled you will be.*

With maturity often comes patience. (Patience, however, often gets the credit that belongs to fatigue!) Patience gives you time to learn, network, and gain wisdom. Humorist Arnold Glasow said, "The key to everything is patience. You get the chicken by hatching the egg—not smashing it."

5. Put the Team Above Your Personal Success

When the stakes are high, good team members put the success of the team ahead of their own personal gains. An excellent example of this can be seen in the actions of two high-profile leaders of the British government during World War II—Winston Churchill and Clement Attlee.

Two leaders could not have been more different. Churchill was a member of the conservative party, Attlee of the labor party. Churchill was fierce, fiery, and proud; Atlee, quiet and unassuming. Churchill is quoted as saying of Attlee: "He is a modest man with much to be modest about." Yet the two men served together admirably during the war for the sake of England. When Churchill was made prime minister of England in 1940, he chose Attlee as a member of his war cabinet, eventually naming him deputy prime minister. In fact, Attlee was the only other person besides Churchill to serve in the war cabinet for the entire war.[3]

One of the keys to England's winning the war was that both leaders put the country's best interest above their own political ambitions. The depth of the two men's differences concerning leadership and government became more obvious after the war in 1945, when the two opposed each other in the election for prime minister, and Churchill was defeated by Attlee.

These two leaders did what they thought was right, both during the war and after it. They put the nation ahead of their personal gain. As a result, the people of Great Britain won. That's what leadership is really all about—it's about helping others to win. That's much more important than where you are in the organizational chart.

Challenge #6

The Vision Challenge:

Championing the Vision Is More Difficult When You Didn't Create It

The Key to Successfully Navigating the Vision Challenge:

The more you invest in the vision, the more it becomes your own.

What would you rather do? See your own vision put into action and come to fruition? Or help others fulfill theirs? For people who want to lead, the answer is usually the former. Leaders see possibilities, and they want to seize them. Most of the time they would rather work to fulfill their own vision than someone else's—unless that other leader's vision is really compelling and captivating. Leading from the middle, however, means that you will be asked to become a champion for a vision other than your own. In fact, the reality is that all the people in an organization other than the top leader are going to be asked to fulfill a vision they didn't generate.

How People Respond to the Vision Challenge

So the natural question is: How are you going to respond to the Vision Challenge? Even though your own vision may excite you more than someone else's, to get the opportunity to pursue your own dreams, you will almost certainly have to succeed in achieving the dreams of others.

There are a number of ways people respond when leaders cast vision and attempt to enlist them. The following responses represent a progression, from most negative to most positive.

1. Attack It—Criticize and Sabotage the Vision

Not everyone is going to buy into the vision of an organization, even if it is compelling, and even if the leader does a fantastic job of communicating it. That's just a fact, and it isn't always because the people are bad followers. Take a look at the most common reasons people fail to adopt a worthy vision:

THEY DIDN'T HELP CREATE IT. Let's face it. Most people don't like change, and whenever someone begins casting a new vision, change is inevitable. I used to think that leaders liked change and followers didn't. But as I've gained maturity, I've come to realize that leaders don't like change any more than followers do—unless, of course, it's their idea!

Leaders don't like change any more than followers do—unless, of course, it's their idea!

People's attitudes toward change are different when they help create it. Participation increases ownership. When you're an owner, you see things differently. You step up. You take better care of whatever it is. If you doubt that, answer this question: When was the last time you waxed a rental car? It just doesn't happen. People are up on things that they're in on.

THEY DON'T UNDERSTAND IT. People don't buy into a vision that they don't understand. It just doesn't happen. And just because leaders have cast a vision in a clear and compelling manner, doesn't mean that their people really understand it. Different kinds and styles of communication don't connect equally for everybody.

Ken Blanchard once asked Max DePree, author of *Leadership Is an Art*, what he thought the leader's role was in an organization. DePree said, "You have to act like a third-grade teacher. You have to repeat the vision over and over and over again until the people get it." And if a leader is really wise, she communicates it in many ways, in many settings, using many methods.

They don't agree with it. Some people react negatively to a vision because they think it's impossible to achieve. Others—though it happens much less often—because they think it's too small. Still others balk because the vision has changed since the time they originally signed on. But more often than not, the real issue has more to do with the leader. If people disagree with the vision, it's often because they have a problem with the person who cast it.

If people disagree with the vision, it's often because they have a problem with the person who cast it.

The Law of Buy-In found in *The 21 Irrefutable Laws of Leadership* says that people buy into the leader, then the vision. If they believe in leaders, then they embrace what those leaders believe in. Even when their leaders promote a vision that isn't compelling, the people who have already bought into them continue to support them. However, this variation on the Law of Buy-In is also true: No matter how good the vision is, if people don't believe in the leader, they will have problems buying in to the vision.

They don't know the vision. When it comes to results, there is absolutely no difference between people not knowing an organization's vision and the organization not having a vision at all. The inevitable result is dissatisfaction and discouragement.

If you have brought new people into an organization since the last time vision was cast, then you have people who don't know your vision. I apologize if this sounds painfully obvious, but this is an issue all the time in organizations. Growing businesses often hire new employees but have nothing in place to make sure that they know and embrace the vision. Every organization needs a built-in process for passing on the vision.

But even if you make sure that every person who becomes a part of your organization hears the vision, that doesn't mean they all know it. Vision leaks. It needs to be communicated clearly, creatively, and continually.

Imagine that every person in your organization has a tank where they keep the vision. Now assume that there is a crack or small hole in that tank. Because everybody is human (and therefore flawed), you can't eliminate these leaks. The best you can do is keep refilling the tanks. Some leaders don't like to keep repeating themselves, but there really is no alternative if you want everyone to know the vision.

Vision leaks. It needs to be communicated clearly, creatively, and continually.

THEY FEEL UNNEEDED TO ACHIEVE IT. There are three different kinds of attitudes when it comes to enlisting people to help fulfill a vision. The first one says, "We're going to do this with or without you." The second says, "We sure would like you to help us do this." The third says, "We can't do this without you." You can guess which one inspires and motivates people to participate and give their best.

Old-style autocratic leaders may have been able to get away with the first type of attitude, but that doesn't fly with people today, at least not in nations where people are free. The second approach sometimes works, but neither is as effective as the third. People who understand how important their part is are motivated to persevere and work with excellence, even in the face of obstacles and problems.

A good example of this occurred during World War II in a parachute factory. Workers made parachutes by the thousands for the war effort, but it was a painfully tedious job. They spent long hours at a sewing machine stitching miles of plain white fabric. Every morning workers were reminded that every stitch was part of a lifesaving operation. Their husbands, brothers, or sons might wear the parachute they sewed that day. Those lives could not be saved without their efforts. The fact that the vision was continually before them and they knew that it would not be completed without them kept them going.

THEY AREN'T READY FOR IT. I love this cartoon by the late Jeff

MacNelly, Pulitzer Prize–winning editorial cartoonist and creator of the comic strip *Shoe*:

It may be sad to say, but some people are not ready—emotionally, intellectually, or professionally—to step up, embrace the vision, and help to make it happen. If they are willing but unable, then they can be trained and developed. If they are neither willing nor able, then there may not be much you can do to help them.

360-Degree Leaders are informational conduits that connect the top and the bottom of the organization. When any one of these six issues is a problem—the people didn't help create it, the people don't understand it, the people don't agree with it, the people don't know the vision, the people feel unneeded to achieve it, or the people aren't ready for it—then the conduit becomes clogged, and the vision cannot flow from the leaders at the top to the people who actually accomplish the work. If the vision fails to connect with the workers, it will never come to fruition.

2. Ignore It—Do Their Own Thing

Some people may not attack the vision, but they don't support it either. Instead, they pretend it doesn't exist and do their own thing. Leaders cannot do this and still maintain their integrity and effectiveness. One leader I spoke to, who for many years worked in the middle of an organization, said that he remembers a time when his boss wanted him to confront an employee on a dress code issue. The problem for this leader was that he didn't agree with the policy. But he believed in the larger vision of the organization and wanted to support his leader, so he followed through with the confrontation. It turned out to be especially difficult because the employee thought the rule was petty. But the mid-level leader firmly supported his leader. The employee never knew that this leader actually agreed with the employee, not with his boss.

3. Abandon It—Leave the Organization

If the vision violates your principles or doesn't speak to what you value deep down, leaving the organization may be the appropriate action. Sometimes that is the best option—leaving with honor. That way the leader in the middle is neither undermining the vision, nor is he endorsing something with which he cannot agree. I must mention one caution, however. If a leader in the middle of the organization bails out for the wrong reasons, he may find himself in a similar situation again in another organization. If you find yourself in a situation where you are considering leaving an organization, make sure you're not doing it because of selfishness or ego.

4. Adapt to It—Find a Way to Align with the Vision

At the very least, a good employee finds a way to align himself with the vision of his organization. David Branker told me the story of Bret, a middle manager whose job was to provide computer support and data tracking for an organization's training department. Bret was frustrated because he didn't think the job he was asked to do was contributing significantly to the company's vision.

Instead of sulking or complaining, he approached his leader to talk about the issue. Together, they discovered how his department might add greater value to the organization by creating systems that used technology to make training faster, more efficient, and more cost-effective. By aligning himself with the vision, Bret not only furthered the mission, added value to the organization, and improved the bottom line, but he also found greater personal fulfillment.

Douglas Randlett, who works with former football coach Pastor Tom Mullins, did his doctoral dissertation on the issue of leading from the middle of an organization. He said that when the vision of the leader in the middle doesn't align with that of the top leadership, low job satisfaction is always the result. When those two factors do align, satisfaction is high, and so is success.

5. Champion It—Take the Leader's Vision and Make It a Reality

Vision may begin with one person, but it is accomplished only through the efforts of many people. Taking the leader's vision and working to fulfill it should be the response of 360-Degree Leaders. They should strive to take the vision from *me* to *we*.

John W. Gardner said, "The prospects never looked brighter and the problems never looked tougher. Anyone who isn't stirred by both of those statements is too tired to be of much use to us in the days ahead."

Vision begins with one person, but it is only accomplished by many people.

During the thirty-five years that I've led organizations, I have always worked hard to transfer the vision I possessed to my staff. Some people embraced it; others didn't.

Those Who Championed the Vision	Those Who Did Not
Placed the organization's needs first	Placed their own needs first
Kept the vision before the people	Kept themselves before the people
Represented me well to others	Represented themselves well to others
Understood their roles	Misunderstood their roles

The people who didn't accept the vision neither championed it nor transferred it to their followers. As a result, the people they led often didn't contribute to the overall success of the organization.

6. Add Value to It

The most positive response to a leader's vision is to go beyond championing it and to actually add value to it. At that point, the vision becomes something more. It has greater value to the leader, greater value to the recipients of the vision, and greater value to the person who contributed to it.

Not everyone gets the opportunity to add value to the vision. There is a prerequisite for getting the opportunity to do it, and that is championing the vision as it already exists. But here's the great thing: Once you have begun to add value to the vision, then you have eliminated the Vision Challenge, because you're no longer championing someone else's vision; you are championing a vision to which you have contributed.

Nobody champions a vision and adds value to it like my team at EQUIP, the faith-based nonprofit organization I founded in 1996. From the very beginning, our mission was to train leaders. Initially, our strategy was to work in three distinct areas: in academia, in urban areas, and internationally. In 2001 we narrowed our focus and refined our vision, deciding to turn every bit of our attention to training leaders overseas. Everyone on the EQUIP team was a vision champion from the start, but key leaders did even more than champion the vision. They were instrumental in helping us recognize the need to focus our attention and try to do one thing with total excellence, not three things merely well.

What emerged was the Million Leaders Mandate, our attempt to train one million spiritual leaders around the world. As I write this, more than 700,000 leaders are in training. By January 2006, when this book goes to print, we will be training on every continent except Antarctica, and we will have reached our goal of training more than one million leaders. Already we are looking toward the goal of training a *second* million leaders!

Every day members of the EQUIP team champion the vision—with the leaders we want to train at no cost, with the associate trainers who donate their money and time to train leaders across the globe, and to the donors, whose every dollar goes to underwriting the project. They are partners championing the vision that we created together. And for that, my gratitude knows no bounds.

Challenge #7

The Influence Challenge:

Leading Others Beyond Your Position Is Not Easy

The Key to Successfully Navigating the Influence Challenge:

Think influence, not position.

As you have read about the previous six challenges, perhaps you have felt that their impact on you is minimal. If so, you can consider yourself fortunate. Nobody, however, escapes the Influence Challenge, no matter how wonderful an organization you work for or how great your boss is. Leading others beyond your position is not easy. If real leadership were easy, anybody would do it, and everyone could excel at it.

Most good leaders believe in themselves and their leadership. They are confident that if others would follow them, then the team would benefit and accomplish its goals. So why doesn't that always happen? Why don't people who report to them line up to follow? Because they don't have to! Leadership is influence. If you have neither position nor influence, people will not follow you. And the further outside your position they are, the less likely they are to let you lead them. That's why 360-Degree Leaders work to change their thinking from *I want a position that will make people follow me* to, *I want to become a person whom people will want to follow.*

People Follow Leaders . . .

It's a fallacy to believe that people would automatically follow you if you were the positional leader. Leaders who have actually been on top know that it doesn't work that way. Do people follow you now? If they follow you today, then they will follow you tomorrow when you have a better position. But if people don't follow you where you are currently, then they won't follow you where you're going either.

> *360-Degree Leaders work to change their thinking from,* I want a position that will make people follow me *to,* I want to become a person whom people will want to follow.

The only solution to the Influence Challenge is to become the kind of leader other people want to follow. And what kind of leader would that be?

People Follow Leaders They Know—Leaders Who Care

Many people try to move others by criticizing them or trying to "power up" on them. People generally respond by becoming defensive, behaving combatively, or isolating themselves. Protestant reformer John Knox said, "You cannot antagonize and influence at the same time."

On the other hand, if leaders care about each individual as a person, then people respond well to them. The greater the depth of their concern, the broader and longer lasting their influence. Bo Schembechler, former head coach of the University of Michigan football team, remarked, "Deep down, your players must know you care about them. This is the most important thing. I could never get away with what I do if the players felt I didn't care. They know, in the long run, I'm in their corner."

People can sense how you feel about them. They can tell the difference between leaders who are using them for their own gain and those who want to help them succeed. People warm up to warm people. They get to know the heart of someone who cares, and they respond well to them. I think of it this way: second-mile leaders produce second-mile followers. If you go out of your way to care about others and help them, then they will go out of their way to help you when you ask them to.

PEOPLE FOLLOW LEADERS THEY TRUST—LEADERS WITH CHARACTER

Political theorist Thomas Paine said, "I love the man that can smile in trouble, that can gather strength from distress, and grow brave by reflection. 'Tis the business of little minds to shrink, but he whose heart is firm, and whose conscience approves his conduct, will pursue his principles unto death." What gives a leader the strength to exhibit such admirable qualities? The answer is *character*.

> *"You cannot antagonize and influence at the same time."*
> —JOHN KNOX

We tend to put a lot of emphasis on intelligence and skill in this country. And while those things are important, they cannot substitute for strong character. As I teach in *The 21 Irrefutable Laws of Leadership*, trust is the foundation of leadership. A leader who understands all too well how character issues impact leadership is Chuck Colson, the former Nixon aide who was imprisoned in the wake of the Watergate scandal. Colson turned his life around after that ordeal and now lectures on leadership and faith issues. He said: "As you go through life, whether it's in the military, in your business, in the church, or whatever walk of life (and certainly in your family), someone is going to depend on your character more than upon your IQ."

Most people would acknowledge that trustworthiness is important in a leader. What some people don't recognize is the importance of trustworthiness in would-be leaders. Rod Loy, who leads a large organization in Little Rock, Arkansas, said:

> Too many middle leaders say, "When I become the leader, I'll change the way I live." I meet with so many people who are second in command

> who don't live according to the character code of top leadership. Their thought is, *I don't have to live by that until I become the visible leader.* My belief is, if I don't live by those high standards, I'll never become the leader. I choose to limit my freedoms—because I understand the sacrifices of the position I one day desire to possess.

If you desire to overcome the influence challenge, then develop and exhibit the kind of character that you would find admirable in a top leader. That will pave the way for relationships with others today and prepare you for nonpositional leadership for tomorrow.

People Follow Leaders They Respect—Leaders Who Are Competent

Respect is almost always gained on difficult ground. A leadership position will help a leader only until difficulties arise. Then the leader must arise to meet those difficulties. Leaders who are incapable of meeting challenges may desire respect from their followers and peers, but they rarely get it. They may be liked if they possess good character and care for others, but they won't be highly respected. People may treat them kindly, but they won't listen to them. Everyone may have the right to speak, but not everyone has earned the right to be heard.

> *While poor leaders demand respect, competent leaders command respect.*

While poor leaders demand respect, competent leaders command respect. Being able to do a job well brings a leader credibility. If you think you can do a job—that's confidence. If you actually can do it—that's competence. And there is no substitute for it.

People Follow Leaders They Can Approach—Leaders Who Are Consistent

One middle leader I interviewed while working on this book, whom I will call Fred, told me he once had a very moody leader as his boss. He never knew whether the "good boss" or the "evil boss" would show up at the office on any given day. But Fred learned how to deal with the issue after following the advice of a fellow staff member.

If Fred had a problem at work that would need the attention of the moody boss, he would add that to a running list he kept and took to their weekly staff meeting. Fred was always very careful never to sit next to his boss during the meeting. That way, he had a chance to observe how he treated others as discussion went from person to person around the table. After the boss talked to two or three employees, Fred could gauge what kind of mood the boss was in that day. If his boss was in a bad mood, Fred would keep his list to himself and save it for another day. But if the boss was in a positive and helpful mood, Fred asked every question on his list and got a good answer for every one. Fred often ended up holding his list for five or six weeks until the boss's mood was right. The bad news was that there was often a delay in resolving some important issues, but the good news was that his moody leader rarely bushwhacked Fred.

A Yiddish proverb states, "If you act like an ass, don't get insulted if people ride you." I guess you could say that is what Fred had to do to get along with his inconsistent leader. Consistency isn't easy for anybody. In fact, writer Aldous Huxley said, "Consistency is contrary to nature, contrary to life. The only completely consistent people are the dead."

If you want to be the kind of leader others want to follow—a 360-Degree Leader—then plan to fight the good fight to be consistent so that you are approachable. Even if you care for people, are honest with them, and can perform your job well, unless you are consistent, people will not depend on you, and they will not trust you.

PEOPLE FOLLOW LEADERS THEY ADMIRE—LEADERS WITH COMMITMENT

I love the story of the farmer who had experienced several bad years and went to see the manager of his bank. "I've got some good news and some bad news to tell you," he told the banker. "Which would you like first?"

"Why don't you tell me the bad news first and get it over with?" the bank manager replied.

"Okay. With the bad drought and inflation and all, I won't be able to pay anything on my mortgage this year; either on the principal or the interest."

"Well, that is pretty bad," responded the banker.

"It gets worse. I also won't be able to pay anything on the loan for all that machinery I bought—not on the principal or interest."

"Wow, that's really bad!"

"It's worse than that," continued the farmer. "You remember I also borrowed to buy seeds and fertilizer and other supplies? Well, I can't pay anything on that either—principal or interest."

"That's awful—and that's enough! Tell me what the good news is," the banker pleaded.

"The good news," replied the farmer with a smile, "is that I intend to keep on doing business with you."[1]

The joke is corny, but it is true that people admire people who exhibit great commitment. Think of some of the great leaders you admire. When I think of people like Winston Churchill, Martin Luther King Jr., and John Wesley, one of the first qualities that comes to mind is their commitment. They gave everything they had to leading according to their principles.

Several years ago, I coauthored a book called *Becoming a Person of Influence* with Jim Dornan. Many people tell me that of all my books, it is their favorite. Why is that? I believe it's because it's a book on leadership for people without leadership positions. It's especially popular among people involved in network marketing, because their business is entirely influence based. The book is based on an acrostic that I will give you now, because it describes the qualities of an influencer and is easy to remember.

Integrity—builds relationships on trust
Nurturing—cares about people as individuals
Faith—believes in people
Listening—values what others have to say
Understanding—sees from their point of view
Enlarging—helps others become bigger
Navigating—assists others through difficulties
Connecting—initiates positive relationships
Empowering—gives them the power to lead

If you work hard to do all of these things with the people in your organization, you will overcome the Influence Challenge. The whole secret is to think *influence*, not *position*. That's what leadership is all about. If you begin to practice the qualities of influence, you will be ready to take on one of the toughest tasks of 360-Degree Leaders: leading up. That's the subject of the next section of this book.

Section II Review
The Challenges 360-Degree Leaders Face

Here is a brief review of the challenges every leader in the middle faces:

1. The Tension Challenge: The Pressure of Being "Caught in the Middle"
2. The Frustration Challenge: Following an Ineffective Leader
3. The Multi-Hat Challenge: One Head . . . Many Hats
4. The Ego Challenge: You're Often Hidden in the Middle
5. The Fulfillment Challenge: Leaders Like the Front More Than the Middle
6. The Vision Challenge: Championing the Vision Is More Difficult When You Didn't Create It
7. The Influence Challenge: Leading Others Beyond Your Position Is Not Easy

If these challenges resonate with you, then you know you need to lead better from the middle in order to handle them most effectively. How well do you do that now? One way to measure your ability is to take the 360-Degree Leadership assessment, offered free of charge to people who have purchased this book. Go to 360DegreeLeader.com for more information.

SECTION III

The Principles 360-Degree Leaders Practice to Lead Up

"Follow me, I'm right behind you."

If you are trying to make an impact from the middle of an organization, then you probably relate to the myths and challenges outlined in the previous two sections of the book. More than likely you have to deal with one or more of them every day. So how do you make the best of your situation while overcoming the challenges and avoiding the myths? You develop the ability to be a 360-Degree Leader by learning to lead up (with your leader), lead across (with your colleagues), and lead down (with your followers). Each of these draws on different principles and requires different skills.

> *"If you want to get ahead, leading up is much better than kissing up."*
> —Dan Reiland

Leading up is the 360-Degree Leader's greatest challenge. Most leaders want to lead, not be led. But most leaders also want to have value added to them. If you take the approach of wanting to add value to those above you, you have the best chance of influencing them. Dan Reiland said as we talked over ideas for this book: "If you want to get ahead, leading up is much better than kissing up."

In the fall of 2004, I got a glimpse of a world that was totally new to me. At "Exchange," an event for executives that I host every year, I invited the attendees to experience a presentation by noted Boston Philharmonic conductor Benjamin Zander along with the Atlanta Symphony Orchestra. It was an interactive leadership experience where we got to sit in among the musicians of the orchestra as they rehearsed, and the conductor gave us insights into communication, leadership, and followership within a world-class team of artists. It was incredible.

That experience prompted me to read the book Zander wrote with his wife, Rosamund Stone Zander, called *The Art of Possibility*. In it, they tell a story that wonderfully illustrates the value of leading up and how it can add value to a leader and an organization. Benjamin Zander wrote:

> One of the most supremely gifted and accomplished artists I have known sat for decades as a modest member of the viola section of one of America's leading orchestras. Eugene Lehner had been the violist of the legendary Kolisch Quartet, and had coached the distinguished Juilliard String Quartet as well as innumerable other ensembles . . . How often I have consulted him on thorny points of interpretation—to have the scales removed from my eyes by his incandescent insight into the music![1]

Zander went on to say that he wondered if any of the other conductors—who have a notorious reputation for being egoists—had consulted him and drawn on his immense knowledge and experience as an artist and leader. Following is Lehner's response:

> One day, during my very first year playing with the orchestra, I remember an occasion when Koussevitsky was conducting a Bach piece and he seemed to be having some difficulty getting the results he wanted—it simply wasn't going right. Fortunately, his friend, the great French pedagogue and conductor Nadia Boulanger, happened to be in

> town and sitting in on the rehearsal, so Koussevitsky took the opportunity to extricate himself from an awkward and embarrassing situation by calling out to her, "Nadia, please, will you come up here and conduct? I want to go to the back of the hall to see how it sounds." Mademoiselle Boulanger stepped up, made a few comments to the musicians, and conducted the orchestra through the passage without a hitch. Ever since that time, in every rehearsal, I have been waiting for the conductor to say, "Lehrer, you come up here and conduct, I want to go to the back of the hall to hear how it sounds." It is now forty-three years since this happened, and it is less and less likely that I will be asked.[2]

I'm sure you don't want to wait forty-three years for an opportunity to lead up. You want to be a person of influence beginning today.

Influencing your leader isn't something you can make happen in a day. In fact, since you have no control over the people above you on the organizational chart, they may refuse to be influenced by you or anyone under their authority. So there's a possibility that you may never be able to lead up with them. But you can greatly increase the odds of success if you practice the principles in this section of the book. Your underlying strategy should be to support your leader, add value to the organization, and distinguish yourself from the rest of the pack by doing your work with excellence. If you do these things consistently, then in time the leader above you may learn to trust you, rely on you, and look to you for advice. With each step, your influence will increase, and you will have more and more opportunities to lead up.

Lead-Up Principle #1

Lead Yourself Exceptionally Well

Every now and then at a conference, sharp young kids will come up to me and tell me how much they want to become great leaders and how hard they're working to learn and grow. But then they'll lament, "I don't have anyone to lead yet."

My response is to tell them, "Lead yourself. That's where it all starts. Besides, if you wouldn't follow yourself, why should anyone else?"

Have you ever worked with people who didn't lead themselves well? Worse, have you ever worked for people in leadership positions who couldn't lead themselves? What do they do other than set a bad example? They're like the crow in a fable I once read. The crow was sitting in a tree, doing nothing all day. A small rabbit saw the crow and asked him, "Can I also sit like you and do nothing all day long?"

"Sure," answered the crow, "why not?" So the rabbit sat on the ground below the crow, following his example. All of a sudden a fox appeared, pounced on the rabbit, and ate him.

The tongue-in-cheek moral of the story is that if you're going to sit around doing nothing all day, you had better be sitting very high up. But if you are down where the action is, you can't afford to be sitting around doing nothing. The key to leading yourself well is to learn self-management. I have observed that most people put too much emphasis on decision making and too little on decision managing. As a result, they lack focus, discipline, intentionality, and purpose.

I believe this so firmly that I wrote an entire book on it called *Today Matters*. The thesis of the book is that successful people make right decisions early and manage those decisions daily. We often think that self-leadership is about making good decisions every day, when the reality is that we need to make a few critical decisions in major areas of life and then manage those decisions day to day.

Here's a classic example of what I mean. Have you ever made a New Year's resolution to exercise? You probably already believe that exercise is important. Making a decision to do it isn't that hard, but managing that decision—and following through—is much more difficult. Let's say, for example, that you sign up for a health club membership the first week of January. When you sign on, you're excited. But the first time you show up at the gym, there's a mob of people. There are so many cars that police are directing traffic. You drive around for fifteen minutes, and finally find a parking place—four blocks away. But that's okay; you're there for exercise anyway, so you walk to the gym.

The key to leading yourself well is to learn self-management.

Then when you get inside the building, you have to wait to even get into the locker room to change. But you think, *That's okay. I want to get into shape. This is going to be great*. You think that until you finally get dressed and discover all the machines are being used. Once again you have to wait. Finally, you get on a machine—it's not the one you really wanted, but hey, you'll take it—and you exercise for twenty minutes. When you see the line for the shower, you decide to skip it, take your clothes, and just change at home.

On your way out, you see the manager of the club, and you decide to complain about the crowds. She says, "Don't worry about it. Come back in three weeks, and you can have the closest parking place and your choice of machines. Because by then, 98 percent of the people who signed up will have dropped out!"

It's one thing to decide to exercise. It's another to actually follow through with it. As everyone else drops out, you will have to decide whether you will quit like everyone else or if you will stick with it. And that takes self-management.

Nothing will make a better impression on your leader than your ability to manage yourself. If your leader must continually expend energy managing you, then you will be perceived as someone who drains time and energy. If you manage yourself well, however, your boss will see you as someone who maximizes opportunities and leverages personal strengths. That will make you someone your leader turns to when the heat is on.

What a Leader Must Self-Manage

In *Today Matters* I reference the dozen things that people who desire to be successful should do. But here I want to focus on leadership alone. So if you want to gain credibility with your boss and others, focus on taking care of business in these seven areas:

1. Manage Your Emotions

I once heard that people with emotional problems are 144 percent more likely to have auto accidents than those who don't have them. The same study evidently found that one out of five victims of fatal accidents had been in a quarrel with another person in the six hours preceding the accident.

It's important for everybody to manage emotions. Nobody likes to spend time around an emotional time bomb who may "go off" at any moment. But it's especially critical for leaders to control their emotions because whatever they do affects many other people.

Good leaders know when to display emotions and when to delay them. Sometimes they show them so that their people can feel what they're feeling. It stirs them up. Is that manipulative? I don't think so, as long as the leaders are doing it for the good of the team and not for their own gain. Because leaders see more than others and ahead of others, they often experience the emotions first. By letting the team know what you're feeling, you're helping them to see what you're seeing.

Good leaders know when to display emotions and when to delay them.

Other times leaders have to hold their feelings in check. In his book *American Soldier*, Gen. Tommy Franks wrote about a devastating incident that occurred in Vietnam when he was a junior officer and the example that was set for him in this area by Lt. Col. Eric Antilla, who put the men he commanded ahead of his own emotional needs:

> I studied Eric Antilla's eyes. I knew he was gripped by anguish, but he never let it show. We were at war; he was commanding troops in combat. And his quiet resolve in meeting this catastrophe gave us all strength. In an hour he would grieve, but now he stood rock solid. In war, it is necessary that commanders be able to delay their emotions until they can afford them.[1]

When I say that leaders should delay their emotions, I'm not suggesting that they deny them or bury them. The bottom line in managing your emotions is that you should put others—not yourself—first in how you handle and process them. Whether you delay or display your emotions should not be for your own gratification. You should ask yourself, *What does the team need?* not, *What will make me feel better?*

2. Manage Your Time

Time management issues are especially tough for people in the middle. Leaders at the top can delegate. Workers at the bottom usually punch a time clock. They get paid an hourly wage, and they do what they can while they're on the clock. Middle leaders, meanwhile, feel the Tension Challenge, and they are encouraged—and are often expected—to put in long hours to get work done.

Time is valuable. Psychiatrist and author M. Scott Peck said, "Until you value yourself, you won't value your time. Until you value your time, you will not do anything with it." In *What to Do Between Birth and Death* (Wm. Morrow & Co., 1992), Charles Spezzano says that people don't pay for things with money; they pay for them with time. If you say to yourself, *In five years, I'll have put enough away to buy that vacation house*, then what you are really saying is that the house will cost you five years—one-twelfth of your adult life. "The phrase *spending your time* is not a metaphor," said Spezzano. "It's how life works."

> *"Until you value yourself, you won't value your time."*
> —M. SCOTT PECK

Instead of thinking about what you do and what you buy in terms of money, instead think about them in terms of time. Think about it. What is worth spending your life on? Seeing your work in that light just may change the way you manage your time.

3. MANAGE YOUR PRIORITIES

The best 360-Degree Leaders are generalists. They know a lot about a lot of things. They often have no choice because of the Multi-Hat Challenge. But at the same time, the old proverb is true: If you chase two rabbits, both will escape.

What is a leader in the middle to do? Since you are not the top leader, you don't have control over your list of responsibilities or your schedule. You should still try to get yourself to the point where you can manage your priorities and focus your time in this way:

80 percent of the time—work where you are strongest
15 percent of the time—work where you are learning
5 percent of the time—work in other necessary areas

This may not be easy to achieve, but it is what you should strive for. If you have people working for you, try to give them the things you aren't good at but they are. Or if possible, trade some duties with your colleagues so that each of you is playing to your strength. Remember, the only way to move up from the middle is to gradually shift from generalist to specialist, from someone who does many things well to someone who focuses on a few things she does exceptionally well.

The secret to making the shift is often discipline. In *Good to Great*, Jim Collins wrote:

> Most of us lead busy, but undisciplined lives. We have ever-expanding "to do" lists, trying to build momentum by doing, doing, doing—and doing more. And it rarely works. Those who build the good-to-great companies, however, made as much use of "stop doing" lists as the "to do" lists. They displayed a remarkable amount of discipline to unplug all sorts of extraneous junk.[2]

You must be ruthless in your judgment of what you should not do. Just because you like doing something doesn't mean it should stay on your to-do list. If it is a strength, do it. If it helps you grow, do it. If your leader says you must handle it personally, do it. Anything else is a candidate for your "stop doing" list.

4. Manage Your Energy

Some people have to ration their energy so that they don't run out. Up until a few years ago, that wasn't me. When people asked me how I got so much done, my answer was always, "High energy, low IQ." From the time I was a kid, I was always on the go. I was six years old before I realized my name wasn't "Settle Down."

Now that I'm fifty-eight, I do have to pay attention to my energy level. In *Thinking for a Change*, I shared one of my strategies for managing my energy. When I look at my calendar every morning, I ask myself,

What is the main event? That is the one thing to which I cannot afford to give anything less than my best. That one thing can be for my family, my employees, a friend, my publisher, the sponsor of a speaking engagement, or my writing time. I always make sure I have the energy to do it with focus and excellence.

The greatest enemy of good thinking is busyness.

Even people with high energy can have that energy sucked right out of them under difficult circumstances. I've observed that leaders in the middle of an organization often have to deal with what I call "the ABCs energy-drain."

Activity Without Direction—doing things that don't seem to matter
Burden Without Action—not being able to do things that really matter
Conflict Without Resolution—not being able to deal with what's the matter

If you find that you are in an organization where you often must deal with these ABCs, then you will have to work extra hard to manage your energy well. Either that or you need to look for a new place to work.

5. MANAGE YOUR THINKING

Poet and novelist James Joyce said, "Your mind will give back to you exactly what you put into it." The greatest enemy of good thinking is busyness. And middle leaders are usually the busiest people in an organization. If you find that the pace of life is too demanding for you to stop and think during your workday, then get into the habit of jotting down the three or four things that need good mental processing or planning that you can't stop to think about. Then carve out some time later when you can give those items some good think-time. That may be thirty minutes at home the same day, or you may want to keep a running list for a whole week and then take a couple of hours on Saturday. Just don't let the list get so long that it disheartens or intimidates you.

I encouraged readers in *Thinking for a Change* to have a place to think, and I wrote about the "thinking chair" I have in my office. I don't use that chair for anything else other than my think-time. I've discovered since the book's publication that I didn't explain clearly enough how to correctly use the thinking chair. People at conferences told me that they sat in their own thinking chairs and nothing happened. I explain to them that I don't sit in that thinking chair without an agenda, just hoping that a good idea hits me. What I usually do is think about the things I've jotted down because I couldn't think about them during a busy day. I take the list to my chair, put it in front of me, and give each item as much think-time as it needs. Sometimes I'm evaluating a decision I've already made. Sometimes I'm thinking through a decision I will have to make. Sometimes I'm developing a strategy. Other times I'm trying to be creative in fleshing out an idea.

A minute of thinking is often more valuable than an hour of talk or unplanned work.

I want to encourage you to try managing your thinking in this way. If you've never done it before, you will be amazed by the payoff. And know this: 1 minute > 1 hour. A minute of thinking is often more valuable than an hour of talk or unplanned work.

6. Manage Your Words

Legendary basketball coach John Wooden said, "Show me what you can do; don't just tell me what you can do." I think just about every leader has said—or at least thought—those words at some time or another when dealing with an employee. Leaders value action. And if they are going to stop what they're doing long enough to listen, the words they hear need to have value. Make them count.

In *The Forbes Scrapbook of Thoughts on the Business Life* (Triumph Books, 1995), Emile de Girardin is quoted as saying, "The power of words is immense. A well-chosen word has often sufficed to stop a flying army, to change defeat into victory, and to save an empire." If you wish to make sure that your words carry weight, then weigh them well. The good news is that if you manage your thinking and take advantage of focused think-time, you will probably see improvement in the area of managing your words too.

David McKinley, a 360-Degree Leader in a large organization in Plano, Texas, told me a story about something that happened in his first job after graduate school. He was preparing to make an important call on someone, and he decided that he should ask the top leader to go with him. When they got there, David, in his enthusiasm, just wouldn't stop talking. He didn't give his leader a chance to do anything but watch until the very end of their visit.

As they returned to the car, David's boss told him, "I might as well have stayed at the office." He went on to explain how his presence was superfluous. David told me, "I learned a huge lesson that day about staying 'in bounds' when I was with the senior leader. His honest counsel and correction strengthened our relationship and has served me well throughout my life." If you have something worthwhile to say, say it briefly and well. If you don't, sometimes the best thing to do is remain silent.

7. MANAGE YOUR PERSONAL LIFE

You can do everything right at work and manage yourself well there, but if your personal life is a mess, it will eventually turn everything else sour. What would it profit a leader to climb to the top of the organizational chart but to lose a marriage or alienate the children? As someone who spent many years counseling people, I can tell you, no career success is worth it.

Success is having those closest to me love and respect me the most.

For years one of my definitions of *success* has been this: having those closest to me love and respect me the most. That is what is most important. I want the love and respect of my wife, my children, and my grandchildren before I want the respect of anyone I work with. Don't get me wrong. I want the people who work with me to respect me too, but not at the expense of my family. If I blow managing myself at home, then the negative impact will spill over into every area of my life, including work.

If you want to lead up, you must always lead yourself first. If you can't, you have no credibility. I've found the following to be true:

If I can't lead myself, others won't follow me.
If I can't lead myself, others won't respect me.
If I can't lead myself, others won't partner with me.

That applies whether the influence you desire to exert is on the people above you, beside you, or below you. The better you are at making sure you're doing what you should be doing, the better chance you have for making an impact on others.

Lead-Up Principle #2

Lighten Your Leader's Load

You've probably heard the saying, "Pass the buck," meaning to duck ownership or shirk responsibility. One source says that the expression comes from when card games were played in the old West, and a Buck knife was used to indicate who was to deal the cards next. If someone didn't want to deal, he could pass the Buck.

When Harry Truman was president of the United States, he used to keep a sign on his desk that said, "The Buck Stops Here." By that he meant that no matter how many people might avoid taking responsibility up and down the chain of command, he would take responsibility. In an address at the National War College on December 19, 1952, Truman said, "You know, it's easy for the Monday morning quarterback to say what the coach should have done, after the game is over. But when the decision is up before you—and on my desk I have a motto which says 'The Buck Stops Here'—the decision has to be made." On another occasion he said, "The president—whoever he is—has to decide. He can't pass the buck to anybody. No one else can do the deciding for him. That's his job."[1]

Responsibility weighs heavily on leaders. The higher they are in an organization, the heavier the responsibility. As president of the United

States, Truman carried the weight of the entire nation on his shoulders. Leaders can give up many things. They can delegate many things. The one thing that the top leader can never let go of is final responsibility.

HOW LIFTING YOUR LEADER LIFTS YOU

As an employee, you can do one of two things for your leader. You can make the load lighter, or you can make it heavier. It's similar to the Elevator Principle in *Winning with People*: "We can lift people up or take people down in our relationships." If you help lift the load, then you help your leader succeed. When the boss succeeds, the organization succeeds. Conversely, it is almost impossible for you to win if your boss fails.

Leaders can give up many things. They can delegate many things. The one thing that the top leader can never let go of is final responsibility.

I should mention that motives do matter when it comes to lifting your leader's load. I'm recommending that you lift up, not suck up. That's not to say that people who are nice to the boss and hope it helps their careers have bad motives or poor character. They have just misplaced their energies. And a good leader can tell the difference between someone who really wants to help and someone who is trying to curry favor.

There are many positive benefits that can come from helping to lift your leader's load. Following are a few of those benefits.

LIFTING SHOWS YOU ARE A TEAM PLAYER

When I think of the consummate team player, I think of Kirk Nowery, the president of Injoy Stewardship Services. When Kirk first began with ISS, he was one of our "road warriors." He consulted with churches and also presented information about ISS and its services to pastors and their lay leaders. But every time I saw Kirk, he used to ask me the same question: "John, is there anything I can do for you?" It was his way of letting me know that he was a team player, willing to do whatever it took for ISS to succeed. Now that Kirk is running the company, he still asks me that question whenever we meet. And if I ask him to do anything, whether it's to accomplish a big company goal or help me with something personal, he completes the task with excellence.

Lifting Shows Gratitude for Being on the Team

A Chinese proverb says, "Those who drink the water must remember those who dug the well." Gratitude is one of the most attractive of all personal attributes; sometimes I think it is one of the least practiced. But I have to say that the people I work with are not remiss in this area. I find them to be very grateful. They continually show their gratitude by lifting my load and taking things off of my shoulders; and because they take good care of me, I try to take good care of them.

Lifting Makes You Part of Something Bigger

In February 2005, a few members of the EQUIP staff, several volunteer leadership trainers, and some current and potential donors made a trip to Europe to launch the Million Leaders Mandate there. It was an amazing experience as we met with national leaders in the United Kingdom, Germany, Ukraine, and Russia.

When you help someone bigger than you, it makes you part of something bigger.

We covered a lot of territory in ten days. Often we flew into a country in the morning, took in some sights in the afternoon, and met with key leaders in the evening or the next day. As we rushed from place to place and traveled together on buses from airport to hotel to meeting hall, Doug Carter, the vice president of EQUIP, continually reminded everyone of the vision of EQUIP and the Million Leaders Mandate—to train and equip a million people on six continents for spiritual leadership.

Doug is a good leader. He was reminding us that what we were doing was a part of something bigger than the events of the moment. It's the truth that when you help someone bigger than you, it makes you part of something bigger. Doesn't just about everyone desire to be part of something significant? There is also another benefit to being part of something bigger; it makes you bigger. You cannot contribute to something significant without being changed. If you want to be better than you are, become part of something bigger than you are.

Lifting Gets You Noticed

When you lift people up, they can't help but notice it. Even if others aren't aware of what you're doing, the person being lifted is. Of course, lifting others isn't meant to be a one-time occurrence. You can't add value to people by helping them once. It needs to be an ongoing process if you want the value you add to come back to you.

How Often You Lift	How the Leader Responds
Once or twice	"Thanks."
Many times	"I need you."
Continually	"Let me help you."

If you continually help others, then others will eventually want to help you. Even if the leader you work for never turns around to lift you up in return, someone who has seen you doing that lifting will extend a hand to you. Just remember: *It's not how heavy the load is. It's how you carry it.*

Lifting Increases Your Value and Influence

Do you have a friend or family member who always makes things better for you, who seems to add value to you every time you are together? If you do, I bet that person has a special place in your heart. Likewise, load lifters have a special place in the hearts of their leaders.

From the perspective of the top leader, the question that must be asked is, "Am I better off with them on the team?" That's really the bottom line for a leader. If you make your leaders feel that they are better off because you are part of the team, then your value goes up, and so does your influence. I ask myself that question about two years after hiring someone. I'm naturally optimistic, so it takes that long for my enthusiasm for them to be tempered enough for me to look at their performance realistically. Other leaders could perhaps make a fair assessment sooner than that, though I also recommend that pessimists wait two years (to get over their skepticism).

The lift you give for the leader often leads to the leader lifting you.

When you lift a leader's load, your load certainly gets heavier. You're taking on more when leading in the middle is already difficult. Know, however, that the lift you give for the leader often leads to the leader lifting you.

How to Lift Your Leader's Load

As you read about the various ways that lifting your leader's load can help you, perhaps several ways you could help came to mind. I recommend that you go with your instincts. But just in case you aren't sure of where to begin, please allow me to give you several suggestions.

1. Do Your Own Job Well First

Hall of Fame baseball player Willie Mays said, "It isn't hard to be good from time to time in sports. What's tough is being good every day." When you are good every day, you do the first important step in lifting your leader's load—you prevent him from having to lift yours.

I once had an employee who continually told me that he wanted to help me. At first, I thought, *What a great attitude!* But then I began to notice something. Despite his constant requests to help, he never seemed to get his own work done. After seeing that this was a pattern, I sat him down and told him that the best way he could help me was to do his job. But guess what? He kept asking to help me but didn't follow through and get his own job done. I finally concluded that what he wanted was to spend time with me, not help me. In time, I had to let him go.

2. When You Find a Problem, Provide a Solution

I love the *Peanuts* comic strip in which Lucy walks up to Charlie Brown, who is leaning against a wall with his head in his hands. She looks at him and says, "Discouraged again, eh, Charlie Brown?"

"You know what your trouble is?" she asks when he doesn't respond. "The whole trouble with you is that you are you!"

"Well, what in the world can I do about that?" he responds in exasperation.

> *"It isn't hard to be good from time to time in sports. What's tough is being good every day."*
>
> —WILLIE MAYS

Lucy answers, "I don't pretend to be able to give advice. I merely point out the trouble."

Load lifters don't follow the path of Lucy. They are more like Henry Ford, who said, "Don't find a fault; find a remedy."

In an organization I led many years ago, I seemed to have a whole bunch of "Lucys" working for me, who seemed to continually dump problems on my desk and then go away to look for more problems. I instituted a rule. Anyone who brought a problem to me wanting help with it had to also come up with three potential solutions before coming to see me. Did I do that because I didn't want to help them? No, I did it because I wanted them to learn to help themselves. They quickly became creative and resourceful. As time went by, they needed less help and became better decision makers and leaders.

3. Tell Leaders What They *Need* to Hear, Not What They *Want* to Hear

Because of their intuition, good leaders often see more than others see, and they see things before others do. Why? Because they see everything from a leadership bias. But if the organization they lead gets large, they often lose their edge. They become disconnected. What is the remedy to this problem? They ask the people in their inner circle to see things for them.

> *"Very few big executives want to be surrounded by 'yes' men."*
>
> —Burton Bigelow

Most good leaders want the perspective of people they trust. Sales expert Burton Bigelow said, "Very few big executives want to be surrounded by 'yes' men. Their greatest weakness often is the fact that 'yes' men build up around the executive a wall of fiction, when what the executive wants most of all is plain facts."

One of the ways to become a person whom leaders trust is to tell them the truth. One of the biggest load lifters in my life is Linda Eggers, my assistant. Every time I meet with Linda, I ask her to keep me on track. And believe me, I trust her in everything. Having Linda work with me is like possessing an extra brain!

Early on in our working relationship, I asked Linda to always be up front with me when it came to bad news. I didn't want her to talk around issues or try to spare my feelings. If I'm going to get bad news, I want it straight and right away. My promise to Linda, in return, was to never shoot the messenger. If you were to talk to Linda, I believe she would confirm that I have kept that promise.

If you've never spoken up to your leaders and told them what they need to hear, then it will take courage. As World War II general and later president Dwight D. Eisenhower said, "A bold heart is half the battle." But if you are willing to speak up, you can help your leaders and yourself. Start small and be diplomatic. If your leader is receptive, become more frank over time. If you get to the point where your leader is not only willing to hear from you but actually wants your perspective, then remember this: Your job is to be a funnel, not a filter. Be careful to convey information without "spinning" it. Good leaders want the truth—even if it hurts.

4. Go the Second Mile

Motivational sales expert Zig Ziglar said, "There are no traffic jams on the extra mile." When you do more than is asked, you will certainly stand out from the crowd. When you have a whatever-it-takes attitude related to helping the organization, then you can emerge as a go-to player. (I address this in greater depth in Chapter 8 of this section.) People who emerge from the crowd often become members of a leader's inner circle. Leaders expect more from their inner circle. They come to expect a second-mile mind-set from them. They expect extra effort, extra responsibility, and extra thinking. But the good leaders also give extra in return.

> *"There are no traffic jams on the extra mile."*
> —Zig Ziglar

5. Stand Up for Your Leader Whenever You Can

Helping your leaders means supporting them and standing up for them whenever you can. Former army general and U.S. secretary of state Colin Powell said, "When we are debating an issue, loyalty means giving me your honest opinion, whether you think I'll like it or not. Disagreement, at this stage, stimulates me. But once a decision has been made, the debate ends. From that point on, loyalty means executing the decision as if it were your own."

6. Stand In for Your Leader Whenever You Can

Every employee in an organization is a representative of that organization. And individuals at all levels also represent the leaders they work for. Accordingly, they can choose to step up and stand in for their leaders, representing them well and serving the organization.

Years ago, I used to tell new leaders I hired that every person in our organization walked around with two buckets. One bucket contained water, and the other gasoline. As leaders, they would continually come across small fires, and they could pour water or gasoline on a fire. It was their choice.

7. Ask Your Leader How You Can Lift the Load

It's good to anticipate what your leader may need or want. It's even better to come right out and ask. If you are doing your own job and doing it well, chances are your leader will be glad to tell you how you can help.

Over the years as I have worked as a consultant and speaker, I have discovered that there are two approaches that people in those industries take. One type of consultant walks into an organization and says, "Here's what I know; sit down and listen." Another says, "What do I need to know? We'll work on this together." Likewise, some speakers arrive at an engagement with the idea that it's their moment to be in the spotlight, and they are quick to tell you what you can do to help them. Other speakers recognize that it's their moment to add value to the leader who invited them.

As I have grown in maturity and experience, I have tried to become like the communicators in that second group. Like many leaders early in their lives, I started out focusing on myself. But in time I came to recognize that when I am invited to speak, I am there to serve the leaders who invited me. I want to add value to them, to lift their load if I can. To do that, I ask them three things:

- "Can I say something that you *have said* before to give you another voice?"
- "Can I say something that you *would like to say but can't*, to give you a needed voice?"
- "Can I say something that you *haven't said yet* to give you the first voice?"

Most of the time, the good leaders say yes to those requests. They are always thinking ahead, thinking about where to take the organization and how they will get there. When someone asks how he can help, they are delighted. All it takes is for someone to ask.

Lead-Up Principle #3

Be Willing to Do What Others Won't

Successful people do the things that unsuccessful people are unwilling to do.

—John C. Maxwell

It's said that an aid group in South Africa once wrote to missionary and explorer David Livingstone asking, "Have you found a good road to where you are? If so, we want to know how to send other men to join you."

Livingstone replied, "If you have men who will come only if they know there is a good road, I don't want them. I want men who will come even if there is no road at all." That's what top leaders want from the people working for them: they want individuals who are willing to do what others won't.

Few things gain the appreciation of a top leader more quickly than an employee with a whatever-it-takes attitude.

Few things gain the appreciation of a top leader more quickly than an employee with a whatever-it-takes attitude. That is what 360-Degree Leaders must have. They must be willing and able to think outside of their job description, to be willing to tackle the kinds of jobs that others are too proud or too frightened to take on. These things are what often elevate 360-Degree Leaders above their peers. And remember, being noticed is one of the first steps to influencing the person above you.

WHAT IT MEANS TO DO WHAT OTHERS WON'T

Perhaps you already possess a whatever-it-takes mind-set, and if a task is honest, ethical, and beneficial, you're willing to take it on. If so, good for you! Now all you need is to know how to direct that attitude into action so that you're doing the things that will make the greatest impact and create influence with others. Here are the top ten things I recommend you do to be a 360-Degree Leader who leads up:

1. 360-DEGREE LEADERS TAKE THE TOUGH JOBS

The ability to accomplish difficult tasks earns others' respect very quickly. In *Developing the Leader Within You*, I point out that one of the quickest ways to gain leadership is problem solving.

> Problems continually occur at work, at home, and in life in general. My observation is that people don't like problems, weary of them quickly, and will do almost anything to get away from them. This climate makes others place the reins of leadership into your hands—if you are willing and able to either tackle their problems or train them to solve them. Your problem-solving skills will always be needed because people always have problems.[1]

You learn resiliency and tenacity during tough assignments, not easy ones. When tough choices have to be made and results are difficult to achieve, leaders are forged.

Not only does taking on tough jobs earn you respect, but it also helps you become a better leader. You learn resiliency and tenacity during tough assignments, not easy ones. When tough choices have to be made and results are difficult to achieve, leaders are forged.

2. 360-Degree Leaders Pay Their Dues

Former U.S. senator Sam Nunn said, "You have to pay the price. You will find that everything in life exacts a price, and you will have to decide whether the price is worth the prize." To become a 360-Degree Leader, you will have to pay a price. You will have to give up other opportunities in order to lead. You will have to sacrifice some personal goals for the sake of others. You will have to get out of your comfort zone and do things you've never done before. You will have to keep learning and growing when you don't feel like it. You will have to repeatedly put others ahead of yourself. And if you desire to be a really good leader, you will have to do these things without fanfare or complaint. But remember, as NFL legend George Halas said, "Nobody who ever gave their best ever regretted it."

3. 360-Degree Leaders Work in Obscurity

I think very highly of the importance of leadership. I guess that's obvious for a guy whose motto is "Everything rises and falls on leadership." Occasionally someone will ask me about how ego fits into the leadership equation. They'll want to know what keeps a leader from having a huge ego. I think the answer lies in each leader's pathway to leadership. If people paid their dues and gave their best in obscurity, ego is usually not a problem.

One of my favorite examples of this occurred in the life of Moses in the Old Testament. Though born a Hebrew, he lived a life of privilege in the palace of Egypt until he was forty years old. But after killing an Egyptian, he was exiled to the desert for forty years. There God used him as a shepherd and father, and after four decades of faithful service in obscurity, Moses was called to leadership. Scripture says by that time he was the most humble man in the world. Bill Purvis, the senior pastor of a large church in Columbus, Georgia, said, "If you do what you can, with what you have, where you are, then God won't leave you where you are, and He will increase what you have."

English novelist and poet Emily Bronte said, "If I could I would always work in silence and obscurity, and let my efforts be known by their results." Not everyone wants to be out of the spotlight as she did. But it's important for a leader to learn to work in obscurity because it is a test of personal integrity. The key is being willing to do something because it matters, not because it will get you noticed.

4. 360-Degree Leaders Succeed with Difficult People

People working at the bottom of an organization usually have no choice concerning whom they work with. As a result, they often have to work with difficult people. In contrast, people at the top almost never have to work with difficult people because they get to choose who they work with. If someone they work with becomes difficult, they often let that person go or move him or her out.

For leaders in the middle, the road is different. They have some choice in the matter, but not complete control. They may not be able to get rid of difficult people, but they can often avoid working with them. But good leaders—ones who learn to lead up, across, and down—find a way to succeed with people who are hard to work with. Why do they do it? Because it benefits the organization. How do they do it? They work at finding common ground and connect with them. And instead of putting these difficult people in their place, they try to put themselves in their place.

You don't have the right to put the organization on the line . . . If you are going to take a risk, you need to put yourself on the line.

5. 360-Degree Leaders Put Themselves on the Line

I mentioned previously that if you want to lead up, you must distinguish yourself from your colleagues. How do you do that, especially while paying your dues or working in obscurity? One way is to take a risk. You cannot play it safe and stand out at the same time.

Here's the tricky thing about taking risks in the middle of the organization. You should never be casual about risking what's not yours. I call that "betting with other people's money." You don't have the right to put the organization on the line. Nor would it be right for you to create high risk for others in the organization. If you are going to take a risk, you need to put *yourself* on the line. Play it smart, but don't play it safe.

6. 360-Degree Leaders Admit Faults but Never Make Excuses

It's easier to move from failure to success than from excuses to success. And you will have greater credibility with your leader if you admit your shortcomings and refrain from making excuses. I guarantee that. Of course, that doesn't mean you don't need to produce results. Baseball coach and tutor McDonald Valentine said, "The higher the level you play, the less they accept excuses."

It's easier to move from failure to success than from excuses to success.

The middle of the organization is a good place to discover your identity and work things out. You can discover your leadership strengths there. If you fall short in an area, you can work to overcome your mistakes. If you keep falling short in the same way, you may learn how to overcome an obstacle, or you may discover an area of weakness where you will need to collaborate with others. But no matter what, don't make excuses. Steven Brown, president of the Fortune Group, summed up this issue: "Essentially there are two actions in life: Performance and excuses. Make a decision as to which you will accept from yourself."

7. 360-Degree Leaders Do More than Expected

Expectations are high for people at the top. And, unfortunately, in many organizations the expectations for people at the bottom are low. But expectations are mixed in the middle. So if you do more than is expected of you, you stand out, and often there can be wonderful, serendipitous results.

When Chris Hodges, a senior pastor who is a donor and volunteer trainer with EQUIP, was working as a staff member at a large church in Baton Rouge, his boss, Larry Stockstill, had the opportunity to become the host of a live television show. Chris had no responsibilities related to the show, and was, in fact, rather low in the organization's hierarchy. But he knew that the show was important to Larry, so Chris took it upon himself to go down to the studio to see the first taping. As it turned out, he was the only staff member to do so.

There was great excitement in the studio as the hour of the first broadcast approached. That excitement quickly turned to panic when the guest who was scheduled to appear on the show called in to say he was having a problem getting there. The guest wasn't worried, because he thought they could just start the taping later. What he didn't realize was that the show was scheduled to go on the air live!

In that moment, Larry looked around, saw Chris, and said, "You're going to be my guest today." The crew scrambled, put a microphone on Chris, slapped some makeup on his face, and sat him down in the chair next to Larry. Then to Chris's great shock, when the lights turned on and the cameras started rolling, Larry introduced Chris as his cohost.

Chris ended up being on that show with Larry every week for two and a half years. The experience changed him forever. Not only did it build his relationship with his leader, but it also made him well-known in the community. More importantly, he learned to think on his feet and become a better communicator, skills that serve him well every day of his life. And it all happened because he decided to do more than was expected of him.

8. 360-Degree Leaders Are the First to Step Up and Help

In *25 Ways to Win with People*, I point out that being the first to help others is a great way to make them feel like a million bucks. It lets them know you care. The kind of influence you gain from helping a peer is also gained with your leader when you step up and help others. Haven't you found the following to be true?

- The first person to volunteer is a hero and is given the "10" treatment.
- The second person is considered a helper and viewed as only slightly above average.
- The third person, along with everyone after, is seen as a follower and is ignored.

It doesn't matter whom you're helping, whether it's your boss, a peer, or someone working for you. When you help someone on the team, you help the whole team. And when you help the team, you're helping your leaders. And that gives them reasons to notice and appreciate you.

9. 360-Degree Leaders Perform Tasks That Are "Not Their Job"

Few things are more frustrating for a leader than having someone refuse to do a task because it is "not his job." (In moments like those, most of the top leaders I know are tempted to invite such people to be without a job altogether!) Good leaders don't think in those terms. They understand the Law of the Big Picture from *The 21 Irrefutable Laws of Leadership*: "The goal is more important than the role."

A 360-Degree Leader's goal is to get the job done, to fulfill the vision of the organization and its leader. That often means doing whatever it takes. As a leader "moves up," that more often takes the form of hiring someone to get it done, but leaders in the middle often don't have that option. So instead, they jump in and get it done themselves.

10. 360-Degree Leaders Take Responsibility for Their Responsibilities

I recently saw a cartoon where a dad is reading a book to his little boy at bedtime. The title on the cover of the book says, *The Story of Job*, and the boy has only one question for his father: "Why didn't he sue someone?"

Isn't that the way a lot of people think these days? Their knee-jerk reaction to adversity is to blame someone else. That's not the case with 360-Degree Leaders. They take hold of their responsibilities and follow through with them 100 percent.

Lack of responsibility can be a deal breaker when it comes to the people who work for me. When my employees don't get the job done, certainly I become disappointed. But I'm willing to work with them to help them improve—if they are taking responsibility for themselves. I know they will work at getting better if they take ownership and have teachable spirits. We have no starting point for improvement, however, if they don't get the job done and they fail to take responsibility. In such cases, it's time to move on and find someone else to take their place.

J. C. Penney said, "Unless you are willing to drench yourself in your work beyond the capacity of the average man, you are just not cut out for positions at the top." I'd say that you're not cut out for leadership in the middle either! People who want to be effective are willing to do what others won't. And because of that, their leaders are willing to resource them, promote them, and be influenced by them.

Lead-Up Principle #4

Do More Than Manage—Lead!

People sometimes ask me to explain the difference between management and leadership. Here's my take on it in a nutshell: Managers work with processes—leaders work with people. Both are necessary to make an organization run smoothly, but they have different functions.

To understand what I mean, think about some of the things that must happen on a military ship for it to function properly. The ship must be navigated, fueled, and supplied. It has various weapons systems that must be kept in good working order. The routine maintenance on a ship is endless, and there are dozens of processes related to the personnel onboard the ship.

All of these are processes that must be overseen. There are procedures that must be followed, schedules that must be created, inventories that must be maintained. These things will never happen without people to manage them. And if they are not managed, the ship will never be capable of fulfilling its purpose.

So what is the role of leaders? Leaders lead the people who manage the processes. If all the work in an organization were performed by machines, and the processes were monitored and controlled by computers, that organization wouldn't need any leaders. But *people* do the work and manage the processes, and people don't function like machines. They have feelings. They think. They have problems, hopes, and dreams. Though people can be managed, they would much rather be led. And when they are led, they perform at a much higher level.

I have yet to meet a good leader who wasn't also a good manager. They begin by managing themselves well. Once they do that well, they learn how to manage within their area of expertise. Then they add to that the skills needed to work with and influence others. They learn to understand the dynamics of leadership. As Tom Mullins said, "Leaders must be good managers, but most managers are not necessarily good leaders."

"Leaders must be good managers, but most managers are not necessarily good leaders."
—TOM MULLINS

Leadership is more than management. Leadership is:

- People more than projects
- Movement more than maintenance
- Art more than science
- Intuition more than formula
- Vision more than procedure
- Risk more than caution
- Action more than reaction
- Relationships more than rules
- Who you are more than what you do

If you want to influence others, then you must learn to lead.

MOVING BEYOND MANAGEMENT

If you are already good at doing your work and managing processes, you're on the road toward leadership. But to move beyond management to leadership, you need to broaden your mind-set and begin thinking like a leader. If you are already leading well, then use this as a checklist to see where you need to keep growing.

1. Leaders Think Longer Term

Many people in organizations don't look ahead. They're like the person who said, "My department has a short-range plan and a long-range plan. Our short-range plan is to stay afloat long enough to start working on our long-range plan." But 360-Degree Leaders focus on more than just the task at hand and see more than just the current moment. They look ahead, whether it be a few hours, a few days, or a few years.

By necessity, managers often have to live in the moment. They are working to keep everything running smoothly. Someone once pointed out that managers are people who do things right, while leaders are people who do the right thing. In other words, leaders have a responsibility to make sure the right things are being done so that the organization will thrive tomorrow as well as today.

Most people evaluate events in their lives according to how they will be personally affected. Leaders think within a broader context.

That requires long-term thinking. While good managers may keep the production line working at low cost and peak efficiency, it would be of no value if that production line was still churning out rotary telephones!

2. Leaders See Within the Larger Context

Most people evaluate events in their lives according to how they will be personally affected. Leaders think within a broader context. They start by asking themselves, *How will this impact my people?* But then they also look at how something will impact those above and beside them. They try to see everything in terms of the entire organization and beyond.

Effective leaders know the answers to the following questions:

- How do I fit in my area or department?
- How do all the departments fit into the organization?
- Where does our organization fit in the market?
- How is our market related to other industries and the economy?

And as industries in our economy become more global, many good leaders are thinking even more broadly!

You don't have to become a global economist to lead effectively from the middle of your organization. The point is that 360-Degree Leaders see their area as part of the larger process and understand how the pieces of the larger puzzle fit together. If you desire to be a better leader, then broaden your thinking and work at seeing things from a larger perspective.

3. Leaders Push Boundaries

People are trained to follow rules from the time they are kids: *Stand in line. Do your homework. Put your hand up to ask a question.* Most rules are good because they keep us from living in chaos. And most processes are governed by rules. You drop a brick from a second-story window, and you know it's going to fall to the ground. You forget to place the order for office supplies, and you run out of staples. It's simple cause and effect.

Managers often rely on rules to make sure the processes they oversee stay on track. In fact, self-management, which I discussed in Principle #1 of this section, is basically having the discipline to follow through with the rules you set for yourself. But to move beyond management, you have to learn to think outside the box.

Leaders push boundaries. They desire to find a better way. They want to make improvements. They like to see progress. All these things mean making changes, retiring old rules, inventing new procedures. Leaders are constantly asking, "Why do we do it this way?" and saying,

"Let's try this." Leaders want to take new territory, and that means crossing boundaries.

4. Leaders Put the Emphasis on Intangibles

The things that people can manage are usually tangible and measurable. They provide concrete evidence. You can logically evaluate them before making decisions.

Leadership is really a game of intangibles. What could be more intangible than influence? Leaders deal with things like morale, motivation, momentum, emotions, attitudes, atmosphere, and timing. How do you measure timing before you do something? How do you put your finger on momentum? It's all very intuitive. To gauge such things, you have to read between the lines. Leaders have to become comfortable—more than that, confident—dealing with such things.

Many times the problems leaders face in organizations are not the real problems. For example, let's say a department is $100,000 over budget at the end of the quarter. Their problem isn't a money problem. The deficit is only evidence of the problem. The real problem may be the morale of the sales force, or the timing of a product launch, or the attitude of the department's leader. A leader needs to learn to focus on such things.

I love the way retired army general Tommy Franks has disciplined himself to look at intangibles and get ready for them. Every day of his career since February 23, 1988, he has approached his work by looking ahead for the day. In the morning, he places a blank three-by-five card near his calendar and writes on one side of it the date and the words "The biggest challenges I may face today." Beneath it he writes the five most important problems he might face. On the back of the card, he writes, "Opportunities that may appear today," and lists those.

Franks said, "Every morning since that Thursday in February 1988, I noted the 'Challenges and Opportunities' that might occur on that day. More than five thousand cards later, I still do. The card itself isn't important; preparing myself for each day definitely is."[1]

5. Leaders Learn to Rely on Intuition

How do leaders learn to work with intangibles? They learn to rely on their intuition. I love what psychologist Joyce Brothers said, "Trust your hunches. They're usually based on facts filed away just below the conscious level." The more you focus your attention on intangibles instead of tangibles, on principles instead of practices, the more information you will be filing away for future use, and the sharper your intuition will become. Intuition alone may not be enough to go on, but you should never ignore your intuition.

> *"Trust your hunches. They're usually based on facts filed away just below the conscious level."*
>
> —Joyce Brothers

Business professor, consultant, and leadership guru Warren Bennis said, "A part of whole-brain thinking includes learning to trust what Emerson called the 'blessed impulse,' the hunch, the vision that shows you in a flash the absolutely right thing to do. Everyone has these visions; leaders learn to trust them."

6. Leaders Invest Power in Others

Management is often about control. Managers have to control costs, control quality, control efficiency. That's one reason why some good managers have a difficult time making the paradigm shift to leadership. Leading isn't about controlling; it's about releasing.

Good leaders give their power away. They look for good people, and they invest in them to the point where they can be released and empowered to perform. That process is not smooth. It is often messy, and it cannot be controlled. The better the leaders, the more delighted they are to see members of the team finding their own new ways to get things done. And in the case of the best leaders . . . if some of the people outshine the leaders who empowered them, then all the better.

7. Leaders See Themselves as Agents of Change

Psychologist and author Charles Garfield said:

> Peak performers . . . do not see accomplishments as a fixed state, nor as a safe haven in which the individual is moored, completed, finished. Not once have I heard a peak performer speak of an end to challenge, excitement, curiosity, and wonder. Quite the contrary. One of the most engaging characteristics is an infectious talent for moving into the future; generating new challenges, living with a sense of "more work to be done."[2]

The same things can be said of leaders. They don't want things to stay the same. They desire innovation. They love new challenges. They want more than just seeing progress—they want to help make it happen.

Leadership is a moving target, and it always will be. If you desire to become a better leader, get comfortable with change. And if you want to lead up, learn to think like a leader. Think people, think progress, and think intangibles.

Lead-Up Principle #5

Invest in Relational Chemistry

All good leadership is based on relationships. People won't *go* along with you if they can't *get* along with you. That's true whether you are leading up, across, or down. The key to developing chemistry with your leaders is to develop relationships with them. If you can learn to adapt to your boss's personality while still being yourself and maintaining your integrity, you will be able to lead up.

I often teach leaders that it is their job to connect with the people they lead. In an ideal world, that's the way it should be. The reality is that some leaders do little to connect with the people they lead. As a 360-Degree Leader, you must take it upon yourself to connect not only with the people you lead, but also with the person who leads you. If you want to *lead up*, you must take the responsibility to *connect up*. Here's how to get started.

People won't go along with you if they can't get along with you.

1. Listen to Your Leader's Heartbeat

Just as a doctor listens to someone's heartbeat to know that person's physical condition, you need to listen to your leader's heartbeat to understand what makes him or her tick. That may mean paying attention in informal settings, such as during hallway conversations, at lunch, or in the meeting that often occurs informally before or after a meeting. If you know your leader well and feel the relationship is solid, you may want to be more direct and ask questions about what really matters to him or her on an emotional level.

If you're not sure what to look for, focus on these three areas:

- What makes them laugh? These are the things that give a person great joy.
- What makes them cry? This is what touches a person's heart at a deep emotional level.
- What makes them sing? These are the things that bring deep fulfillment.

All people have dreams, issues, or causes that connect with them. Those things are like the keys to their lives. Think about it from your own point of view for a moment. Are you aware of the things that touch you on a deep emotional level? What are the signs that they "connect" for you? Do you see those signs in your leader? Look for them, and you will likely find them.

Many leaders are very wary about letting the people who work for them see the keys to their heart because they feel it makes them vulnerable. So don't approach it casually, and never treat the subject flippantly. To do so would be a violation of trust. And never try to "turn the key" manipulatively for personal gain.

2. Know Your Leader's Priorities

The heartbeat of leaders is what they *love* to do. The priorities of leaders are what they *have* to do—and by that I mean more than just their to-do lists. All leaders have duties that they must complete or they will fail in fulfilling their responsibility. It's the short list that your boss's boss would say is do-or-die for that position. Make it your goal to learn what those priorities are. The better acquainted you are with those duties or objectives, the better you will understand and communicate with your leader.

3. Catch Your Leader's Enthusiasm

It's much easier to work with someone when you share an enthusiasm. When you and a friend are excited about something, such as a common hobby, don't you often lose track of time when you're engaged in it? You can spend hours talking about it and never grow tired. If you can catch your leader's enthusiasm, it will have a similarly energizing effect. And it will create a bond between you and your leader. If you can share in that enthusiasm, you will pass it on because you will not be able to contain it.

4. Support Your Leader's Vision

When top leaders hear others articulate the vision they have cast for the organization, their hearts sing. It's very rewarding. It represents a kind of tipping point, to use the words of author Malcolm Gladwell. It indicates a level of ownership by others in the organization that bodes well for the fulfillment of the vision.

Each time another person in the organization embraces the vision and passes it on, it's like giving the vision "fresh legs."

Leaders in the middle of the organization who are champions for the vision become elevated in the estimation of a top leader. They get it. They're on board. And they have great value. Each time another person in the organization embraces the vision and passes it on, it's like giving the vision "fresh legs." In other words, when the vision gets handed off, the next person is able to run with it.

You should never underestimate the power of a verbal endorsement of the vision by a person with influence. The same kind of power can be seen in the business world. For example, I've observed that with most books, the sales that occur during the first six months are due to the marketing, distribution, and promotion done by the publisher (and sometimes the author). After that, the sales are almost entirely a result of word of mouth. If people like the book, they talk about it with others. They are, in essence, passing on the vision of the author and testifying to the value of the book.

As a leader in the middle, if you are unsure about the vision of your leader, then talk to him. Ask questions. Once you think you understand it, quote it back to your leader in situations where it's appropriate to make sure you're in alignment. If you've got it right, you will be able to see it in your leader's face. Then start passing it on to the people in your sphere of influence. It will be good for the organization, your people, your leader, and you. Promote your leader's dreams, and he will promote you.

Promote your leader's dreams, and he will promote you.

5. Connect with Your Leader's Interests

One of the keys to building relational chemistry is knowing and connecting with the interests of your leader. Have you identified the pet projects that your leader really cares about at work? If so, that's good, but how about her interests outside of work? Can you name them?

It's important to know enough about your leader to be able to relate to him as an individual beyond the job. If your boss is a golfer, you may want to take up the game—or at least learn some things about it. If he collects rare books or porcelain, then spend some time on the Internet finding out about those hobbies. If she builds fine furniture on the weekends, then subscribe to a woodworking magazine. You don't have to take up the hobby yourself or become an expert. Just learn enough to relate to your boss and talk intelligently about the subject.

Leaders sometimes feel isolated and find themselves wondering, *Does anyone else understand?* Though you may not be able to understand your leader's work situation, you can at least understand him or her on some level. When leaders feeling isolated experience a genuine connection with someone "under" them, they often find it very rewarding. And if you feel isolated in the middle, that connection just might be rewarding for you too.

6. Understand Your Leader's Personality

Two staff members were discussing the president of their company, and one of them said, "You know, you can't help liking the guy."

To which the other replied, "Yeah, if you don't, he fires you."

Leaders are used to having others accommodate their personalities. As you lead down from the middle of the organization, don't you expect others to conform to your personality? I don't mean that in an unreasonable or spiteful way—not that you would fire someone who didn't like you, as in the joke. If you are simply being yourself, you expect the people who work *for* you to work *with* you. But when you are trying to lead up, you are the one who must conform to your leader's personality. It's a rare great leader who conforms down to the people who work for him.

It's wise to understand your leader's style and how your personality type interacts with his. If you study some of the materials designed to reveal personality, such as DISC, Myers-Briggs, and Littuaer's Personality Plus, you will gain greater insight into the way your leader thinks and works. Most of the time, personality opposites get along well as long as their values and goals are similar. Cholerics work well with phlegmatics; sanguines and melancholics appreciate each other's strengths. Trouble can come when people with like personality types come together. If you find that your personality is similar to your boss's, then remember that you're the one who has to be flexible. That can be a challenge if yours is not a flexible personality type!

7. Earn Your Leader's Trust

When you take time to invest in relational chemistry with your leader, the eventual result will be trust—in other words, relational currency. For years I've taught the concept of relational "change in your pocket." When you do things that add to the relationship, you increase the change in your pocket. When you do negative things, you spend that change. If you keep dropping the ball—professionally or personally—you harm the relationship, and you can eventually spend all the change and bankrupt the relationship.

People with a lot of history who have invested in relational chemistry build up a lot of change. As a result, the relationship can weather many problems or mistakes. For example, Doug Carter, the vice president of EQUIP, is constantly directing me to potential donors for the organization. Doug and I have a lot of relational chemistry. I've known him for a long time, we have worked together for years, and he is an absolute all-star at his job. When he is occasionally mistaken in his assessment of people and asks me to spend a lot of time with someone who is ultimately uninterested in EQUIP, it doesn't harm our relationship; Doug has a tremendous amount of relational currency "in the bank" with me.

"Loyalty publicly results in leverage privately."
—Andy Stanley

Andy Stanley, who is a fantastic 360-Degree Leader, said, "Loyalty publicly results in leverage privately." If you earn your leader's trust over time by giving him public support, then you will gain change with him privately. And you will have opportunities to lead up.

8. Learn to Work with Your Leader's Weaknesses

Sales expert and author Les Giblin said, "You can't make the other fellow feel important in your presence if you secretly feel that he is a nobody." Likewise, you can't build a positive relationship with your boss if you secretly disrespect him because of his weaknesses. Since everybody has blind spots and weak areas, why not learn to work with them? Try to focus on the positives, and work around the negatives. To do anything else will only hurt you.

9. Respect Your Leader's Family

I'm almost reluctant to introduce the concept of family in the context of leading up with someone at work, but I think it bears mentioning. If you do all of the other things I have recommended, but your boss's spouse doesn't like or trust you, the relationship between the two of you will always be strained. You, of course, have no real control over this. The best you can do is to be kind and respectful to your boss's family members and try to connect with them in an appropriate way. Just be aware that if you sense key members of your boss's family don't like you, even though it may be through no fault of your own, it may lessen your influence and maybe even hinder your career.

The thesis of *Winning with People* is that people can usually trace their successes and failures to the relationships in their lives. The same is true when it comes to leadership. The quality of the relationship you have with your leader will impact your success or failure. It is certainly worth investing in.

Lead-Up Principle #6

Be Prepared Every Time You Take Your Leader's Time

As I write this chapter, on my desk is a recent issue of *Time* magazine with an article about Bill Gates and the Xbox 360 gaming system that Microsoft has been working on. I'm not a video-game player, so that doesn't hold much personal interest for me. The opening sentences of the article about Gates caught my attention, however, because they highlighted the importance of a leader's time.

> Bill Gates' time is valuable. There are Microsoft employees who wait their whole career to be alone with Gates for 45 minutes. As the richest man in the world and, arguably, the greatest philanthropist in history, at any given moment Gates could and probably should be off feeding the hungry or curing some horrible disease.[1]

Every leader values time. British essayist William Hazlitt wrote, "As we advance in life, we acquire a keener sense of the value of time. Nothing else, indeed, seems of any consequence; and we become misers in this respect." But what makes the time of Gates, a fairly young man, valuable is that he is a leader who could be using his time to do things that can change the lives of thousands of people.

For all leaders, time is precious. Time is the one commodity that cannot be increased, no matter what a leader does. And it is the necessary component for the leader to do anything. For that reason, you must always be prepared when you take any of your leader's time. Though you may have latitude in how you spend your employees' or peers' time, when dealing with those above you, the amount of time you can spend is limited. If you desire to lead up, you need to act accordingly.

Hopefully, you won't have to wait an entire career to have a few minutes of your leader's time, as some people apparently must at Microsoft. But whether you have unlimited access to your boss or you only get a few minutes on rare occasions, you need to follow the same guidelines.

1. Invest 10X

You show your value when you show that you value your leader's time. The best way to do that is to spend ten minutes preparing for every minute that you expect to meet. Management author Charles C. Gibbons confirmed this when he advised, "One of the best ways to save time is to think and plan ahead; five minutes of thinking can often save an hour of work."

In *Today Matters*, I wrote about the lunch I had with John Wooden, legendary former coach of the UCLA Bruins basketball team. Before I went, I spent hours preparing.

> *"One of the best ways to save time is to think and plan ahead; five minutes of thinking can often save an hour of work."*

Let me say one more thing about preparing before taking your leader's time. Most top leaders are good decision makers. (If they're not, they rarely get the opportunity to lead from the top of the organization.) But many of the times they are unable to make decisions, it is because they don't have enough information. I know that's true with me. When my assistant cannot get a quick answer from me on an issue, it's usually because she hasn't done enough homework on the front end. That's not to say that it happens very often.

Linda is awesome, and 99 percent of the time she doesn't even ask me a question until she's put in the groundwork. She easily invests ten times, putting in ten minutes of preparation for every minute of my time.

The less relational connection you have with your leaders, the more time you ought to put in on the front end preparing. The less your leaders know about you, the smaller the window of time you have to prove yourself. But if you prepare well, chances are you will get other opportunities. British prime minister Benjamin Disraeli said, "The secret of success in life is for a man to be ready for his time when it comes."

2. Don't Make Your Boss Think for You

Not all bosses make themselves inaccessible. As a leader, you may have an open-door policy that makes it easy for the people you lead to come to you when they need to ask questions. But have you ever had an employee who seemed to ask questions constantly without ever taking the time to think for himself? It can be very frustrating, can't it?

In a question-and-answer session, Jack Welch talked about how important it is for someone starting out to be a good thinker. He said it's one of the things that distinguishes a person from the rest of the people on the same level.

Leaders in the middle should ask questions of their bosses only when they cannot answer those questions. Here's how leaders at the top think when they receive questions from leaders in the middle:

- *If they ask questions because they can't think, then we're in trouble.*
- *If they ask questions because they're lazy, then they are in trouble.*
- *If they ask questions so that everyone can move faster, then we're headed for success.*

While bad questions have a negative impact, good questions actually do several positive things: They clarify objectives; they speed up the process of completion; and they stimulate good thinking. All of these things will benefit the organization and help you stand out in a positive way with your leader.

3. Bring Something to the Table

For years I have used the expression "bring something to the table" to describe a person's ability to contribute to a conversation or to add value to others at a meeting. Not everyone does that. In life, some people always want to be the "guest." Wherever they go, they are there to be served, to have their needs met, to be the recipient. Because they possess that attitude, they never bring anything to the table for anyone else. After a while, that can really wear out the person who is always playing host.

People who become 360-Degree Leaders don't work that way. They have a totally different mind-set. They are constantly looking for ways to bring something to the table for their leaders, their peers, and their employees—whether it's resources, ideas, or opportunities. They recognize the wisdom found in the proverb: "A gift opens the way for the giver and ushers him into the presence of the great."[2]

As the leader of an organization, I am always looking for people who bring something to the table in the area of ideas. If they can be creative and generate ideas, that's great. But I also highly value people who are constructive, who take an idea that someone puts on the table and make it better. Often the difference between a good idea and a great idea is the value added to it during the collaborative thinking process.

Some leaders aren't very tactful when it comes to letting others know that they are not adding value to them in the way they would desire. Several years ago I toured Hearst Castle, the home of media magnate William Randolph Hearst in San Simeon, California. Hearst was well-known for the celebrity guests he invited to his estate. But once he became bored with a guest, he let him know it was time for him to go. The guests who were being asked to leave would find a note in their room at bedtime saying that it had been nice to have them as a visitor.

If you always try to bring something of value to the table when you meet with your boss, you may be able to avoid a similar fate at work. If you don't, at the end of the day you just may get a note from the boss. Only yours will be a pink slip.

4. When Asked to Speak, Don't Wing It

I admire people who can think on their feet and handle tough situations, but I have little respect for people who don't prepare. I've found that the first time a person wings it, people usually cannot tell, but by the third or fourth meeting when a person talks without thinking, everybody knows it. Why? Because it all starts to sound the same. If people have little professional depth, they use everything they know as they wing it. The next time they try it, you hear the same kinds of things you heard the last time. After a while, they lose all credibility.

Former world championship boxer Joe Frazier said, "You can map out a fight plan or a life plan. But when the action starts, you're down to your reflexes. That's where your roadwork shows. If you cheated on that in the dark of the morning, you're getting found out now under the bright lights."[3] If you don't put in the work, you always eventually get found out.

5. Learn to Speak Your Boss's Language

When Charlie Wetzel, my writer, and I first started working together back in 1994, I spent a good deal of time working with him to help him understand how I think and learn how I speak. Charlie already had his master's degree in English and was a good writer, but he wasn't yet on my wavelength. The first thing I did was get him recordings of the first one hundred lessons on leadership I taught so that he got a better feel for my communication.

Next, I took him on the road with me when I was speaking. After a presentation when we were on the plane or at dinner, I would ask him to identify what parts of the session connected with the audience and where he thought the high points were. We would discuss it so that I could sense whether he was getting it. I would also occasionally pass along a bunch of quotes and illustrations to him and ask him to mark what he thought were the good ones. Then we would compare notes.

All of the things I did with Charlie were to help him learn to speak my language. That was critical if he was to write for me, but it's also important for any employee, and especially important for 360-Degree Leaders in the middle of an organization. Learning their boss's language will help them not only to communicate with their boss, but also to communicate with others on behalf of their boss. The goal isn't to become a yes man, but to be able to connect.

6. Get to the Bottom Line

Playwright Victor Hugo said, "Short as life is, we make it still shorter by the careless waste of time." I haven't met a good leader yet who didn't want to get quickly to the bottom line. Why? Because they want results. Their motto is, "Never mind about the delivery; just show me the baby."

When you first begin working with a leader, you may need to spend some time giving insight into the process by which you came to a decision. Early on in the relationship, you have to earn your credibility. But as time goes by and the relationship builds, just get to the point. Just because you possess all the data needed to explain what you're doing doesn't mean you need to share it. If your leader wants more detail or wants to know about the process you used, she can ask you for it.

7. Give a Return on Your Leader's Investment

When you are continually prepared every time you take your leader's time, there is a good chance that he will begin to see the time he spends with you as an investment. And nothing is as rewarding to leaders who invest in others as seeing a positive return on what they give.

One mid-level leader I interviewed said that every year he writes a list of everything his leader taught him the previous year and gives that list to him. He explained, "[It's] to document my appreciation and let him know his input was valuable and resulting in growth. I have learned that when I am open about my growth and learning, people are willing to invest more into my growth and learning."

I mentor about half a dozen people drawing on my thirty-plus years of leadership experience. One of the people I love spending time with is Courtney McBath, pastor of a church in Norfolk, Virginia. Every time I meet with him, in one way or another he says:

> Here's what you said the last time we met.
> Here's what I learned.
> Here's what I did.
> Did I do it right?
> Can I ask you more questions?

How can a leader not love that?

Recently I received the following e-mail from Courtney:

> Dr. Maxwell,
>
> You've often commented that the greatest joy of a leader/teacher is seeing their students utilizing what they've learned. Last night I had the honor of speaking in a large, orthodox Jewish synagogue for their Sabbath celebration. I was the first African-American Christian man to ever do so and it was a tremendous experience and success. An older Jewish couple told me they wished I could go to their seminaries and teach their young rabbis how to communicate!
>
> Your investment in me has taught me so much about how to cross

cultural, religious, and social boundaries and communicate truth to all people. God was glorified last night and you were a significant part of it all. Thank you for being my leader and friend.

I love you dearly, and I'm not just a better leader, I'm a better man because of you.

Thanks,
Courtney

Not only is Courtney always prepared every time he takes my time, but he also takes the counsel I give him and runs with it! What a delight he is to spend time with. And let me tell you something. Because he is so good, when he speaks, I listen. He is leading up, and ours is a relationship where we add value to each other, and that's what 360-Degree Leadership is really all about.

Lead-Up Principle #7

Know When to Push and When to Back Off

Make hay when the sun shines—that's smart;
Go fishing during the harvest—that's stupid.

—Proverbs 10:5, The Message

In February of 2005, I visited Kiev, Ukraine, to conduct a leadership seminar, visit and teach at Europe's largest church, and launch the Million Leaders Mandate for EQUIP in that country. One of the exciting things I got to do while I was there was walk down the main street just a few blocks from our hotel to the city's Independence Square, site of the Orange Revolution that had occurred just three months before we visited.

As we walked down the wide boulevard, which was closed to vehicular traffic that afternoon, our guide, Tatiana, told us about how the people reacted to the news of the bogus election results that were threatening to keep the government-supported candidate, Viktor Yanukovych, in power. Common people began flooding the downtown area, and they staged peaceful protests in the square. They created a tent city right on the boulevard where we were walking, and they refused to leave until the government relented and ordered a new and fair election.

Later in our visit, I talked to Steve Weber, EQUIP's country coordinator for Ukraine, about the extraordinary events that occurred in Kiev and led to the election of reformer Viktor Yushchenko as the nation's president. In years past, such a demonstration would have been crushed, and that could have been the case in this instance, were it not for the behavior of the common people of Ukraine. Following is Steve's summary of the events.

> The Orange Revolution was an incredible moment in the history of the Ukrainian people. The masses gathered, not knowing for sure what they would encounter in the city's center . . . Momentum built as multitudes of people came out to not only see but also to participate in the protest. The student organizations held their ground and hundreds decided to pitch tents till the truth was acknowledged. So in the freezing weather, the true heart of Ukraine came alive . . .
>
> The kindness and goodwill expressed during the revolution was fresh and something never previously experienced by most Ukrainians. Normal citizens pouring out their practical support for the protesters was unprecedented. Water, food, hot drinks, winter boots, coats, and much more were flooding the city center. This attitude was almost unheard of in the past. "Give to others? Why? I have needs too" has been the norm—but on that square a better nation was being reborn in the hearts of the people. Even people who came from other cities to support the government-backed candidate couldn't stand against the momentum of the revolution. Upon arrival, they were met with friendliness and generosity from their countrymen that they hadn't expected. Could this really be their Ukraine? Would it be possible to live in a country where all people are valued, respected? . . . People were simply believing, hoping, and longing for a better country.
>
> The government-supported candidate was heavily endorsed by the current regime, and their intimidations backfired . . . The nation woke up and said, "Enough! We don't want to live in that kind of country any longer," and their cries were heard.

> The consciousness of the nation stirred and the people voted for change . . . The true Ukrainian soul was lifted out of the mire of corruption to a place of dignity and freedom, and the country looks to the future with reclaimed hope.

The common people of Ukraine—those at the bottom of society—led up and took their entire nation with them. And they chose a unique time in history to do it, a time when they could push because of the advances in modern communication. Steve told me, "At the beginning, the national television stations refused to even acknowledge the mass protest going on. But soon they could ignore it no longer, for news was getting around their false ploys. They didn't consider the new day of technology and communication."

The Ukrainian people influenced each other, the government that was attempting to manipulate them and the political process, and even the opposition leader, Victor Yushchenko. After the new elections were over, during his victory speech, Yushchenko wisely acknowledged the leadership of the people and actually bowed to them in respect and thanks.

When Should I Push Forward?

Timing is critically important to leadership. If the people of Ukraine had not recognized that it was time to push for honest elections, they would probably still be living under the same corrupt government led by Yanukovych. And if they had tried to push free elections thirty years ago while under communist rule, they likely would have been crushed. To be successful, you have to know when to push and when to back off.

When it comes to gaining influence with your boss, timing is equally important. Poet Ralph Waldo Emerson said, "There are but ten minutes in the life of a pear when it is perfect to eat." It's wise to wait for the right moment to speak up. A great idea at the wrong time will be received just the same as a bad idea. Of course, there are times when you must speak up, even if the timing doesn't seem ideal. The trick is knowing which is which.

Here are four questions you can ask to help determine if it is time to push:

1. Do I Know Something My Boss Doesn't but Needs To?

Every leader in the middle of an organization knows things that the boss doesn't. Not only is that normal, but it's also good. There are times when you may know something your boss doesn't, but you need to communicate it to her because it can hurt the organization or her.

> *"There are but ten minutes in the life of a pear when it is perfect to eat."*
> —RALPH WALDO EMERSON

My brother Larry, who is an excellent leader and very successful businessman, tells his staff that he needs to be informed in two kinds of situations: when there is a great problem or when there is a great opportunity. He wants to know about great problems because of their potential to negatively impact the organization. And he wants to know about the great opportunities for a similar reason—they can also impact the organization, but in a positive direction. Either way, he wants to be involved in how the organization and its leaders will address those situations.

How do you know whether you need to bring something to your boss? I know of only two ways to go about figuring that out. You can ask specific questions up front, requesting that your leader spell out when you should bring him in, as Larry has done. Or you can play it by ear and find out by trial and error, using your best judgment and continuing to communicate until the issues are identified.

2. Is Time Running Out?

There's an old saying, "Better one word in time than two afterward." If that was true in ages past, it is even more applicable today in our fast-paced society where information and markets move so quickly.

Constantine Nicandros, president of Conoco, said, "The competitive marketplace is strewn with good ideas whose time came and went because inadequate attention was given to moving rapidly and hitting an open window of opportunity. The same marketplace is strewn with broken glass of windows of opportunities hit after they were slammed shut."

If waiting will make it impossible for your organization to seize an opportunity, take a risk and push forward. Your leader can always choose not to take your advice, but no leader wants to hear, "You know, I thought that might happen" after it's too late. Give your leader the chance to decide.

3. Are My Responsibilities at Risk?

When your leader entrusts you with tasks, you have a responsibility to follow through and get them done. If you are having difficulty with that, most leaders I know would rather know about it and have an opportunity to help you accomplish them than see you work all by yourself but fail.

This is an issue I've had to work on with Charlie Wetzel. Most of the time Charlie is an all-star. In eleven years of working together, we've completed more than thirty books. One of Charlie's weaknesses is that he is slow to ask for help. If he's facing a problem as he's writing, he'll work too long trying to solve it himself instead of picking up the phone and asking me to lend him a hand. His intentions are good; he wants to lighten my load. And he has a very strong sense of responsibility. (It's one of his strengths according to the self-assessment created by the Gallup Organization.) But that sense of responsibility can also work against him. I don't want him to be perfect; I want us to be effective.

4. Can I Help My Boss Win?

Successful leaders make the right move at the right moment with the right motive. There will be times when you recognize opportunities for your leader to win that she doesn't see. When that is the case, it's time to push forward. How do you know what your boss considers a win? Go back to what you learned when you discovered your leader's heartbeat and priorities. If you see a way for her to accomplish something related to one of those, you can be sure she will consider it a win.

When Should I Back Off?

Knowing when to push is important, since you want to initiate to create wins or avoid losses. Possibly more important is knowing when to back off. Leaders may not always be aware of a missed opportunity because you failed to push, but they will definitely notice if you ought to back off but don't. If you push your boss inappropriately too often, your boss might push you right out the door.

Successful leaders make the right move at the right moment with the right motive.

If you're not sure whether it's time to back off, ask these six questions:

1. Am I Promoting My Own Personal Agenda?

From the perspective of leaders at the top, organizations have two kinds of leaders in the middle: those who ask, "What can you do for me?" and those who ask, "What can I do for you?" The first are trying to ride their leaders—and any colleagues or employees they find useful—to the top. The second are trying to carry their organization—along with its leaders and others they can help—to the top.

Just as there are sometimes selfish leaders at the top of an organization, which I described in the Frustration Challenge, there are also selfish leaders in the middle. They see everything in light of their personal agenda instead of their professional responsibilities.

In contrast, 360-Degree Leaders back off if they realize that they are beginning to promote their own agenda instead of what's good for the organization. Not only that, but they are willing to sacrifice their own resources for the greater good of the organization when necessary.

2. Have I Already Made My Point?

Investment expert Warren Buffet said, "Sometimes it's not how hard you row the boat. It's how fast the stream is going." Whenever you're dealing with your leader, you need to pay attention to the flow of the stream.

It is very important to learn to communicate your point of view clearly to your leader. It is your responsibility to communicate what you know and give your perspective on an issue. But it's one thing to communicate and another to coerce your leader. The choice your leader makes is not your responsibility. Besides, if you have made your point clearly, you are unlikely to help your cause by continuing to hammer away at it with your leader. President Dwight D. Eisenhower said, "You do not lead by hitting people over the head—that's assault, not leadership." If you keep repeating yourself after your point's been made, you're just trying to get your own way.

"Sometimes it's not how hard you row the boat. It's how fast the stream is going."
—WARREN BUFFET

David Branker, the executive director of a large organization, said that he had a hard time learning the lesson of when to back off, but it paid dividends in his leadership. He said:

> Learning to back off once you've made your point can make the most foolish person appear wise. When I was a rookie leader I had a tough time learning this. My boss at the time became more and more infuriated [with me when I didn't back off] especially when she disagreed with my point of view and could not understand why I wasn't dropping the issue. I was helped in this issue by a gracious colleague who was much more seasoned in leadership at the time. He said, "I will cue you when you need to drop an issue by simply looking down." Thanks to him and his creative idea, I learned to read when an issue needed to be dropped for a more opportune time.

The next time you are in a meeting with your boss, pay attention to the way you handle the presentation of your point of view. Do you state it clearly as a contribution to the discussion? Or do you hammer away at it to try to "win"? Trying to win your point at all costs with your boss can be like trying to do the same with your spouse. Even if you win, you lose.

3. Must Everyone but Me Take the Risk?

As I've already mentioned, it's easier to risk someone else's resources than your own. And if you keep pushing when you don't share in the risk, you will inevitably alienate the people who must shoulder the risk. People don't want to enter a partnership with someone when they have all the risk and their partner has none.

People don't want to enter a partnership with someone when they have all the risk and their partner has none.

Leaders in the middle who distinguish themselves usually do so because they have "skin in the game." If they are willing to risk their resources, opportunities, and success, then they win the respect of their leaders.

4. Does the Atmosphere Say "No"?

Kathie Wheat, a former employee who worked for Walt Disney World right out of college, said that Disney employees are trained to be sensitive to the emotional atmosphere and dynamics of the guests in their parks. One of the things they teach employees is to never approach a family that is arguing. That makes good sense.

Effective 360-Degree Leaders are like weather forecasters. They are able to read the atmosphere of their workplaces—and especially of their bosses. Take a look at this "weather chart" for leaders in the middle of an organization.

Forecast	Outlook	Action
Sunny	Visibility is clear and the sun is shining	Move forward
Foggy	No way to read weather conditions	Wait for the fog to lift
Partly cloudy	Sunny one minute, cloudy the next	Wait for the right moment
Rainy	Steady rain but no thunder or lightning	Move only in an emergency
Thunderstorms	Lightning could strike anywhere	Wait for the storm to pass
Hurricane	Gale force winds, damage is unavoidable	Run for cover

Obviously I'm having a little fun with this, but it really is important that you read what's going on around you and pay attention to your boss's mood. Don't let a great idea get rained on because you picked the wrong day to introduce it.

5. Is the Timing Right Only for Me?

Emperor Hadrian said, "To be right too soon is to be wrong." Let's face it. Leaders in the middle can be in a tough spot when it comes to timing. People at the top often get to choose the timing for what they do. It may not be as simple as saying, "Let's go," because they do have to prepare the people to move. But they get to decide when the timing is right. On the other hand, people at the bottom have little choice concerning when to go. They either keep up or get left behind.

Effective 360-Degree Leaders are like weather forecasters. They are able to read the atmosphere of their workplaces.

When Titus was emperor of Rome, he had the coins of the empire struck with the image of a dolphin curled around an anchor. At the time, the dolphin was considered the swiftest and most playful of marine animals. The anchor represented steadiness and unchanging conviction. Together they symbolized the balance between initiative and wisdom, progress and caution. A family crest years later used the same symbol with the motto *festina lente*, meaning "hasten slowly."

That's what 360-Degree Leaders must do. They must hasten slowly. If the timing is right for everyone, then move forward. But if it is right only for them, they should back off and move more slowly.

6. Does My Request Exceed Our Relationship?

One of my favorite stories from the Old Testament is the story of Esther. It's a tremendous lesson in leadership. When Xerxes was ruler of Persia, one day he summoned his queen, Vashti, but she refused to come, which was unthinkable in those times. As a result, Xerxes stripped her of her position and prohibited her from ever seeing him again. Meanwhile, he sought to find someone else to take her place, and after a long and elaborate process, Esther, a Hebrew, became his queen.

All was well until a member of Xerxes' court convinced the ruler to let him have all the Jews in the kingdom executed. Esther faced a dilemma. Though her life probably would have been spared, could she stand by and watch her fellow Hebrews die? If she approached Xerxes to ask him to spare her countrymen when he didn't wish to see her, he could order her to be executed. Her relationship with Xerxes was tenuous, and she knew it. If her request exceeded that relationship, she was doomed.

In the end, with faith and courage, Esther approached the king, her request was granted, and the Jews were spared. It was a great challenge for this leader in the middle, but she was successful in leading up.

Leaders in the middle of an organization don't have a lot of authority, and they don't hold a lot of cards. Often their only "ace" is the relationship they have with the leaders above them. They must play that ace carefully. If they push and their request exceeds the relationship, they are asking for their ace to be trumped.

You can tell a lot about the character and motives of people in the middle of an organization by watching when they push and when they back off. My wife, Margaret, and I enjoy visiting presidential libraries. Recently, while visiting the George H. W. Bush museum, we read a story about the actions of Vice President George H. W. Bush the day President Ronald Reagan was shot in 1981. Bush said that when he got the news, the enormity of the incident came upon him, and right then he prayed for the president.

Since Reagan was in surgery, Bush was really the acting executive of the country, but he deliberately backed off to make sure that he didn't appear to challenge or displace the president. For example, when Bush went to the White House, he refused to land on the south lawn, because by tradition only the president lands there. And at seven o'clock that night when Bush presided over an emergency cabinet meeting, he sat in his normal seat, not in the president's.

Reagan, of course, recovered and resumed his duties, and also went on to be reelected as president in 1984. Bush was content to stay in the background, serving his leader and his country—until the time was right and the American people elected him their leader.

Lead-Up Principle #8

Become a Go-To Player

If you found yourself in a situation at work where you were on a deadline and trying to finish a project that was critical for the success of the organization, and then suddenly, with almost no time left, you were handed another critical task that had to be completed at the same time, what would you do? In this case, let's assume that delaying the deadline beyond today was not a possibility. It's do or die. How do you respond? If you're like most good leaders, you hand one of the tasks to a go-to player.

The Law of the Catalyst in *The 17 Indisputable Laws of Teamwork* states that winning teams have players who make things happen. That's always true—whether in sports, business, government, or some other arena. Those team members who can make things happen are their go-to players. They demonstrate consistent competence, responsibility, and dependability.

If that is what you do in a crunch—or would do if you trusted one of your players to consistently deliver—then why would *your* leaders do any differently? They wouldn't. All leaders are looking for people who can step up and make a difference when it matters. When they find such people, they come to rely on them and are inevitably influenced by them.

GO-TO PLAYERS PRODUCE WHEN . . .

Few things elevate a person above his peers the way becoming a go-to player does. Everyone admires go-to players and looks to them when the heat is on—not only their leaders, but also their followers and peers. When I think of go-to players, I mean people who always produce.

1. GO-TO PLAYERS PRODUCE WHEN THE PRESSURE'S ON

There are many different kinds of people in the workplace, and you can measure them according to what they do for the organization:

WHAT THEY DO	KIND OF PLAYER
Never deliver	Detrimental
Sometimes deliver	Average
Always deliver when in their comfort zone	Valuable
Always deliver regardless of the situation	Invaluable

Go-to players are the people who find a way to make things happen no matter what. They don't have to be in familiar surroundings. They don't have to be in their comfort zones. The circumstances don't have to be fair or favorable. The pressure doesn't hinder them either. In fact, if anything, the more pressure there is, the better they like it. They always produce when the heat is on.

Go-to players are the people who find a way to make things happen no matter what. They don't have to be in familiar surroundings. They don't have to be in their comfort zones.

2. GO-TO PLAYERS PRODUCE WHEN THE RESOURCES ARE FEW

In 2004 when *Today Matters* came out and I was frequently being asked to speak on the subject, I was once booked to do back-to-back sessions in Little Rock, Arkansas. After the first session, the site ran out of books. When the leader of the organization I was speaking for found out, he mobilized some of his people and sent them out to all the bookstores in town to buy more copies of the book so that his people could have access to them right after my second speaking session. I think he ended up buying every copy in town.

The thing I loved about it was that he wanted his people to benefit from the book, and he knew that if he didn't have it there after I spoke, they probably wouldn't get a copy. So he made it happen—even though he had to buy the books at full retail and resell them for that same amount. It took a lot of effort and provided no financial return. What a leader!

3. Go-To Players Produce When the Momentum Is Low

Organizations have only three kinds of people when it comes to momentum. There are momentum breakers—people who sabotage the leader or organization and actually sap momentum as a result. These people have terrible attitudes and represent the bottom 10 percent of the organization. (At General Electric, Jack Welch made it his goal every year to identify and fire these people.) The second group is comprised of the momentum takers—people who merely take things as they come. They neither create nor diminish momentum; they simply flow with it. These people represent the middle 80 percent.

The final group is the momentum makers—the people who move things forward and create momentum. These are the leaders in the organization and comprise the top 10 percent. These momentum makers make progress. They overcome obstacles. They help move others along. They actually create energy in the organization when the rest of the team is feeling tired or discouraged.

4. Go-To Players Produce When the Load Is Heavy

Good employees always have the desire to be helpful to their leaders. I've worked with many of them over the years. I always appreciate it when someone who works with me says, "I've finished my work. Can I do something for you?" But there is another level of play that some go-to players reach, and you can see it in their ability to carry a heavy load anytime their leader needs it. They don't help the leader with a heavy load only when theirs is light. They do it anytime their leader's load is heavy.

Linda Eggers, Tim Elmore, and Dan Reiland are examples of heavy load lifters for me. For years, when I've been pressed, they've taken tasks from me and completed them with excellence. Dan Reiland is so incredible at this that he continues to do it even now—and he doesn't even work for me anymore. He does it as a friend.

If you have the willingness and capacity to lift the load of your leaders when they need it, you will have influence with them.

The keys to becoming this kind of player are availability and responsibility. Being a heavy load lifter is really an attitude issue, not a position issue. If you have the willingness and capacity to lift the load of your leaders when they need it, you will have influence with them.

5. Go-To Players Produce When the Leader Is Absent

The greatest opportunity for a leader in the middle of an organization to distinguish himself is when the leader is absent. It is at those times that a leadership vacuum exists, and leaders can rise up to fill it. True, when leaders know they will be absent, they usually designate a leader to stand in for them. But even then, there are still opportunities for people to step up, take responsibility, and shine.

If you step forward to lead when there is a leadership vacuum, you may have a very good chance of distinguishing yourself. You should also know, however, that when people step up to fill that vacuum, it almost always exposes their true colors. If their motives are good, and they desire to lead for the good of the organization, it will show through. If they are attempting a power grab for personal gain and their own advancement, that will show through too.

6. Go-To Players Produce When the Time Is Limited

I love a sign I saw at a small business called "The 57 Rules to Deliver the Goods." Beneath the title it read:

Rule 1: Deliver the Goods
Rule 2: The Other 56 Don't Matter

That's the philosophy of go-to players. They deliver no matter how tough the situation is.

As I was working on this chapter, Rod Loy told me a story about when he was a leader in the middle of an organization. At a large meeting, his leader announced a new program that he said was in place. Roy listened with interest, because he had not been aware of it. It sounded great, but then his leader announced that Rod would be leading the program, and anyone who was interested in it could talk to him about it after the meeting.

Rod had not been informed of his role in this program, but that didn't matter. During the rest of the meeting while his leader spoke, Rod quickly sketched out the design and action plan for the program. When the meeting was over and people approached him, he communicated his plan and launched it. Rod said it may not have been his best work, but it was good work under the circumstances. It created a win for the organization, preserved his leader's credibility, and served the people well.

You may never find yourself in the kind of situation Rod did. But if you adopt the positive attitude and tenacity of a go-to player, and take every opportunity to make things happen, you will probably perform as he did under similar circumstances. If you do, your leader will come to rely on you, and the people we rely on increase their influence and credibility every day we work with them.

Lead-Up Principle #9

Be Better Tomorrow Than You Are Today

A turkey was chatting with a bull. "I would love to be able to get to the top of that tree," sighed the turkey, "but I haven't got the energy."

"Well," replied the bull, "why don't you nibble on some of my droppings? They're packed with nutrients."

The turkey pecked at a lump of dung and found that it actually gave him enough strength to reach the lowest branch of the tree. The next day, after eating some more dung, he reached the second branch. Finally after a fourth night, there he was proudly perched at the top of the tree. But he was promptly spotted by a hunter, who shot him down out of the tree.

The moral of the story: BS might get you to the top, but it won't keep you there.

How Growth Helps You Lead Up

I've met a lot of people who have destination disease. They think that they have "arrived" by obtaining a specific position or getting to a certain level in an organization. When they get to that desired place, they stop striving to grow or improve. What a waste of potential!

There's certainly nothing wrong with the desire to progress in your career, but never try to "arrive." Instead, intend your journey to be open-ended. Most people have no idea how far they can go in life. They aim way too low. I know I did when I first started out, but my life began changing when I stopped setting goals for *where* I wanted to be and started setting the course for *who* I wanted to be. I have discovered for others and me that the key to personal development is being more *growth* oriented than *goal* oriented.

The key to personal development is being more growth *oriented than* goal *oriented.*

There is no downside to making growth your goal. If you keep learning, you will be better tomorrow than you are today, and that can do so many things for you.

The Better You Are, the More People Listen

If you had an interest in cooking, with whom would you rather spend an hour—Mario Batali (chef, cookbook author, owner of Babbo Ristorante e Enoteca and other restaurants in New York City, and host of two shows on the Food Network) or your neighbor who loves to cook and actually does it "every once in a while"? Or if you were a leadership student, as I am, would you rather spend that hour with the president of the United States or with the person who runs the local convenience store? It's no contest. Why? Because you respect most and can learn best from the person with great competence and experience.

Competence is a key to credibility, and credibility is the key to influencing others. If people respect you, they will listen to you. President Abraham Lincoln said, "I don't think much of a man who is not wiser today than he was yesterday." By focusing on growth, you become wiser each day.

The Better You Are, the Greater Your Value Today

If you were to plant fruit and nut trees in your yard, when could you expect to start harvesting from them? Would you be surprised to learn that you had to wait years—three to seven years for fruit, five to fifteen years for nuts? If you want a tree to produce, first you have to let it grow. The more the tree has grown and has created strong roots that can sustain it, the more it can produce. The more it can produce, the greater its value.

People are not all that different. The more they grow, the more valuable they are because they can produce more. In fact, it's said that a tree keeps growing as long as it is living. I would love to live in such a way that the same could be said for me—"he kept growing until the day he died."

I love this quote from Elbert Hubbard: "If what you did yesterday still looks big to you, you haven't done much today." If you look back at past accomplishments, and they don't look small to you now, then you haven't grown very much since you completed them. If you look back at a job you did years ago, and you don't think you could do it better now, then you're not improving in that area of your life.

If you're not moving forward as a learner, then you are moving backward as a leader.

If you are not continually growing, then it is probably damaging your leadership ability. Warren Bennis and Bert Nanus, authors of *Leaders: The Strategies for Taking Charge*, said, "It is the capacity to develop and improve their skills that distinguishes leaders from followers."[1] If you're not moving forward as a learner, then you are moving backward as a leader.

The Better You Are, the Greater Your Potential for Tomorrow

Who are the hardest people to teach? The people who have never tried to learn. Getting them to accept a new idea is like trying to transplant a tomato plant into concrete. Even if you could get it to go into the ground, you know it isn't going to survive anyway. The more you learn and grow, the greater your capacity to keep learning. And that makes your potential greater and your value for tomorrow higher.

Indian reformer Mahatma Gandhi said, "The difference between what we do and what we are capable of doing would suffice to solve most of the world's problems." That is how great our potential is. All we have to do is keep fighting to learn more, grow more, become more.

One leader I interviewed for this book told me that when he was in his first job, his boss would sit him down after he made a mistake and talk it through with him. Every time before he left one of those meetings, his boss asked, "Did you learn something from this?" and he would ask him to explain. At the time, this young leader thought his boss was being pretty tough on him. But as he progressed through his career, he discovered that many of his successes could be traced back to practices he adopted as a result of those talks. It made a huge positive impact on him because it kept making him better.

If you want to influence the people who are ahead of you in the organization—and keep influencing them—then you need to keep getting better. An investment in your growth is an investment in your ability, your adaptability, and your promotability. No matter how much it costs you to keep growing and learning, the cost of doing nothing is greater.

How to Become Better Tomorrow

Founding father Ben Franklin said, "By improving yourself, the world is made better. Be not afraid of growing too slowly. Be afraid only of standing still. Forget your mistakes, but remember what they taught you." So how do you become better tomorrow? By becoming better today. The secret of your success can be found in your daily agenda. Here is what I suggest you do to keep growing and leading up:

1. Learn Your Craft Today

On a wall in the office of a huge tree farm hangs a sign. It says, "The best time to plant a tree is twenty-five years ago. The second best time is today." There is no time like the present to become an expert at your craft. Maybe you wish you had started earlier. Or maybe you wish you had found a better teacher or mentor years ago. None of that matters. Looking back and lamenting will not help you move forward.

A friend of the poet Longfellow asked the secret of his continued interest in life. Pointing to a nearby apple tree, Longfellow said, "The purpose of that apple tree is to grow a little new wood each year. That is what I plan to do." The friend would have found a similar sentiment in one of Longfellow's poems:

> Not enjoyment and not sorrow
> Is our destined end or way;
> But to act that each tomorrow
> Find us further than today.[2]

You may not be where you're supposed to be. You may not be what you want to be. You don't have to be what you used to be. And you don't have to ever arrive. You just need to learn to be the best you can be right now. As Napoleon Hill said, "You can't change where you started, but you can change the direction you are going. It's not what you are going to do, but it's what you are doing now that counts."

> *"You can't change where you started, but you can change the direction you are going. It's not what you are going to do, but it's what you are doing now that counts."*
>
> —NAPOLEON HILL

2. TALK YOUR CRAFT TODAY

Once you reach a degree of proficiency in your craft, then one of the best things you can do for yourself is talk your craft with others on the same and higher levels than you. Many people do this naturally. Guitarists talk about guitars. Parents talk about raising children. Golfers talk about golf. They do so because it's enjoyable, it fuels their passion, it teaches them new skills and insights, and it prepares them to take action.

Talking to peers is wonderful, but if you don't also make an effort to strategically talk your craft with those ahead of you in experience and skill, then you're really missing learning opportunities. Douglas Randlett meets regularly with a group of retired multimillionaires so that he can learn from them. Before he retired, Major League Baseball player Tony Gwynn was known to talk hitting with anybody who had knowledge about it. Every time he saw Ted Williams, they talked hitting.

I enjoy talking about leadership with good leaders all the time. In fact, I make it a point to schedule a learning lunch with someone I admire at least six times a year. Before I go, I study up on them by reading their books, studying their lessons, listening to their speeches, or whatever else I need to do. My goal is to learn enough about them and their "sweet spot" to ask the right questions. If I do that, then I can learn from their strengths. But that's not my ultimate goal. My goal is to learn what I can transfer from their strength zones to mine. That's where my growth will come from—not from what they're doing. I have to apply what I learn to my situation.

The secret to a great interview is listening. It is the bridge between learning about them and learning about you. And that's your objective.

3. Practice Your Craft Today

William Osler, the physician who wrote *The Principles and Practice of Medicine* in 1892, once told a group of medical students:

> Banish the future. Live only for the hour and its allotted work. Think not of the amount to be accomplished, the difficulties to be overcome, or the end to be attained, but set earnestly at the little task at your elbow, letting that be sufficient for the day; for surely our plain duty is, as Carlyle says, "Not to see what lies dimly at a distance, but to do what lies clearly at hand."

The only way to improve is to practice your craft until you know it inside and out. At first, you do what you know to do. The more you practice your craft, the more you know. But as you do more, you will also discover more about what you ought to do differently. At that point you have a decision to make: Will you do what you have always done, or will you try to do more of what you think you should do? The only way you improve is to get out of your comfort zone and try new things.

People often ask me, "How can I grow my business?" or, "How can I make my department better?" The answer is for you personally to grow. The only way to grow your organization is to grow the leaders who run it. By making yourself better, you make others better. Retired General Electric CEO Jack Welch said, "Before you are a leader, success is all about growing yourself. When you become a leader, success is all about growing others."[3] And the time to start is today.

Section III Review
The Principles 360-Degree Leaders Need to Lead Up

Before you begin to learn what it takes to lead across, review the nine principles you need to master in order to lead up:

1. Lead yourself exceptionally well.
2. Lighten your leader's load.
3. Be willing to do what others won't.
4. Do more than manage—lead!
5. Invest in relational chemistry.
6. Be prepared every time you take your leader's time.
7. Know when to push and when to back off.
8. Become a go-to player.
9. Be better tomorrow than you are today.

How well are you doing those nine things? If you're not sure where you stand, take the 360-Degree Leadership assessment, offered free of charge to people who have purchased this book. For more information, go to 360DegreeLeader.com.

SECTION IV

The Principles 360-Degree Leaders Practice to Lead Across

"Follow me, I'll walk with you."

What distinguishes a merely competent leader from one who goes to the next level? Competent leaders can lead followers. They can find, gather, recruit, and enlist them. This is no easy task, but a leader who can lead only followers is limited. To make it to the next level of leadership, a leader must be able to lead other leaders—not just those below them, but also those above and alongside them.

Leaders who work really hard and exhibit very high competence can influence their bosses. So in that respect, they have become leaders of leaders. But leading peers is another kind of challenge. In fact, for highly productive people who create feelings of jealousy or resentment because of their relationship with their bosses, leading peers can be especially difficult. If the leaders in the middle who lead up are seen as political or as brownnosers, then their peers may reject any overtures toward leading across.

To succeed as a 360-Degree Leader who leads peer-to-peer, you have to work at giving your colleagues reasons to respect and follow you. How do you do that? By helping your peers win. If you can help them win, you will not only help the organization but will also help yourself.

The people who find it most difficult to lead across are those who don't excel at building relationships. If you look back at the Five Levels of Leadership in "The Position Myth," you'll see that after the first level, which is position, the second and third levels are permission and production. Leaders who excel at production but neglect permission may be able to influence their bosses, but they will have a nearly impossible time trying to influence their peers. If you want to lead across, you need to work for and win your peers' permission. That can be a great challenge, but it is definitely one worth accepting.

Lead-Across Principle #1

Understand, Practice, and Complete the Leadership Loop

Many people who have difficulty leading across have trouble because their approach is too shortsighted. They try to gain influence too quickly. Leading is not a one-time event; it's an ongoing process that takes time—especially with peers.

If you want to gain influence and credibility with people working alongside you, then don't try to take shortcuts or cheat the process. Instead, learn to understand, practice, and complete the leadership loop with them.

The Leadership Loop

Take a look at the following graphic, which will give you an idea of what the leadership loop looks like:

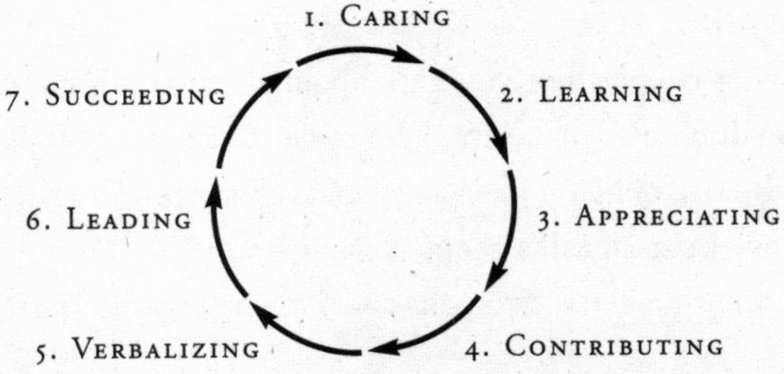

You can see that it's a cycle that starts with caring and ends with succeeding. Here's how each of these steps in the loop works.

1. Caring—Take an Interest in People

This may sound too simple, but it really all starts here. You have to show people that you care about them by taking an interest in them. Many leaders are so action oriented and agenda driven that they don't make people a high enough priority. If that describes you, then you need to turn that around.

I don't mean to sound crass, but it helps if you like people. If you're not a people person, that may be the first step you need to take. Look for value in every person. Put yourself in others' shoes. Find reasons to like them. You won't take an interest in people if deep down you care nothing about them. And if you care nothing about them, that flaw will always be a hindrance to your ability to lead people.

People always move toward someone who increases them and away from anyone who decreases them.

If this is an area of challenge for you, then you may want to take a look at *25 Ways to Win with People: How to Make Others Feel Like a Million Bucks*, which I coauthored with Les Parrott; or read the classic *How to Win Friends and Influence People*, by Dale Carnegie. However you go about developing people skills, just remember that people always move toward someone who increases them and away from anyone who decreases them.

2. Learning—Get to Know People

Showing people that you care about them is always a good thing. But if you don't also make an effort to get to know them as individuals, you run the risk of being like the *Peanuts* character, Charlie Brown, who said, "I love mankind. It's people I can't stand."

Take the time to talk to your peers in the organization. Ask to hear their stories. Try to discover their best skills. Learn to appreciate their differences. Ask for their opinions on work-related issues. And as much as you can, try to put yourself in their shoes.

There are also structured ways to learn about your coworkers. I often speak for Maximum Impact, a company I founded that is now owned and led by Todd Duncan. One of the exercises the organization offers to clients involves Value Cards. Participants are asked to thumb through a stack of forty-plus cards, each printed with a value, such as integrity, commitment, wealth, faith, creativity, and family. They are asked to choose their top six values, the ones they consider nonnegotiable. Then they are asked to eliminate two cards, and then another two. It prompts people to weigh what matters and make some tough choices.

Recently Rick Packer, a corporate trainer, shared an e-mail with me that he had received from John Farrell of PrintingHouse Press. In it he raved about the Value Card experience and how he used it to get to know the people in his organization better. John said:

> A few weeks after I got back [from the workshop], I sat with each of my twenty-five employees—two at a time—so they could take part in the Maximum Impact Value Cards exercise. I told them I thought it would be a great experience, and that they may find out something more about each other than they knew before. I wasn't disappointed. Each one of the twenty-five enjoyed it so much that they were all eager for me to publicly post the values of each one of their coworkers. So by unanimous vote, I had my graphic designer create and print a 30 x 24-inch poster displaying our top three values. Today it has been officially posted in our office for all to see.

John went on to say that the camaraderie that already existed among his people had gotten even better. He also included a miniature version of the poster his artist created.

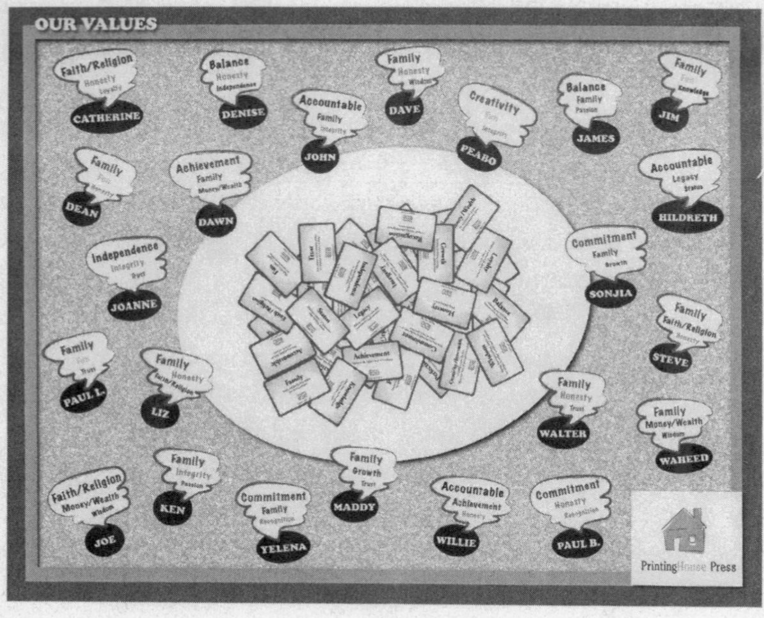

Not only does he now know his people better, but they are also in a better position to know, appreciate, and influence each other.

3. Appreciating—Respect People

We tend to appreciate people who can do things we admire. That's only natural. But if we only appreciate people like ourselves, we're missing so much. We should strive to see others' unique experiences and skills as a resource and try to learn from them.

Dennis Bakke, chief executive of AES and author of *Joy at Work,* has an interesting take on this. He intentionally makes positive assumptions about people and strives to live them out in his desire to respect people. Bakke states his philosophy by describing the people at AES. He says they:

- are creative, thoughtful, trustworthy adults, capable of making important decisions;

- are accountable and responsible for their decisions and actions;
- are fallible (make mistakes, sometimes on purpose);
- are unique; and
- want to use our talents and skills to make a positive contribution to the organization and the world.[1]

If you treat your peers (and your employees) with this kind of respect, appreciating them for who they are, then they will be more likely to respect and listen to you in return.

4. Contributing—Add Value to People

Few things increase the credibility of leaders more than adding value to the people around them. That is especially true when they are neither obligated to do it nor likely to receive any kind of direct benefit from it. When you go out of your way to add value to your peers, they understand that you really want them to win with no hidden agenda of your own.

Few things increase the credibility of leaders more than adding value to the people around them.

Here are some suggestions for how to get started:

Don't keep your best stuff to yourself. Our natural tendency is to protect what's ours, whether it's our turf, our ideas, or our resources. But if you share what you have when it can help others, you really send a positive message to the people who work with you.

Fill in their gaps. I love that in the movie *Rocky*, Sylvester Stallone's character says of his fiancée Adrian: "I got gaps, she's got gaps, together we don't got gaps." That could be said of our coworkers and us. Instead of exploiting other people's gaps to get ahead of them, why not fill in each other's gaps and both get ahead?

Invest in their growth. I suggested in Challenge #2 (The Frustration Challenge: Following an Ineffective Leader) that you share resources with your leader. Why not do the same with your peers? As the saying goes, when you light another's candle, you lose nothing of your own. You just produce more light.

Take them along. Many times when we get an opportunity to do something exciting or special, we soak up the experience and enjoy it, but we keep it to ourselves; 360-Degree Leaders always think in terms of who they can take along with them at those times. If you want to influence your peers, share the good things you're doing with them.

At first it may feel a little awkward to add value to people on your own level. If you work in a hostile or highly competitive environment, your peers may at first look at you with suspicion. But persevere. If you give with no strings attached and try to help others win, they will, in time, come to trust your motives.

5. Verbalizing—Affirm People

Take a moment to think about the teachers you've had in your life. Who were your favorites? Why did you like those teachers more than the dozens of others? If you're like most people, you revered them because they affirmed you and made you feel good about yourself.

Few things build a person up like affirmation. According to *Webster's New World Dictionary, Third College Edition* (Simon and Schuster, 1991), the word *affirm* comes from *ad firmare*, which means "to make firm." So when you affirm people, you make firm within them the things you see about them. Do that often enough, and the belief that solidifies within them will become stronger than the doubts they have about themselves.

If you want to influence your peers, become their best cheerleader. Praise their strengths. Acknowledge their accomplishments. Say positive things about them to your boss and peers. Sincerely compliment them at every opportunity, and someday you may have the opportunity to influence them.

6. Leading—Influence People

After taking the previous five steps—caring, learning, appreciating, contributing, and verbalizing—now you are finally ready to start leading your peers. The things you've done up to now have served to build your relationship with them, give you credibility, and display that your motives are good. With that kind of history, you will have earned the opportunity to influence them.

Some leaders are able to go through all the steps quickly, while others need quite a bit of time to complete them. The greater the natural leadership gifting you have, the more quickly you will be able to do it. But influencing others is not the end of the road. If your sole motivation is merely to get people to listen to you or do what you want, then you've really missed the boat. If you desire to become a 360-Degree Leader, then you need to take the next step. You need to help them win!

7. Succeeding—Win with People

I know that you have the desire to lead others, or you would not have come this far in the book. But I don't know if you've given much thought to why you want to lead. I believe that good leaders balance two very important motivations. The first is to fulfill their vision. All leaders have inside of them a dream, a vision they want to see come to fruition. For some it's modest; for others it's huge. The second motivation is to see others succeed. Great leaders don't use people so that they can win. They lead people so that they all can win together. If that is truly your motivation, you can become the kind of person others want to follow—whether they are beside, above, or below you in the organizational hierarchy.

Great leaders don't use people so that they can win. They lead people so that they all can win together.

The wonderful thing about helping others succeed is that it earns you more opportunities to help an even greater number of people. Haven't you seen that in every area of life? A winning coach or business leader has a much easier time recruiting potential players than someone without a winning track record. Once leaders prove that they can help make people's dreams come true, others seek them out so that they, too, can be helped to win.

And that's what starts the cycle over again. If you help others succeed, additional people will come into your life whom you will have an opportunity to help succeed. Every time that happens, you must choose to go through the process again, beginning with caring and ending with succeeding. You can't take shortcuts. True, if you help others win consistently for a long time, they will allow you to go through the process more quickly with them, but you still have to take each step.

When Lou Holtz was coaching Notre Dame's football team, he was quoted as saying, "Do what's right! Do the best you can and treat others the way you want to be treated, because they will ask three questions: (1) Can I trust you? (2) Do you believe in this? Are you committed to this—have a passion for this? (3) Do you care about me as a person?" If the people around you can answer yes to all of those questions, then you have a very good chance of making an impact on their lives.

Lead-Across Principle #2

Put Completing Fellow Leaders Ahead of Competing with Them

Chris Hodges, a good leader who is a native of Baton Rouge, is well-known for telling Boudreaux jokes, a type of humor popular in Louisiana. Recently on a trip for EQUIP, he told me this one (I'll try to capture the accent in writing as best I can—just think Justin Wilson):

> A group of Cajuns was sitting around bragging about how successful they were. Thibideaux says, "I just bought me another shrimp boat, yeah, and I got me a crew of ten people workin' for me."
>
> "Dat ain't nottin'," says Landry, "I been promoted at the refinery, and now I got fifty men workin' for me."
>
> Boudreaux hears this, and he doesn't want to look bad in front of his friends, so he says, "Oh yeah, well I got three hundred people under me."
>
> Thibideaux says, "What you talkin' 'bout, Boudreaux? You mow lawns all day."
>
> "Dat's true," says Boudreaux, "but now I'm cuttin' da grass at the cemetery, and I got three hundred people under me."

There's nothing wrong with competition. The problem for many leaders is that they end up competing against their peers in their own organization in a way that hurts the team and them. It all depends on how you handle competition and how you channel it. In healthy working environments, there is both competition and teamwork. The issue is to know when each is appropriate. When it comes to your teammates, you want to compete in such a way that instead of *competing* with them, you are *completing* them. Those are two totally different mind-sets.

Winning at all costs will cost you when it comes to your peers.

Competing vs. Completing

Competing	Completing
Scarcity mind-set	Abundance mind-set
Me first	Organization first
Destroys trust	Develops trust
Thinks win–lose	Thinks win–win
Single thinking (my good ideas)	Shared thinking (our great ideas)
Excluding others	Including others

Winning at all costs will cost you when it comes to your peers. If your goal is to beat your peers, then you will never be able to lead across with them.

How to Balance Competing and Completing

The bottom line is that the success of the whole team is more important than any individual wins. Organizations need both competition and teamwork to win. When those two elements exist in the right balance, great team chemistry is the result.

So how do you balance competing and completing? How do you learn to easily shift from one to the other? Here's what I recommend.

1. Acknowledge Your Natural Desire to Compete

About four or five years after I graduated from college, I went back to play in an alumni basketball game against the college's then-current team. Back when I played for the team, I had been a shooting guard, but this time they assigned me to cover the team's point guard. As I watched him in warm-ups, I knew I was in trouble. He was a lot faster than I was. So I quickly developed a strategy.

The first time he tried to take the ball inside to the hoop, I fouled him. I don't mean I tapped his hand as he shot the ball. I mean I really fouled him—hard. He got up, limped to the line for his free throws, and clanged both of them off the back of the rim. So far, so good.

The next time his team came down the floor and he tried to set up a shot from outside, I fouled him hard again. As he got up, he started grumbling under his breath.

Soon after that when there was a loose ball, I dove after it, but I also made sure I landed right on top of him. I wasn't as big then as I am now, but I was heavier than he was.

He popped up and barked at me, "You're playing too hard. It's only a game."

"Okay," I said with a grin, "then let me win."

It doesn't matter who you are or what you do, competitiveness is a natural leadership instinct. I haven't met a leader yet who didn't like to win. I look back now and recognize that I wasn't very mature. The good news is that the alumni team won the game. The bad news is that I didn't make a friend that day.

The key to being competitive is channeling it in a positive way. If you squash it, you lose an edge that motivates you to do some of your best work. If you let it run wild, you run over your teammates and alienate them. But if you control it and direct it, competitiveness can help you succeed.

2. Embrace Healthy Competition

Every winning team I've ever seen or been a part of experienced healthy competition among team members. Healthy competition does so many positive things for a team, many of which cannot be achieved through anything else.

Healthy competition helps bring out your best. How many world records do you suppose are set when a runner runs alone? I don't know of one! People function at peak capacity when they have someone else pushing them. That's true whether you're learning, practicing, or playing in the game.

Healthy competition promotes honest assessment. What is the quickest way for you to measure your effectiveness in your profession? Maybe you have long-term measurements in place, such as monthly or yearly goals. But what if you want to know how you're doing today? How would you go about measuring it? You could look at your to-do list. But what if you set the bar too low for yourself? You could ask your boss. But maybe the best way would be to see what others in your line of work are doing. If you are significantly behind or ahead of them, wouldn't that tell you something? And if you were behind, wouldn't you try to figure out what you're doing wrong? It may not be the only way to assess yourself, but it certainly can provide a good reality check.

Healthy competition creates camaraderie. When people compete together, it often creates a connection between them, whether they are on the same team or opposing teams. When competition is ongoing and friendly on the same team, it creates an even stronger bond that can lead to great camaraderie.

Healthy competition doesn't become personal. Competition between teammates is ultimately about having fun. When competition is healthy, teammates remain friends when the game is done. They play against each other for the thrill of it, and when they're done, they can walk away together without hard feelings.

I love the joke about the rooster who dragged an ostrich egg into the henhouse. He laid it down for all the hens to see and said, "I don't want to intimidate you girls, but I just want to show you what they're doing up the road." Competition can definitely help motivate a team to get going.

3. Put Competition in Its Proper Place

The whole goal of healthy competition is to leverage it for the corporate win. Competition in practice helps teammates to improve one another for game day. If it is channeled correctly, it is used to beat the other team.

The whole goal of healthy competition is to leverage it for the corporate win.

Of course, some leaders can take this to the extreme. Tommy Lasorda, former manager of the Los Angeles Dodgers, has told the story about the day his team was scheduled to play on the road against the Cincinnati Reds. In the morning, Lasorda went to mass. As he settled into his pew, the manager of the Reds, Johnny McNamara, happened to come into the same church and sit down in the same pew.

The men eyed one another, but neither spoke.

When mass was over, they had begun to walk out when Lasorda discovered that the other manager had paused to light a candle. He figured that gave the Reds an edge. "When he left, I went down and blew that candle out," Lasorda said. "All throughout the game, I kept hollering to him, 'Hey, Mac, it ain't gonna work. I blew it out.' We clobbered them that day, 13–2."

4. Know Where to Draw the Line

No matter how much you desire to win, if you want to cultivate the ability to compete in a healthy way, you must make sure you never cross the line by "going for the throat" with your peers, because if you do, you will alienate them. And that line is not difficult to define. I'd say that when competitiveness raises the bar and makes others better, that's healthy. Anytime it lowers morale and hurts the team, it's unhealthy and out of line.

When I was leading Skyline Church in the San Diego area, my staff was very competent and very competitive. The core group who always led the charge consisted of Dan Reiland, Sheryl Fleisher, and Tim Elmore. They all had their own departments and own areas of expertise, but they were always competing, always trying to one-up each other. Their friendly competition kept them on their toes, and it inspired the rest of the staff to join in and do their best. But as hard-driving and competitive as they were, if any one of them had a problem, the others were right there, ready to jump in and lend a hand. They always put the team's win ahead of their own.

Today those three leaders are out doing different things in different organizations across the country, but they remain friends. They keep in touch, share stories, and still help one another whenever they can. The kind of bond that develops when you compete together doesn't die easily. They have a deep respect for each other that continues to give them credibility—and influence—with one another.

Lead-Across Principle #3

Be a Friend

We often consider ourselves to be many things to the people who work alongside us—coworkers, teammates, contributors, competitors—but we often forget to be the one thing that every person wants: a friend. Poet Ralph Waldo Emerson wrote, "The glory of friendship is not in the outstretched hand, nor the kindly smile, nor the joy of companionship; it is in the spiritual inspiration that comes to one when he discovers that someone else believes in him and is willing to trust him."

No matter how driven or competitive your coworkers appear to be, they will enjoy having a friend on the job. Some people don't look to the workplace for friendship, but they will certainly benefit from finding it there. When a job is especially tough or unpleasant, having a friend is sometimes the only thing a person has to look forward to when going to work. And when the job is good, then having a friend is icing on the cake.

To Teamwork, Add Friendship

Why do I recommend that you work to develop friendships on the job?

Friendship Is the Foundation of Influence

President Abraham Lincoln said, "If you would win a man to your cause, first convince him that you are his sincere friend." Good relationships make influence possible, and friendship is the most positive relationship you can develop on the job with your coworkers.

Friendship Is the Framework for Success

I believe long-term success is unachievable without good people skills. Theodore Roosevelt said, "The most important single ingredient in the formula of success is knowing how to get along with people." Without it, most achievements are not possible, and even what we do achieve can feel hollow.

Friendship Is the Shelter Against Sudden Storms

If you're having a bad day, who can make you feel better? A friend. When you have to face your fears, who would you rather do it with? A friend. When you fall on your face, who can help pick you up? A friend. Aristotle was right when he said, "True friends are a sure refuge."

How to Be a Friend

Undoubtedly, you already have friends, so you know how to develop friendships. But relationships at work can often be different, and I want to suggest a specific way that you should approach friendship within your organization. Make it your goal to be a friend, not to find a friend.

When most people approach friendships, they look for people who will reciprocate their efforts at relationship building, and if they don't sense any kind of mutual effort, they abandon their efforts with that individual and move on. At work, if you want to lead across, you need to keep working at being a friend—even with people who don't initially put any effort into being a friend back.

As you reach out to your coworkers, I want to encourage you to include the following steps in the approach you take:

1. LISTEN!

Author Richard Exley once said:

> A true friend is one who hears and understands when you share your deepest feelings. He supports you when you are struggling; he corrects you, gently and with love, when you err; and he forgives you when you fail. A true friend prods you to personal growth, stretches you to your full potential. And most amazing of all, he celebrates your successes as if they were his own.

That entire process begins with listening.

Many people on the job just want to be left alone so that they can get their work done. If they do desire to interact with others, it's often to jockey for position or to get others to listen to what they have to say. How rare it is when people go out of their way and make it a point to listen to others.

Ralph Nichols said, "The most basic of all human needs is the need to understand and be understood. The best way to understand people is to listen to them." If you become a consistently good listener to your coworkers, they will want to spend time with you. They will begin to seek you out. And if they develop a rapport with you, they will probably also begin asking advice from you. That is the starting point for influence with them.

2. FIND COMMON GROUND NOT RELATED TO WORK

Frank A. Clark said, "To enjoy a friend, I need more in common with him than hating the same people." Unfortunately, for many people who work together, that's all they seem to have in common. So what's the solution if you don't seem to share common ground with someone at work? Try to discover what you have in common outside of the job.

If you see everyone as a potential friend, and look for connection points inside and outside of work, you have a good chance of finding common ground. And that is where friendships are built.

3. Be Available Beyond Business Hours

Just as you need to find common ground outside of work to become a friend to coworkers, you also need to make yourself available outside of business hours. True friendship means being available.

If you won't do anything outside of work hours, then your relationship will probably never evolve beyond the confines of the work arena. The moment you take your relationship with a coworker outside of the work environment, it instantly begins to change. Think about the first time you had lunch with a coworker off-site. Even if you talked about work the entire time, didn't it change the way you saw that person from then on? How about if you've ever played in a work softball league or played golf with coworkers? Didn't you learn many things about people that you never knew before? Didn't you gain insights into personalities that were unrevealed until then? Think about the first time you went to a coworker's house, and consider the personal connection you felt with that person afterward.

True friendship isn't on the clock. When a friend is in need, real friends don't say, "It's after five. Can you call me back tomorrow?" Obviously, you want to respect people's privacy, and you don't want to violate anybody's personal boundaries. But because leadership isn't limited to nine to five, friendship can't be either.

4. Have a Sense of Humor

Comic pianist Victor Borge said, "Laughter is the closest distance between two people." I have often found that to be true. Humor can quickly bond people who might not otherwise have a lot in common.

Charlie Wetzel said that when he went to graduate school to work on his master's degree at age twenty-four, he was a painfully serious person. He took himself—and everything else in life—way too seriously.

But during his second year in school, he became a teaching assistant, and he got to know some of his fellow graduate students who were also teaching English composition classes for the University of New Orleans. One of those people was Homer Arrington.

Homer had grown up in Southern California, gone to school at Berkeley, and then done a variety of interesting jobs, including driving a cab in New York City for a couple of years. As all fourteen of the grad students would gather in their communal office, they would trade stories of their experiences in class and the troubles they were dealing with. Homer was a good student and an intellectual, but he also had a great sense of humor. When Charlie would tell a story about something that had really irritated him, Homer would see the humor in it, make jokes, and they both would end up laughing.

Though the two men initially had little in common, they quickly became friends. Now, twenty years later, Charlie credits Homer with helping him not take himself so seriously and with reawakening his sense of humor, something for which he continues to be grateful.

If you maintain a sense of humor—even when times are tough, the job gets rough, and your coworkers are feeling out of sorts—you will help to create a positive atmosphere and will appear approachable and accessible to your coworkers. And that certainly will help your chances of making a friend.

> *"Your best friend is he who brings out the best that is within you."*
>
> —Henry Ford

5. Tell the Truth When Others Don't

Once when Henry Ford was having lunch with a man, he asked, "Who is your best friend?" When the man responded that he wasn't sure, Ford exclaimed, "I will tell you!" He took out a pencil and wrote his answer on the tablecloth: "Your best friend is he who brings out the best that is within you."

That is what friends do for one another. They bring out their best.

Often their best is brought out by encouragement, but sometimes the best thing you can do for friends is tell them the truth. Not everybody is willing to do that, because they don't want to risk the relationship, or they really don't care enough to make the effort.

An eastern proverb says, "A friend is one who warns you." When you're headed for trouble, a friend lets you know. When you're blinded by your emotions, a friend tells you. When the quality of your work is hurting the organization or may hurt your career, a friend tells you the truth.

Stepping forward and telling people hard truths can be a risky thing. The irony is that in order for someone to listen to what you have to say about such things, you first need to have relational credibility with them. So it's kind of a catch-22. If you don't tell them, you're not really being a friend. But in order to tell them, you must already be a friend, or they won't accept what you have to say. The more relational currency you have deposited with them, the better the chance they will listen to what you have to say.

Charles Schwab, who started out as a stake driver and worked his way up to the job of president of Carnegie Steel (and later U.S. Steel) was said to be an incredible leader and a master motivator. He saw the value of friendship in every aspect of life, including work. Schwab said:

> Be friends with everybody. When you have friends you will know there is somebody who will stand by you. You know the old saying, that if you have a single enemy you will find him everywhere. It doesn't pay to make enemies. Lead the life that will make you kind and friendly to everyone about you, and you will be surprised what a happy life you will live.

And you will also be surprised by the influence you will earn with your peers.

Lead-Across Principle #4

Avoid Office Politics

A politician arrived late for a speaking engagement where he was scheduled as the keynote speaker. Usually he did his homework on the area and the organization, but because of his busy schedule, he had not been able to do it. He was rushed in as the attendees were finishing their dessert and taken immediately to the podium without having the chance to speak to anyone.

When he was introduced to the crowd, there was nothing he could do but dive in. With the bright lights shining in his eyes, he immediately launched into one of the main issues of the campaign and spoke at length. When he paused for a moment, the gentleman who had introduced him whispered that the group to whom he was speaking was on the opposite side of the issue.

Without missing a beat, the politician said, "My friends. Now that I have explained the opposition's position in great detail, I will tell you the truth."

Some people seeking public office may be able to get away with such tactics—though usually it backfires on them—but people in a working environment where their peers know them certainly cannot. Playing politics at work is a surefire way to alienate your peers.

I would define "playing politics" as changing who you appear to be or what you normally do to gain an advantage with whoever currently has power. Among those who run for public office, that often means changing their position on issues depending on which group they're speaking to. In work environments, it may mean sucking up to the boss, constantly changing positions to get on the winning side, or using people for personal gain without regard for how it affects them. Political people are fickle and opportunistic, doing what's expedient in the moment to win, regardless of what's best for their peers, their employees, or the organization.

Two Ways to Get Ahead

There seem to be two main paths for people to get ahead in organizations. One way is to try to get ahead by doing the work. The other is to try to get ahead by working an angle. It's the difference between production and politics.

People Who Rely on Production	People Who Rely on Politics
Depend on how they grow	Depend on who they know
Focus on what they do	Focus on what they say
Become better than they appear	Appear better than they are
Provide substance	Take shortcuts
Do what's necessary	Do what's popular
Work to control their own destiny	Let others control their destiny
Grow into the next level	Hope to be given the next level
Base decisions on principles	Base decisions on opinions

The bottom line is that people who might be described as "political" are ruled by their desire to get ahead instead of a desire for excellence, productivity, teamwork, or consistency. Whatever values and skills they have are secondary to their ambition. And while they sometimes appear to get ahead, their gains are always temporary. In the long run, integrity, consistency, and productivity always pay off—in better teamwork and a clear conscience.

If you have played politics at work in the past, perhaps you saw others do it and you thought that was what you had to do to advance in your career. Or maybe you didn't have confidence in yourself because you weren't growing, and your skills were not advancing. You may not have done it maliciously, but whatever the reason, if you have played politics, you can be certain that you have betrayed the trust of some of your coworkers. And you will probably have to go to those people to apologize and seek reconciliation. That may be hard, but if you desire to lead across, you will need to do it to regain credibility with your peers.

If you are not a political person by nature, I still recommend that you exercise caution. Some working environments seem to draw people toward behavior that will ultimately damage peer-to-peer relationships. To avoid such difficulties, do the following:

1. Avoid Gossip

It's been said that great people talk about ideas, average people talk about themselves, and small people talk about others. That's what gossip does. It makes people small. There really is no upside to gossip. It diminishes the person being talked about. It diminishes the person who is saying unkind things about others, and it even diminishes the listener. That's why you should avoid not only spreading gossip but also being a recipient of it. If you stop people from unloading gossip on you, it will make you feel better about the person who's being talked about, as well as about yourself. Besides, whoever gossips to you will gossip about you.

British prime minister Winston Churchill said, "When the eagles are silent, the parrots begin to jabber." 360-Degree Leaders are like eagles: they soar; they inspire; they fly high. And they don't talk just to hear themselves. They don't vent about someone to others to make themselves feel better. If they have a problem with a person, they go to that individual and address the issue directly—never through a third party. They praise publicly and criticize privately. And they never say anything about others that they wouldn't want them to hear—because they probably will.

Great people talk about ideas, average people talk about themselves, and small people talk about others.

2. STAY AWAY FROM PETTY ARGUMENTS

In most places where people work, there are past grudges, ongoing feuds, and petty arguments that run like currents through the organization. Wise leaders in the middle of an organization avoid getting sucked into these easily, even if they think they can resolve them. As the saying goes, a bulldog can beat a skunk in a fight anytime, but he knows it's just not worth it. That's also the attitude of 360-Degree Leaders.

Recently I received an e-mail from Marvin "Skip" Schoenhals, chairman and president of Wilmington Savings Fund Society, whom I had met while I was speaking at a CEO forum in Dallas, Texas. When I met Skip, he told me a little bit about himself, and I asked him to write me and share more of his story. He wrote about how he once lived in Owosso, Michigan, and served on the seven-member city council. Skip said he had a knack for seeing the big picture and synthesizing many points of view. He wrote:

> I was often able to summarize issues quickly and move the group to a higher, less detailed level of discussion. As a result, fellow council members increasingly sought my opinion on various matters coming before the council.

> While I recognized that this was happening, I never attempted to capitalize on it. I was willing to speak my mind, but I would in the end defer to the mayor. Further, I would also pick my spots. Sometimes even if I thought that the council was not on the right big-picture item, I didn't always jump in. I let some issues go, even though I did not agree with them. I realized I gained credibility by not having an opinion on everything.

Skip went on to tell about how in a year's time, he became the informal leader of the council and then later the mayor.

It is a sign of maturity when someone knows what's petty and what's not—when to jump in, and when to sit back and listen. If you desire to become effective as a 360-Degree Leader, you will need to cultivate that kind of ability.

3. Stand Up for What's Right, Not Just for What's Popular

While I believe that wise leaders often sit back and listen, I also believe that leaders must stand up for what's right, even when such a stand will be unpopular. How do you do that? How do you know when to stand up and when not to, especially in a culture where many people see truth as subjective? My answer is that you use the Golden Rule: in everything, do to others what you would have them do to you.[1]

In *Ethics 101*, I explained that a form of the Golden Rule is accepted by nearly every culture in the world. Besides Christianity, the religions that have some version of the Golden Rule include Judaism, Islam, Buddhism, Hinduism, Zoroastriansim, Confucianism, Baha'i, and Jainism, among others. When someone is being treated in a way that you would not want to be treated, then it's time to stand up.

4. Look at All Sides of the Issue

I love this piece of business advice: before you have an argument with your boss, take a good look at both sides—his side and the outside.

While seeing things from multiple points of view with your peers may not have as important stakes as seeing things from your boss's point of view, there is still great value in seeing issues from as many sides as possible. It always pays to avoid being dogmatic or stuck in one box in your thinking.

One of the advantages of leading from the middle of an organization is that you have the opportunity to see things from perspectives that many others don't. Leaders at the top of the organization often have a difficult time seeing anything other than the big picture or the bottom line. Those on the bottom are equally limited, often seeing only the issues of their area. But leaders in the middle have a better perspective. They see how any given issue impacts them, but they are also able to look up and down. They are close to the people in the trenches and can see things from their point of view, and they are close enough to the top to see at least some of the big picture. 360-Degree Leaders make the most of this perspective to lead not only up and down, but also across.

Before you have an argument with your boss, take a good look at both sides—his side and the outside.

5. Don't Protect Your Turf

Politics is often about power. Political leaders protect whatever is theirs because they don't want to lose power. If they lose power, then they might not win. And as I already mentioned, winning is their primary motivation. People who want to win at all costs fight and scrap to keep everything that belongs to them. They fight for their budget. They fight for office space. They guard their ideas. They hoard their supplies. If it belongs to them, they protect it.

People who want to lead across take a broader view. They look at what's best for the team. If they have to give up some space to help the organization, they do it. If it makes more sense for another leader to accomplish a task they've done in the past—and if some of the dollars from their budget also go to that leader—they deal with it. What matters is the team.

6. Say What You Mean, and Mean What You Say

Like every other kind of leadership, becoming a 360-Degree Leader is about building trust with people. When asked what he considered the most essential qualification for a politician, Winston Churchill said, "It's the ability to foretell what will happen tomorrow, next month, and next year—and to explain afterward why it did not happen." Churchill understood the dynamics of politics as well as anyone in the twentieth century. Political leaders find themselves under tremendous pressure. Maybe that's why some of them crack under it and tell people what they want to hear rather than what the politicians really believe. And those who do crack create a negative reputation that all politicians have to labor under.

If you want to develop trust with others, you must be more than competent. You must also be credible and consistent. The way to achieve those qualities is to make sure that what you *say*, what you *do*, and what you *say you do* all match. If you do that, the people who work with you will know they can depend on you.

I don't mean to cast a negative light on everyone involved in politics. I've known many candidates for public office who displayed the highest integrity and truly wanted to serve the people. But the word *politician*, which once conjured positive images, brings to mind negative ones for most people.

Instead of trying to be a politician, strive to be a statesman. *Webster's New Universal Unabridged Dictionary* states:

> These terms differ particularly in their connotations; *Politician* suggests the schemes and devices of a person who engages in (esp. small) politics for party ends or for one's own advantage; a dishonest politician.

> *Statesman* suggests the eminent ability, foresight, and unselfish patriotic devotion of a person dealing with (esp. important or great) affairs of state: a distinguished statesman.[2]

Becoming a statesman for your organization is an excellent idea. If you continually keep the big picture in mind, remain unselfish in your efforts, and try to be a diplomat with your peers, you will distinguish yourself, gain credibility, and improve your effectiveness and that of the team. And you will also increase your influence.

Lead-Across Principle #5

Expand Your Circle of Acquaintances

In 1997, I relocated my companies from San Diego, California, to Atlanta, Georgia. In the wake of that move, I felt that I needed to expand my circle of acquaintances into the African-American community, which was really a new world for me.

I grew up in a small town in Ohio in the 1950s and '60s where not many people of color lived. The first ten years of my career I worked primarily in rural Indiana and Ohio—middle America. The next fifteen years I worked in Southern California. There I was introduced to the Hispanic culture and its people, and I led a church that included persons of many backgrounds; but once again, there were not a lot of African-Americans. Even in the conferences I taught around the country, only a small percentage of participants were African-American. So when I got to Atlanta, in the heart of the Deep South, I knew it was time for me to expand my horizons and grow in this area.

I knew someone in Atlanta who I hoped would help me with this: Dr. Samuel Chand. Sam is the chancellor of Beulah Heights Bible College, a multiracial college with a student population that is predominantly African-American. I asked Sam if he would be willing to introduce me to influential African-American leaders from the area, which he said he would gladly do. From then on, every other month I attended a lunch that he arranged with different leaders from that community.

It has been a wonderful growing experience for me. I've met a lot of terrific people, such as Bishop Eddie Long, an excellent leader of one of Atlanta's largest churches; Corretta Scott King and her children; and many others. A few people knew me by reputation, but most of these leaders did not. I've had a great time connecting with them. I could tell that a few people wondered if I had some kind of unspoken agenda, but I think they quickly accepted that my desire was to learn—and to add value to them if I could. That is my mind-set anytime I meet someone new. At times during those lunches I was taken out of my comfort zone, yet I'm glad to say I learned much about the African-American community and have developed wonderful relationships with many of my new friends.

It's always easier to stay within environments where we are comfortable and secure. In fact, that's what most people do. They avoid change and remain where it's safe. But you can't grow and avoid change at the same time. It just doesn't work that way. If you want to expand your influence, you have to expand your circle of acquaintances.

Expanding your circle of acquaintances may be uncomfortable, but it can do a lot for you. First, it helps you improve. Expanding your circle will expose you to new ideas. It will prompt you to see things from a different point of view, which will help you generate new ideas of your own. It will help you to learn new working methods and pick up additional skills. And it will help you to become more innovative.

Expanding your circle also has another valuable benefit. It expands your network, putting you into contact with more people and giving you potential access to their networks, something Yahoo chief solutions officer Tim Sanders describes in *Love Is the Killer App*. Sanders wrote:

> In the twenty-first century, our success will be based on the people we know. Everyone in our address book is a potential partner for every person we meet . . . Relationships are nodes in our individual network that constitute the promise of our bizlife and serve as a predictor of our success. Some of the brightest new-economy luminaries, such as Kevin Kelly (*New Rules for the New Economy*), or Larry Downes and Chunka Mui (*Unleashing the Killer App*), argue that companies, organizations, and individuals comprise, and are most highly valued for, their web of relationships. If you organize and leverage your relationships as a network, you will generate long-lasting value (and peace of mind) beyond your stock options, mutual funds, and bank accounts. You will also create a value proposition for new contacts, which in turn drives membership in that network—the prime law of business ecosystems, known as the Law of Network Effects. Value explodes with membership . . . When we are fully and totally networked, we are powerful.[1]

Sanders believes that along with knowledge and compassion, your network is your most valuable asset.

How to Expand Your Circle

Each of us has a natural circle of people we're comfortable with. Those people comprise our relational comfort zone. Perhaps you enjoy meeting people and already make it a practice to get out and connect with individuals outside of your circle. If that is the case, keep it up. The more broadly you connect with people, the greater your potential to influence—and be positively influenced by—others.

If you are not inclined to stretch yourself relationally, then think about this. People are like rubber bands. They are most valuable when they are stretched, not when they are at rest. Your value as a leader in the middle will increase as you stretch and get out of your comfort zone relationships, which are usually comprised of:

- People that you've known for a long time;
- People with whom you have common experiences; and
- People that you know like you.

What would happen if the number of people in your circle expanded from five to fifty or from a dozen to more than a hundred? When you had a question your coworkers and you couldn't answer, how quickly do you think you could get it from someone you know? If a friend were looking for a job, how much more likely would it be for you to help her connect with someone who might be looking for help? If you were trying to break into a new market, wouldn't it be likely that you could call an acquaintance and get a quick overview of that industry—or at least call someone who has a friend in that industry? You would even have quicker access to information on the best restaurants in town, the best vacation spots, or where to buy a car. And with every quick connection you are able to make or share with a colleague, the more value you would have—and more influence you would gain—with your peers.

If you desire to expand your circle of acquaintances, all you need are a strategy and a will to do it. You must provide the effort, but I will be glad to give you the following ideas to help you with the strategy.

1. Expand Beyond Your Inner Circle

To get outside of your comfort zone, why not start with those in your comfort zone? Every friend you have has a friend you don't have. Begin with your inner-circle friends, and expand the pool. What businesses are your closest friends in? Whom do they know who might benefit you? Think about the interesting people you've heard friends talk about. Also consider their interests. Who have they connected with through their hobbies and travels?

To get outside of your comfort zone, why not start with those in your comfort zone? Every friend you have has a friend you don't have.

I bet for each of your friends, you could come up with a list of at least three or four—and in some cases as many as a dozen—people you would have interest in meeting through them. And chances are they would have just as much interest in meeting you! Why not start asking your friends to introduce you to some of them? Ask them to set up a lunch, as I did with Sam Chand. Or ask if you can tag along as friends engage in their hobbies. Or simply ask for a phone number and make contact yourself.

You'll be amazed by how quickly your circle expands in this first round. You can double, triple, or quadruple your circle of acquaintances almost overnight. And once you do expand the pool of people you know, be sure to touch base with your new contacts periodically so that you remain connected.

2. Expand Beyond Your Expertise

I obviously value people who have experience in my field. In fact, I recommend that you "talk your craft" with others who share expertise in your area. But you should never limit yourself to connecting with people within your department or profession.

If you work in an organization of any size, one large enough to have multiple departments, then I recommend that you start by connecting with people in the other departments. It doesn't matter what kind of an organization you're in, when there is connection and understanding between departments, everyone wins. When the sales and accounting people develop relationships and grasp what each other does, when the waitstaff and the cooks get along in a restaurant, when marketing department workers and engineers appreciate each other, it helps them, their customers, and the organization. Everybody wins.

3. Expand Beyond Your Strengths

Even outside of work, I think we all tend to respect and gravitate to people whose strengths are like our own. Sports stars hang out together.

Actors marry other actors. Entrepreneurs enjoy trading stories with other entrepreneurs. The problem is that if you spend time only with people like yourself, your world can become terribly small and your thinking limited.

If you are a creative type, go out of your way to meet people who are analytical. If you have a type-A personality, then learn to appreciate the strengths of people who are more laid back. If your thing is business, spend time with people who work in nonprofit environments. If you are white-collar, learn to connect with blue-collar people. Anytime you get a chance to meet people with strengths very different from your own, learn to celebrate their abilities and get to know them better. It will broaden your experience and increase your appreciation for people.

4. Expand Beyond Your Personal Prejudices

French novelist André Gide said that "an unprejudiced mind is probably the rarest thing in the world." Unfortunately, that is probably true. I think all human beings have prejudices of some sort. We prejudge people we haven't met because of their race, ethnicity, gender, occupation, nationality, religion, or associations. And it really does limit us.

If we desire to grow beyond not only our circle of acquaintances but also some of the limitations created by our own thoughts, then we need to break down the walls of prejudice that exist in our minds and hearts. Novelist Gwen Bristow said, "We can get the new world we want, if we want it enough to abandon our prejudices, every day, everywhere. We can build this world if we practice now what we said we were fighting for."

What group of people do you find yourself disliking or mistrusting? Why do you hold such views? Has your vision been obscured by the actions of one or more individuals? The way to change your blanket likes and dislikes is to reach out to people of that group and try to find common ground with them. This may be the most difficult of all circles to break out of, but it is well worth doing.

5. Expand Beyond Your Routine

One of the greatest impediments to meeting new people is routine. We often go to the same places all the time—the same gas stations, coffee shop, grocery store, and restaurants. We employ the same providers of services. We use the same companies for our business. It's just easy. But sometimes we need to shake things up and try something new. It's all about getting outside of your comfort zone.

There are even times when getting out of your routine helps you stay connected with people you already know. In the spring of 2005, my companies, EQUIP and ISS, moved their offices to a new facility. In the past, both companies used office space that was separate, but well connected to each other though common halls. They also shared some work rooms, conference rooms, a lunchroom, and so forth.

The offices in their new location still occupy the same building, but they have become much more separate. They occupy two different suites, each with all of its own supporting spaces. A few weeks after the move, I was talking to Linda Eggers, my assistant who has worked with me for nearly twenty years, and she told me that the changes in the office had caused her to change her routine.

Whenever I talk to Linda, I ask her how things are going at work, because she always has a good feel for the atmosphere at the office, and she is usually aware of any issues that are occurring. But after the move, she remarked that EQUIP was so far removed from her normal routine, that she didn't have any idea how everybody was doing over on that side of the building. So Linda, who is very relational, made it her goal to break from her routine at least once a day to touch base with somebody on the EQUIP team. It's extra work, but she knows how valuable it can be.

I know that my ideas for expanding one's circle of influence may not be revolutionary. They're really just practical thoughts. But the whole point of this chapter is to remind you that you can't wait for life to come to you. You need to initiate, invest, and do what's right when you don't feel like it—especially when it comes to cultivating relationships.

I can't remember a single time I've regretted getting outside of my comfort zone and trying to get acquainted with someone I didn't know. Even if I failed to connect, or if there was no chemistry, or if the person turned out to be unpleasant, it always yielded some kind of benefit, either because I had a new experience, learned something new, or received an introduction to someone else I enjoyed meeting. It's an investment in time—and influence—that is always worth making.

Lead-Across Principle #6

Let the Best Idea Win

Imagine that you're getting ready to go into an important project meeting that will be attended by your boss and several people who are on the same level as you in the organization. Let's say that you were picked from among your peers by your boss to lead the meeting, and you see this time as your chance to shine. You've done your homework and then some. You've spent countless hours thinking through the project, brainstorming, planning, and endeavoring to foresee any obstacles that could be ahead. Based on your preliminary discussions with your staff and your peers, you feel that your ideas are better than anything you've heard from anyone else.

So you begin the meeting with great confidence. But before long, the agenda is not proceeding the way you expected or planned. Your boss makes a comment and sends the flow of the discussion in an entirely new direction. At first you think, *That's okay. I can salvage this. My ideas will still work; I just need to steer everyone back around to them.*

And then one of your peers launches in with an idea. You don't think much of it, but everyone else seems to think it's wonderful. A couple of other people in the room springboard off of that initial idea and begin to build on it. You can feel the energy in the room starting to build. Ideas are sparking. And everyone is clearly moving away from everything you've spent weeks planning—the idea that was your "baby."

What do you do?

For most people in those circumstances, their natural instinct would be to fight for their ideas. After all, by then they would have made quite an investment in them, such as the following:

- *The Intellectual Investment*—it takes hours of thinking, planning, and problem solving spent to gather, create, and refine an idea.

- *The Physical Investment*—getting ready for an important meeting or presentation usually takes a lot of time, effort, and resources.

- *The Emotional Investment*—when people come up with something they see as a good idea, it's hard to keep themselves from thinking about not only what the idea could do for the company but also what it could do for them and their careers.

By this time, they become pretty attached to their ideas, and it becomes difficult to let those ideas die, especially when someone else who didn't do any work may come in and get all the credit.

IDEAS: THE LIFEBLOOD OF AN ORGANIZATION

If you desire to become a 360-Degree Leader, then you need to resist the temptation to fight for your idea when it's not the best idea. Why? Because good ideas are too important to the organization. Harvey Firestone, founder of the Firestone Tire and Rubber Company, said, "Capital isn't so important in business. Experience isn't so important.

If you desire to become a 360-Degree Leader, then you need to resist the temptation to fight for your idea when it's not the best idea.

You can get both of these. What is important is ideas. If you have ideas, you have the main asset you need, and there isn't any limit to what you can do with your business and your life. They are any man's greatest asset—ideas."

Great organizations possess leaders throughout the organization who produce great ideas. That is how they become great. The progress they make and the innovations they create don't come down from on high. Their creative sessions are not dominated by top-down leaders. Nor does every meeting become a kind of wrestling match to see who can dominate everyone else. People come together as teams, peers work together, and they make progress because they want the best idea to win.

> *"Capital isn't so important in business. Experience isn't so important. You can get both of these. What is important is ideas."*
>
> —HARVEY FIRESTONE

Leaders in the middle of the organization who help to surface good ideas are creating what an organization needs most. They do that by producing synergy among their peers. And they will develop influence with their peers because when they are present, they make the whole team better.

WHAT LEADS TO THE BEST IDEAS?

To let the best idea win, you must first generate good ideas. And then you must work to make them even better. How do 360-Degree Leaders do that? How do they help the team find the best ideas? I believe 360-Degree Leaders follow this pattern:

1. 360-DEGREE LEADERS LISTEN TO ALL IDEAS

Finding good ideas begins with an open-minded willingness to listen to all ideas. Mathematician and philosopher Alfred North Whitehead said, "Almost all really new ideas have a certain aspect of foolishness when they are first produced." During the brainstorming process, shutting down any ideas might prevent you from discovering the good ones.

In *Thinking for a Change*, one of the eleven thinking skills I recommend people learn is shared thinking. It is faster than solo thinking, is more innovative, and has greater value. Most important, I believe, is the fact that great thinking comes when good thoughts are shared in a collaborative environment where people contribute to them, shape them, and take them to the next level. A 360-Degree Leader helps to create such an environment.

> *"Almost all really new ideas have a certain aspect of foolishness when they are first produced."*
> —Alfred North Whitehead

2. 360-Degree Leaders Never Settle for Just One Idea

I think many times leaders are too quick to settle on one idea and run with it. That is because leaders are so action oriented. They want to go. They want to make something happen. They want to take the hill! The problem is that they sometimes fight their way to the top of the hill only to find that it's not the right one.

One idea is never enough. Many ideas make us stronger. I once heard an analyst say he thought that was the reason the communist bloc fell at the end of the twentieth century. Communism created a system based primarily on only one idea. If anyone tried to do things a different way, they were knocked down or shipped out.

In contrast, democracy is a system based on a multitude of ideas. If people want to try something different, they have the chance to float their idea and see what happens. If it catches on, it moves forward. If not, it is replaced by another idea. Because of that freedom, in democratic countries creativity is high, opportunities are unlimited, and the potential for growth is astounding. The democratic system can be messy, but that is also true of any endeavor that's creative and collaborative.

The same kind of free-market mentality that drives the largest economy in the world can also drive organizations. If people are open to ideas and options, they can keep growing, innovating, and improving.

3. 360-Degree Leaders Look in Unusual Places for Ideas

Good leaders are attentive to ideas; they are always searching for them. And they cultivate that attentiveness and practice it as a regular discipline. As they read the newspaper, watch a movie, listen to their colleagues, or enjoy a leisure activity, they are always on the lookout for ideas or practices they can use to improve their work and their leadership.

If you desire to find good ideas, you have to search for them. Rarely does a good idea come looking for you.

4. 360-Degree Leaders Don't Let Personality Overshadow Purpose

When someone you don't like or respect suggests something, what is your first reaction? I bet it's to dismiss it. You've heard the phrase, "Consider the source." That's not a bad thing to do, but if you're not careful, you may very likely throw out the good with the bad.

Don't let the personality of someone you work with cause you to lose sight of the greater purpose, which is to add value to the team and advance the organization. If that means listening to the ideas of people with whom you have no chemistry, or worse, a difficult history, so be it. Set aside your pride and listen. And in cases where you must reject the ideas of others, make sure you reject only the idea and not the person.

5. 360-Degree Leaders Protect Creative People and Their Ideas

Ideas are such fragile things, especially when they first come to light. Advertising executive Charlie Brower said, "A new idea is delicate. It can be killed by a sneer or a yawn; it can be stabbed to death by a quip and worried to death by a frown on the right man's brow."

If you desire the best idea to win, then become a champion of creative people and their contributions to your organization. When you discover peers who are creative, promote them, encourage them, and protect them. Pragmatic people often shoot down the ideas of creative people. 360-Degree Leaders who value creativity can help the creative people around them to thrive and keep generating ideas that benefit the organization.

6. 360-Degree Leaders Don't Take Rejection Personally

When your ideas are not received well by others, do your best not to take it personally. When someone in a meeting does that, it can kill the creative process, because at that point the discussion is no longer about the ideas or helping the organization; it becomes about the person whose feelings are hurt. In those moments if you can stop competing and focus your energy on creating, you will open the way for the people around you to take their creativity to the next level.

When I give this advice, I'm not just offering up platitudes. I've had to adopt the right attitude when it comes to ideas, and I can give you an example of where I've had to set aside my own wants and desires and accept the creativity of others. If you don't have any personal experience in the publishing world, then I'm guessing that you believe authors always select the titles of their books. While that may be the way it works for some authors, it has not been the case for me. I've written more than forty books, yet I think I've selected the titles for about a dozen of them. Following is a list of the last nine trade books I've written. Of those, I've selected the title of only one.

The 360-Degree Leader	I wanted to call it *Leading from the Middle of the Pack.*
25 Ways to Win with People	Les Parrott came up with the concept and title.

Winning with People	Charlie Wetzel came up with that title.
Today Matters	I wanted to call it *The Secret of Your Success*.
Thinking for a Change	I wanted to call it *Thinking Your Way to the Top*.
The 17 Essential Qualities of a Team Player	The team at Thomas Nelson picked that title.
The 17 Indisputable Laws of Teamwork	I got to pick the title of this book!
The 21 Indispensable Qualities of a Leader	The concept and title were developed in a joint marketing meeting.
The 21 Irrefutable Laws of Leadership	The concept and title came from Victor Oliver, my editor.

A book is a pretty personal thing for an author. Why would I allow someone else to pick the title? Because I know my ideas aren't always the best ideas. I often think they are, but when everyone in the room has a different opinion, it pays to listen. That's why I've adopted the attitude that the company owner doesn't need to win—the best idea does.

Mel Newhoff is executive vice president of Bozell Worldwide, a top advertising agency. In his industry, ideas are everything. Newhoff has some good advice about the big picture concerning ideas and how to approach your interaction with others in relation to them:

Be passionate about your work and have the integrity to stand up for your ideas. But also know when to compromise.

Without passion you will not be taken seriously. If you don't defend your ideas, no one else will either. When principle is involved, don't budge.

But there is another side to this also. There are very few real "absolutes" in life. Most matters involve taste or opinion, not principle. In these areas recognize that you can compromise. If you become someone who can never compromise, you will forfeit opportunities to those who can.

Being a 360-Degree Leader and leading across is not about getting your own way. It's not about winning at all costs. It's about winning respect and influence with your peers so that you can help the whole team win. Should you be passionate and determined, believing in yourself and your ability to contribute? Definitely. Should you hold on to your deeply held values and stand on principle when those are in jeopardy? Absolutely. But never forget that having a collaborative spirit helps the organization. When you think in terms of *our* idea instead of *my* idea or *her* idea, you're probably on track to helping the team win. That should be your motivation, not just trying to win friends and influence people. But I think you'll find that if you let the best idea win, you will win friends and influence people.

Lead-Across Principle #7

Don't Pretend You're Perfect

Nothing would get done at all if a man waited until he could do something so well that no one could find fault with it.

—John Henry Cardinal Newman

A man who had been suffering from constant headaches finally went to see his doctor.

"I don't know why I keep getting these terrible headaches," he lamented. "I don't drink like so many other people do. I don't smoke like so many other people do. I don't run around at night like so many other people do. I don't overeat like so many other people do. I don't—"

At this point, the doctor interrupted him. "Tell me," the physician asked, "this pain you complain of, is it a sharp shooting pain?"

"Yes," the man answered.

"And does it hurt here, here, and here?" the doctor asked indicating three places around his head.

"Yes," the man replied hopefully, "that's it exactly."

"Simple," the doctor said, rendering his diagnosis. "Your problem is that you have your halo on too tight."

Many leaders are similar to the man in that joke. They try so hard to make others think they're perfect that it about kills them. The problem, to quote Norman Cousins, longtime editor of the *Saturday Review*, is that "to talk about the need for perfection in man is to talk about the need for another species."

How to Be "Real" in a Competitive Environment

One of the worst things leaders can do is expend energy on trying to make others think they're perfect. That's true whether the leader is CEO or functioning in the middle of the organization. It's a crock. The closest to perfection people ever come is when they write their resumés. Since nobody is perfect—not you, not your peers, not your boss—we need to quit pretending. People who are real, who are genuine concerning their weaknesses as well as their strengths, draw others to them. They engender trust. They are approachable. And they are a breath of fresh air in an environment where others are scrambling to reach the top by trying to look good.

Here's how I recommend you approach "getting real" to become a more effective 360-Degree Leader:

1. Admit Your Faults

Recently at a forum for CEOs where I was invited to speak, I suggested to the leaders in attendance that they be honest about their weaknesses and admit their faults to the people they work with when they returned to their companies. After I was done speaking, a CEO approached me because he wanted to talk about that remark.

"I can't believe you're suggesting we talk about our weaknesses with our people," he said. "I think that's a really bad idea."

When I asked him why, he answered, "A leader should never show weakness or fear. He should always be in control, in command. Otherwise his people lose confidence in him."

"I think you're laboring under a false assumption," I replied.

"What's that?" he said.

"You think your people don't know your weaknesses," I explained.

"I'm not suggesting that you admit your faults to give your people information they don't already have. I'm suggesting it because it lets them know that you know your faults."

The people who work alongside you know your weaknesses, faults, and blind spots. If you doubt that—and you have great courage—just ask them! When you get real and admit your shortcomings, what you're doing is making yourself approachable and trustworthy. And when you make mistakes, admit them and quickly ask for forgiveness. Nothing is more disarming, and nothing does a better job of clearing the decks relationally.

2. Ask for Advice

It has been said that advice is what we ask for when we already know the answer but wish we didn't. Isn't that often the case? Some people won't ask for advice when they don't have an answer because they are afraid it will make them look bad; they only ask advice if they can't make up their minds. How much more quickly would people get things done if they asked for help when they needed it instead of trying to fake it until they make it?

3. Worry Less About What Others Think

James C. Humes, in *The Wit and Wisdom of Winston Churchill* (Harper Perennial, 1994), told about an incident that occurred one day at the House of Commons. It is customary for members of parliament to expound, and then the prime minister is given an opportunity to respond to their comments. On this day, a member of the Socialist party railed against Prime Minister Churchill, pouring out abusive words against him. While the man spoke, Churchill remained impassive. He seemed almost bored. When the man was finished, Churchill rose and said, "If I valued the opinion of the honorable gentleman, I might get angry."

People who consider the opinions of others too much often perform too little. They get caught up in pleasing others. I know, because I used to be a people pleaser. Early in my career I was often more worried about what others thought of me than I was about doing what I knew to be best. But in the end, each of us has to live with ourselves. It took me a while, but I finally grasped that knowing in my heart I did right was more important than pleasing or impressing others. Failure is inevitable, so I might as well act in a way that allows me to sleep well at night. Besides, one of the nice things about being imperfect is the joy that it brings to others!

One of the nice things about being imperfect is the joy that it brings to others!

If you want to gain credibility with your peers, you've got to be yourself. If you're genuine, will everyone like you? No. But pretending to be something you're not won't make everyone like you either. It will actually make you less likable.

4. Be Open to Learning from Others

Have you ever met someone who felt compelled to play the expert all the time? Such people aren't much fun to be around after a while, because the only input they seem open to is their own. And as the saying goes, people won't go along with you unless they can get along with you.

I love the way President Abraham Lincoln is said to have handled a person who had a know-it-all attitude. Lincoln asked, "How many legs will a sheep have if you call the tail a leg?"

"Five," the man answered.

"No," replied Lincoln, "he'll still have four, because calling a tail a leg doesn't make it one."

If you really desire others to see you as an approachable person, go a step beyond just willingness to admit your weaknesses. Be willing to learn from them. One of the things I teach in *Winning with People* is the Learning Principle, which states, "Each person we meet has the potential to teach us something." I really believe that. If you embrace that idea, I believe you will discover two things. First, you will learn a lot, because every time you meet someone, it is a learning opportunity. Second, people will warm up to you. Complete strangers often treat me like an old friend, simply because I am open to them.

5. Put Away Pride and Pretense

Too often we think that if we can impress others, we will gain influence with them. We want to become others' heroes—to be larger than life. That creates a problem because we're real live human beings. People can see us for who we really are. If we make it our goal to impress them, we puff up our pride and end up being pretentious—and that turns people off.

If you want to influence others, don't try to impress them. Pride is really nothing more than a form of selfishness, and pretense is only a way to keep people at arm's length so that they can't see who you really are. Instead of impressing others, let them impress you.

It's really a matter of attitude. The people with charisma, those who attract others to themselves, are individuals who focus on others, not themselves. They ask questions of others. They listen. They don't try to be the center of attention. And they never try to pretend they're perfect.

Poet and Harvard professor Robert Hillyer said, "Perfectionism is a dangerous state of mind in an imperfect world. The best way is to forget doubts and set about the task at hand . . . If you are doing your best, you will not have time to worry about failure." That's good advice. If you always do your best, your peers will respect you. And if they respect you, they will listen to you and give you a chance. And that's where leadership starts.

Section IV Review
The Principles 360-Degree Leaders Need to Lead Across

Before you begin learning about leading down the 360-Degree Leader way, review the seven principles you need to master in order to lead across:

1. Understand, practice, and complete the leadership loop.
2. Put completing fellow leaders ahead of competing with them.
3. Be a friend.
4. Avoid office politics.
5. Expand your circle of acquaintances.
6. Let the best idea win.
7. Don't pretend you're perfect.

How well are you doing those seven things? If you're not sure, take the 360-Degree Leadership assessment, offered free of charge to people who have purchased this book. Go to 360DegreeLeader.com for more information.

SECTION V

The Principles 360-Degree Leaders Practice to Lead Down

"Follow me, I'll add value to you."

Leadership is traditionally thought of as a top-down activity. The leader leads; the followers follow. Simple. If you have been leading others for any length of time, you may be tempted to skip this section of the book, thinking, *I already know how to do that.* I don't want you to miss something really important, however. Because 360-Degree Leaders are by definition nonpositional, they lead through influence, not position, power, or leverage. And they take that approach not only with those above and alongside them, but also with those who work under them. This is what makes 360-Degree Leaders unique—and so effective. They take the time and effort to earn influence with their followers just as they do with those over whom they have no authority.

360-Degree Leaders take the time and effort to earn influence with their followers just as they do with those over whom they have no authority.

At the heart of this approach with followers is the desire to add value to them. Retired Admiral James B. Stockdale said:

> Leadership must be based on goodwill. Goodwill does not mean posturing and, least of all, pandering to the mob. It means obvious and wholehearted commitment to helping followers. We are tired of leaders we fear, tired of leaders we love, and tired of leaders who let us take liberties with them. What we need for leaders are men of the heart who are so helpful that they, in effect, do away with the need of their jobs. But leaders like that are never out of a job, never out of followers. Strange as it sounds, great leaders gain authority by giving it away.

As a 360-Degree Leader, when you lead down, you're doing more than just getting people to do what you want. You're finding out who they are. You're helping them to discover and reach their potential. You're showing the way by becoming a model they can follow. You're helping them become a part of something bigger than they could do on their own. And you're rewarding them for being contributors on the team. In short, you are endeavoring to add value to them in any way you can.

Lead-Down Principle #1

Walk Slowly Through the Halls

One of the greatest mistakes leaders make is spending too much time in their offices and not enough time out among the people. Leaders are often agenda driven, task focused, and action oriented because they like to get things done. They hole up in their offices, rush to meetings, and ignore everyone they pass in the halls along the way. What a mistake! First and foremost, leadership is a people business. If you forget the people, you're undermining your leadership, and you run the risk of having it erode away. Then one day when you think you're leading, you'll turn around and discover that nobody is following and you're only taking a walk.

First and foremost, leadership is a people business.

Relationship building is always the foundation of effective leadership. Leaders who ignore the relational aspect of leadership tend to rely on their position instead. Or they expect competence to do "all the talking" for them. True, good leaders are competent, but they are also intentionally connected to the people they lead.

One of the best ways to stay connected to your people and keep track of how they're doing is to approach the task informally as you move among the people. As you see people in the parking lot, chat with them. Go to meetings a few minutes early to see people, but don't start in on the agenda until you've had time to catch up. And, as the title of this chapter suggests, take time to walk slowly through the halls. Connect with people and give them an opportunity to make contact with you.

When it comes to connecting informally, leaders in the middle of an organization often have a distinct advantage over their leadership counterparts at the top. Leaders in the middle are viewed as more accessible than top leaders. They are perceived as having more time (even if it's not true). And they are seen as more approachable. Their people don't worry about "bothering them," and are less reluctant to take their time, unlike people who report directly to the top leader.

Walking slowly through the halls is a useful skill for leading down no matter where you are in an organization, but the best time to master it is while you're in the middle, not after you get to the top. To help you develop this skill successfully, here are a few suggestions.

1. Slow Down

To connect with people, you travel at their speed. When connecting with your leader, chances are you need to speed up. Though it is not always true, in general the higher you go in an organization's hierarchy, the faster the leaders travel. The leader at the top often has boundless energy and is very quick mentally.

To connect with people, you travel at their speed.

Conversely, when you move down, people move more slowly. Once again, not everyone will be slower, but in general it is true. People at the bottom don't process information as quickly, and they don't make decisions as fast. Part of that is due to having less information. Some of it comes from having less experience.

Most people who want to lead are naturally fast. But if you want to become a better leader, you actually need to slow down. You can move faster alone. You can garner more individual honors alone. But to lead others, you need to slow down enough to connect with them, engage them, and take them with you.

If you have children, you instinctively understand this. The next time you need to get something done around the house, try doing it two ways. First, have your kids help. That means you need to enlist them. You need to train them. You need to direct them. You need to supervise them. You need to redirect them. You need to recapture and reenlist them when they wander off. Depending on the ages of your children, it can be pretty exhausting, and even when the work is completed, it may not be to the standard you'd like.

Then try doing the task alone. How much faster can you go? How much better is the quality of the work? How much less aggravation is there to deal with? No wonder many parents start off enlisting their children in tasks to teach and develop them but then throw in the towel after a while and do the work themselves.

Working alone is faster (at least in the beginning), but it doesn't have the same return. If you want your children to learn, grow, and reach their potential, you need to pay the price and take the time and trouble to lead them through the process—even when it means slowing down or giving up some of your agenda. It's similar with employees. Leaders aren't necessarily the first to cross the finish line—people who run alone are the fastest. Leaders are the first to bring all of their people across the finish line. The payoff to leadership—at work or home—comes on the back end.

2. Express That You Care

When you go to your mailbox at home, I bet one of the first things you do is shuffle through the various items. What are you on the lookout for? You're probably looking for something with a handwritten envelope, because it's usually a sign that what's inside is something personal from someone you know. We all desire a personal touch from someone who cares about us.

I read somewhere that the United States Postal Service delivers 170 billion pieces of mail every year. Yet in this vast sea of mail, less than 4 percent of the total is comprised of personal letters. That means you have to sort through one hundred bills, magazines, bank statements, credit card offers, ads, and other pieces of junk mail to find just four items from someone who knows and actually cares about you.

The people who follow you also desire a personal touch. They want to know that others care about them. Most would be especially pleased to know that their boss had genuine concern about them and valued them as human beings, not just as workers who can get things done for them or the organization.

3. Create a Healthy Balance of Personal and Professional Interest

Leaders who show interest in the individuals who work for them need to find the balance between personal and professional interest. Professional interest shows that you have the desire to help them. That is something all good leaders share. Personal interest goes deeper—it shows your heart.

When you take interest in your people as human beings, you need to be sure not to cross the line. There is a point at which interest becomes inappropriate. You mustn't be nosy. Your desire should be to help, not to invade someone's privacy or make them feel uncomfortable.

Start by asking fairly neutral questions. You can safely ask how someone's spouse or children are doing. You can ask about people's hobbies or other outside interests. Or you can ask a very general question such as, "How is everything else going?" Then pay attention to not only the content of their answer, but also for any kind of emotional reaction. If you sense that there might be something there, then ask a nonthreatening follow-up question that asks if everything is okay—but don't push. If they choose to talk, don't judge, don't interrupt, and don't be too quick to offer advice unless they specifically ask for it.

Why should you take the time to do this? The reality is that when employees' personal lives are going well, their professional lives often follow suit. What happens at home colors every aspect of people's lives, including their work. If you have an idea where people are personally, you can know what to expect from them at work, and you may get the opportunity to help them along.

4. Pay Attention When People Start Avoiding You

If you make it a habit to walk slowly through the halls, you will get to know your people and the organization better. You will know when things are working. Your leadership intuition will increase, and when something is wrong, you will pick up on it much more quickly.

Most people are creatures of habit. They fall into patterns and do things the same way most of the time. As you walk around, you will get used to seeing people. Because you will be seen as approachable, people will come out of their offices or cubicles to chat with you. They'll be visible. If something is wrong with somebody who is normally communicative, that person will suddenly avoid you. So as you walk around, you have to ask yourself, *Who am I not seeing?*

Often it's not what people say; it's what they're not saying that is a tip-off that something isn't right. People are always quick to bring good news, but they avoid bringing bad news. I see examples of this all the time in my consulting company, ISS. When we are working with a leader to try to develop a partnership, if that leader intends to sign with us, we hear about it right away. If that leader doesn't, she takes quite a while to make contact with us. A good 360-Degree Leader always slows down enough to be looking, listening, and reading between the lines.

5. Tend to the People, and They Will Tend to the Business

A 360-Degree Leader has many exceptional qualities. In fact, Value #5 of the next section of the book outlines those characteristics. But one thing they all have in common is that despite their passion for the vision and their love of action, they give the majority of their effort to the people. Leaders who tend only to business often end up losing the people *and* the business. But leaders who tend to the people usually build up the people—and the business.

As you strive to walk slowly through the halls, I want to encourage you to find your own unique way of doing it. Look for practices that fit your personality, working situation, and leadership style. One evening in the fall when I was watching *Monday Night Football*, I saw a wonderful example of a leader who was doing just that. The halftime feature was about NFL coach Dick Vermeil. He was being interviewed in a studio about his team, the Kansas City Chiefs, and how his season was going, but that's not what intrigued me.

Leaders who tend only to business often end up losing the people and *the business.*

Between interview questions, they were showing Vermeil and his team during a practice. As the players stretched during warm-ups, the veteran coach walked up and down the rows of players, chatting with them. He stopped next to one player, and I could hear him ask, "How's your wife doing?" And they dialogued for a while.

The interviewer asked Vermeil about his interaction, and he explained that the wife of that player had been fighting lupus. He went on to say that he cares about more than how his players catch the ball or tackle. He interacts with them as people first, then as football players. I've since talked to Dick Vermeil, and he told me that he often has players over to his house so that they can get to know each other better.

What's interesting to me is that when Vermeil came out of retirement to coach the St. Louis Rams in 1997, after a fourteen-year hiatus, I remember hearing reports that players were skeptical of Vermeil's methods and thought that he was old-fashioned and out of touch. And he kept telling them to just hang in there with him and see what happened. What happened was the team won the Super Bowl in 1999.

Will Vermeil win another Super Bowl? I don't know. But I do know this: he has found his own way of walking slowly through the halls that keeps him visible, available, and connected. And because of that, his players respect him and work hard for him because they know he cares about them. A leader can hardly ask for more than that.

Lead-Down Principle #2

See Everyone As a "10"

I want to ask you a question: Who is your favorite teacher of all time? Think back through all your years in school, from kindergarten to the last year of your education. Who stands out? Is there a teacher who changed your life? Most of us have one. Mine was actually a Sunday school teacher named Glen Leatherwood. Who was yours?

What made that teacher different? Was it subject knowledge? Was it teaching technique? Though your teacher may have possessed great knowledge and mastered outstanding technique, I'm willing to bet that what separated that teacher from all of the others was his or her belief in you. That teacher probably saw you as a 10. The teacher who browbeats you and tells you how ignorant or undisciplined you are isn't the one who inspires you to learn and grow. It's the one who thinks you're wonderful and tells you so.

Now I'd like you to think about your working life and the leaders you've worked for over the years. As you think about them, ask yourself the following questions:

- Who gets my best effort? The leader who believes I'm a 10 or the leader who believes I'm a 2?

- Who do I enjoy working with? The leader who believes I'm a 10 or the leader who believes I'm a 2?
- Who is the easiest for me to approach? The leader who believes I'm a 10 or the leader who believes I'm a 2?
- Who wants the best for me? The leader who believes I'm a 10 or the leader who believes I'm a 2?
- Who will I learn the most from? The leader who believes I'm a 10 or the leader who believes I'm a 2?

360-Degree Leaders get more out of their people because they think more of their people. They respect and value them, and as a result, their people want to follow them. The positive, uplifting attitude that they bring to leadership creates a positive working environment where everyone on the team has a place and purpose—and where everyone shares in the win.

For some leaders, this is easy and natural, especially if they have positive personalities. I find that people who were greatly encouraged and valued as children often build up others almost instinctively. But it is a skill that can be learned by anyone, and it is a must for anyone who desires to become a 360-Degree Leader.

If you want to really shine in this area, apply the following suggestions when working with your people:

1. See Them as Who They Can Become

Author Bennett Cerf wrote that J. William Stanton, who served many years as a representative from Ohio in the United States Congress, treasured a letter he received from the Chamber of Commerce in Painesville, Ohio, dated 1949. The letter declined Stanton's offer to bring a new congressman as the featured speaker for a fund-raising dinner. The missive reads: "We feel that this year we really need a big-name speaker who'll be a drawing card so we're hoping to bag the head football coach at John Carroll University. Thanks anyhow for suggesting

Representative John F. Kennedy."[1] Do you have any idea who that coach might have been? I certainly don't.

Do you have a potential JFK in your midst? Or a Jack Welch? Or a Mother Teresa? It's easy to recognize great leadership and great talent once people have already blossomed, but how about before they come into their own?

Look for the great potential that is within each person you lead. When you find it, do your best to draw it out. Some leaders are so insecure that when they see a potential all-star, they try to push that person down because they worry that his or her high performance will make them look bad. But 360-Degree Leaders reach down to lift those people up. They recognize that people with huge potential are going to be successful anyway. The best role they can assume is that of discoverer and encourager. In that way, they add value to them and get to be a positive part of the process of their emergence as leaders.

2. Let Them "Borrow" Your Belief in Them

In 1989, Kevin Myers moved from Grand Rapids, Michigan, to Lawrenceville, Georgia, to plant a church. Kevin was a sharp young leader whose future looked bright, and his sponsoring organization, Kentwood Community Church, was glad to support his efforts.

Kevin did all the right things as he prepared for the first service of Crossroads Community Church. He spent weeks talking to people in the community, he selected a good location, and he got his volunteers ready. When he opened the doors for the first time, his hopes were crushed as only about ninety people showed up—about a third of what he had expected. It was a major disappointment, because Kevin had been on staff at a large, dynamic growing church, and he had little desire to lead a small congregation. He was determined to persevere, however, figuring that in a year or two, he would get over the hump and build the kind of church that matched his vision.

After three years of struggle and little growth, Kevin was ready to throw in the towel. He made a trip to Michigan to meet with Wayne Schmidt, his former boss at Kentwood and the original sponsor of Kevin's church-planting endeavor. Feeling like a failure, Kevin explained to Wayne that he needed a job, because he was planning to close down the church in Georgia. Wayne's response changed Kevin's life. He said, "Kevin, if you've lost faith, borrow mine."

Uncertain about his future, but grateful to Wayne for his faith in him, Kevin returned to Georgia and didn't give up. Slowly, as Kevin grew in his leadership, so did his congregation. As I write this, Kevin leads 3,400 people every week, putting his congregation in the top 1 percent in the United States.

When the people you lead don't believe in themselves, you can help them believe in themselves, just as Wayne did for Kevin. Think of it as a loan, something you are giving freely, but that will later return with dividends as that person succeeds.

3. Catch Them Doing Something Right

If you desire to see everyone as a 10 and help them believe in themselves, you need to encourage them by catching them doing something right. And that is really countercultural. We are trained our whole lives to catch people doing something wrong. If our parents and teachers caught us doing something, you can bet it was something wrong. So we tend to think in those same terms.

When you focus on the negative and catch people doing something wrong, it has no real power to make them any better. When we catch people doing something wrong, they become defensive. They make excuses. They evade. On the other hand, if we catch people doing something right, it gives them positive reinforcement. It helps them tap into their potential. It makes them want to do better.

Make it part of your daily agenda to look for things going right. They don't have to be big things, though of course you want to praise those things as well. It can be almost anything, as long as you are sincere in your praise.

4. Believe the Best—Give Others the Benefit of the Doubt

When we examine ourselves, we naturally give ourselves the benefit of the doubt. Why? Because we see ourselves in the light of our intentions. On the other hand, when we look at others, we usually judge them according to their actions. Think about how much more positive our interaction with others would be if we believed the best in them and gave them the benefit of the doubt, just as we do for ourselves.

Many people are reluctant to adopt this attitude because they fear that others will consider them naive or will take advantage of them. The reality is that trustful people are not weaker than distrustful ones; they are actually stronger. As evidence, I offer the following trust fallacies and the facts that refute them, researched by sociology professor Morton Hunt.

Fallacy: Trustful people are more gullible.
Fact: Trustful people are no more likely to be fooled than mistrustful ones.

Fallacy: Trustful people are less perceptive than mistrustful people of what others are really feeling.
Fact: People who scored high on trust are actually better than others at reading people.

Fallacy: People with a poor opinion of themselves are more trustful than people with a good opinion of themselves.
Fact: The opposite is true. People with high self-esteem are more willing to take emotional risks.

Fallacy: Stupid people are trustful; smart people are mistrustful.
Fact: People with high aptitude or scholastic scores are no more mistrustful or skeptical than people judged to be less intelligent.

Fallacy: Trustful people rely on others to direct their lives for them; mistrustful people rely on themselves.

Fact: The opposite is true. People who feel controlled by outside persons and forces are more mistrustful, while those who feel in charge of their lives are more trustful.

Fallacy: Trustful people are no more trustworthy than mistrustful people.

Fact: Mistrustful people are less trustworthy. Research validates what the ancient Greeks used to say: "He who mistrusts most should be trusted least."[2]

I'm not saying that you should become like an ostrich and stick your head in the sand. All I'm suggesting is that you give others the same consideration you give yourself. It's not a lot to ask, and the dividends it will pay you relationally can be huge.

5. Realize That "10" Has Many Definitions

What does it mean to be a 10? When you started reading this chapter and I suggested that you see everyone as a 10, did a certain image of a 10 come to mind? And did you immediately start comparing the people who work for you to that image and find them coming up short? I wouldn't be surprised if that were the case, because I think most of us have a pretty narrow view of what constitutes a 10.

When it comes to improving in skills, I believe that most people cannot increase their ability beyond about two points on a scale of 1 to 10. So, for example, if you were born a 4 when it comes to math, no matter how hard you work at it, you will probably never become better than a 6. But here's the good news. Everybody is exceptional at something, and a 10 doesn't always look the same.

In their book *Now, Discover Your Strengths* (Free Press, 2001), Marcus

Buckingham and Donald O. Clifton identify thirty-four areas of strength that they believe people exhibit—anything from responsibility to WOO (the ability to **w**in **o**ver **o**thers). And the authors assert that everyone has at least one skill they can perform better than the next ten thousand others. That means they believe everyone can be a 10 in some area. You can always focus on that area when encouraging one of your employees.

But let's say you employ someone who does not have any skill that is a 10 or could be developed into a 10. Does that mean you write him off as hopeless? No. You see, there are other non-skill areas where a person can grow into a 10 no matter what his or her starting point is—areas such as attitude, desire, discipline, and perseverance. If you don't see 10 potential anywhere else, look for it there.

6. Give Them the "10" Treatment

Most leaders treat people according to the number that they place on them. If employees are performing at an average level—let's say as a 5—then the boss gives them the 5 treatment. But I believe people always deserve their leader's best, even when they are not giving their best. I say that because I believe every person has value as a human being and deserves to be treated with respect and dignity. That doesn't mean you reward bad performance. It just means that you treat people well and take the high road with them, even if they don't do the same for you.

People usually rise to the leader's expectations—if they like the leader.

It's been my observation that people usually rise to the leader's expectations—if they like the leader. If you have built solid relationships with your employees and they genuinely like and respect you, they will work hard and give their best.

I've learned a lot of things about leadership from many leaders over the years, but the one I still admire most is my father, Melvin Maxwell. In December 2004, I visited my parents in the Orlando area, and while

I was there, I was scheduled to participate in a conference call. Because I needed a quiet place to do it, my dad graciously let me use his office.

As I sat at his desk, I noticed a card next to the phone with the following words written in my father's hand:

#1 Build people up by encouragement.
#2 Give people credit by acknowledgment.
#3 Give people recognition by gratitude.

I knew in a second why it was there. My father had written it to remind him of how he was to treat people as he spoke on the phone with them. And I was instantly reminded that Dad, more than anyone else, taught me to see everyone as a 10.

Begin today to see and lead people as they can be, not as they are, and you will be amazed by how they respond to you. Not only will your relationship with them improve and their productivity increase, but you also will help them rise to their potential and become who they were created to be.

Lead-Down Principle #3

Develop Each Team Member as a Person

When Jack Welch was the CEO of General Electric, he famously sought to cut the bottom 10 percent of performers from his workforce every year. That practice has been criticized by many of his detractors, but isn't it clear why he would do such a thing? It wasn't to be cruel. It was to try to improve the organization.

Laying off poor performers is one way to try to help the organization. Recruiting top performers from other organizations is another. Leaders are beginning to see that those are not always the best methods for improvement. A few years ago I read an article in *USA Today* that indicated leaders were beginning to see the value of the solid team members they had who were neither stars nor duds. The article termed them "B players." It said:

> When employers aren't busy weeding out the bottom 10% of their workforce, they've been trying to steal the A players from the competition in a battle to lure the best. But some of those employers are coming around to the realization that failure and success might not lie among the weakest and strongest links, but in the solid middle, the B players . . . the 75% of workers who have been all but ignored.[1]

The article went on to say that people in the middle are the backbone of every organization and that they should be valued, which I agree with. But I believe leaders need to take that concept one step further. How do you give your team an edge, helping the B players to perform at their highest level and helping the A players to elevate their game even further? You develop them!

There's a lot more to good leadership than just getting the job done. Getting the job done makes you a success. Getting the job done through others makes you a leader. But developing the people while helping them get the job done at the highest level makes you an exceptional leader. When you develop others, they become better, they do the job better, and both you and the organization benefit. Everybody wins. The result? You become the kind of leader that others seek out and want to follow because of the way you add value to people.

HOW TO DEVELOP YOUR PEOPLE

Before I make a few recommendations about how to develop others, I need to make clear the difference between equipping people and developing them. When you equip people, you teach them how to do a job. If you show someone how to use a machine or some other device, that's equipping. If you teach someone how to make a sale, that's equipping. If you train them in departmental procedures, that's equipping. You should already be providing training to your people so that they know how to do their jobs. Equipping should be a given (although I know that not all leaders do this well).

Development is different. When you develop people, you are helping them to improve as individuals. You are helping them acquire personal qualities that will benefit them in many areas of life, not just their jobs. When you help someone to cultivate discipline or a positive attitude, that's development. When you teach someone to manage their time more effectively or improve their people skills, that's development.

When you teach leadership, that's development. What I've found is that many leaders don't have a developmental mind-set. They expect their employees to take care of their developmental needs on their own. What they fail to realize, however, is that development always pays higher dividends than equipping because it helps the whole person and lifts him to a higher level.

When you equip people, you teach them how to do a job. When you develop them, you are helping them to improve as individuals.

Development is harder to do than equipping, but it is well worth the price. Here's what you need to do as you get started:

1. See Development as a Long-Term Process

Equipping is usually a fairly quick and straightforward process. Most people can learn the mechanics of their job very rapidly—in a matter of hours, days, or months, depending on the type of work. But development always takes time. Why? Because it requires change on the part of the person being developed, and you just can't rush that. Like the old saying goes, it takes nine months to produce a baby—no matter how many people you put on the job.

As you approach the development of your people, think of it as an ongoing process, not something you can do once and then be done. When I led Skyline Church in the San Diego area, I made the development of my staff one of my highest priorities. Some of it I did one-on-one. But I also scheduled a time of teaching for the entire staff every month on topics that would grow them as leaders. It's something I did consistently for a decade.

You cannot give what you do not have. In order to develop your staff, you need to keep growing yourself.

I recommend that you plan to develop the people who work for you. Make it a consistent, regularly scheduled activity. You can ask your staff to read a book every month or two and discuss it together. You can teach a lesson. You can take them to conferences or seminars. Approach the task with your own unique spin. But know this: you cannot give what you do not have. In order to develop your staff, you must keep growing yourself.

2. Discover Each Person's Dreams and Desires

When you equip people, you base what you do on your needs or those of the organization. You teach people what you want them to know so that they can do a job for you. On the other hand, development is based on their needs. You give them what they need in order to become better people. To do that well, you need to know people's dreams and desires.

Walter Lippmann, founder of *The New Republic*, said, "Ignore what a man desires and you ignore the very source of his power." Dreams are the generators of energy with your people. If they have high passion for their dreams, they have high energy. If you know what those dreams are and you develop them in a way that brings those dreams within reach, you not only harness that energy, but you also fuel it.

> *"Ignore what a man desires and you ignore the very source of his power."*
> —Walter Lippmann

Unfortunately, some leaders don't like to see others pursuing their dreams because it reminds them of how far they are from living their dreams. As a result, these types of leaders try to talk people out of reaching for their dreams, and they often do it using the same excuses and rationalizations they give themselves.

If you have found yourself resenting the dreams of others and trying to talk them out of pursuing them, then you need to rekindle the fire you have for your own dreams and start pursuing them again. When a leader is learning, growing, and pursuing his own dreams, he is more likely to help others pursue their own.

3. Lead Everyone Differently

One of the mistakes rookie leaders often make is that they try to lead everyone the same way. But let's face it. Everyone doesn't respond to the same kind of leadership. You should try to be consistent with everyone. You should treat everyone with kindness and respect. But don't expect to use the same strategies and methods with everyone.

You have to figure out what leadership buttons to push with each individual person on your team. One person will respond well to being challenged; another will want to be nurtured. One will need the game plan drawn up for him; another will be more passionate if she can create the game plan herself. One will require consistent, frequent follow-up; another will want breathing room. If you desire to be a 360-Degree Leader, you need to take responsibility for conforming your leadership style to what your people need, not expecting them to adapt to you.

If you desire to be a 360-Degree Leader, you need to take responsibility for conforming your leadership style to what your people need, not expecting them to adapt to you.

4. Use Organizational Goals for Individual Development

If you have to build a mechanism that is entirely separate from the actual work that needs to get done in order to develop your people, it's probably going to wear you out and frustrate you. The way to avoid that is to use organizational goals as much as possible for people's individual development. It's really the best way to go.

- When it's bad for the individual and bad for the organization—everyone loses.
- When it's good for the individual but bad for the organization—the organization loses.
- When it's bad for the individual but good for the organization—the individual loses.
- When it's good for the individual and good for the organization—everyone wins.

I know this may seem a little simplistic, but I want you to notice one thing. The only scenario where there are no losses is when something is good for the organization *and* the individual. That's a recipe for long-term success.

The way to create this kind of win is to match up three things:

- A Goal: Find a need or function within the organization that would bring value to the organization.
- A Strength: Find an individual on your team with a strength that needs developing that will help to achieve that organizational goal.
- An Opportunity: Provide the time, money, and resources the individual needs to achieve the goal.

The more often you can create alignments like this, the more often you will create wins for everyone—the organization, the individual to be developed, and you.

5. Help Them Know Themselves

I always operate on the basic principle that people don't know themselves. A person can't be realistic about his potential until he is realistic about his position. In other words, you have to know where you are before you can figure out how to get someplace else.

A person can't be realistic about his potential until he is realistic about his position.

Max DePree, chairman emeritus of Herman Miller, Inc. and a member of *Fortune* magazine's National Business Hall of Fame, said that it is the first responsibility of a leader to define reality. I believe it is the first responsibility of a leader who develops others to help them define the reality of who they are. Leaders help them recognize their strengths and weaknesses. That is critical if we want to help others.

6. Be Ready to Have a Hard Conversation

There is no development without hard lessons. Almost all growth comes when we have positive responses to negative things. The more difficult the thing is to deal with, the more we need to push in order to grow. The process is often not very pleasant, but you always have to pay a price for growth.

Good leaders are willing to have hard conversations to start the growth process for the people under their care. A friend told me the story of a former U.S. Army officer who was working in a Fortune 500 company. The man was repeatedly passed over when the organization's leaders were seeking and recruiting employees with leadership potential to advance in the organization, and he couldn't understand why. His performance record was good, his attitude was positive, and he possessed experience. So what was the problem?

The former officer possessed some peculiar personal habits that made others uncomfortable around him. When he became stressed, he hummed. When he became especially agitated, he sat on his hands. He wasn't aware that he did these things, and nobody ever pointed out the distracting and unprofessional nature of these peculiar habits. People simply wrote him off as being odd.

Fortunately, the man finally worked for a leader who was willing to have a hard conversation with him. The leader made him aware of the problem, he broke the habit, and today he is a senior leader in that organization.

When you don't want to have a difficult conversation, you need to ask yourself: *Is it because it will hurt them or hurt me?* If it is because it will hurt you, then you're being selfish. Good leaders get past the discomfort of having difficult conversations for the sake of the people they lead and the organization. The thing you need to remember is that people will work through difficult things if they believe you want to work with them.

7. Celebrate the Right Wins

Leaders who develop others always want to help their people get wins under their belts, especially when they are just starting out. But a strategic win always has greatest value. Try to target wins based on where you want people to grow and how you want them to grow. That will give them extra incentive and encouragement to go after the things that will help them improve.

It really does matter how you set up these wins. A good win is one that is not only achieved but also approached in the right way. If someone you're leading goes about an activity all wrong but somehow gets the right results—and you celebrate it—you're setting up that person to fail. Experience alone isn't a good enough teacher—evaluated experience is. As the leader, you need to evaluate what looks like a win to make sure it is actually teaching what your employee needs to learn in order to grow and develop.

Experience alone isn't a good enough teacher—evaluated experience is.

8. Prepare Them for Leadership

In an organizational context, no development process would be complete without the inclusion of leadership development. The better your people are at leading, the greater potential impact they will have on and for the organization. But that means more than just teaching leadership lessons or asking people to read leadership books. It means taking them through a process that gets them ready to step in and lead.

The best process I know is like on-the-job training where people work side by side. Imagine that I wanted to prepare you for leadership. This is how we would proceed:

I DO IT. The process begins with my knowing how to do something myself. I cannot give what I do not possess myself.

I DO IT AND YOU WATCH. After I have mastered the process, I take you with me and ask you to watch. I explain what I'm doing. I encourage you to ask questions. I want you to see and understand everything I'm doing.

YOU DO IT AND I WATCH. You can only learn so much from watching. At some point you have to jump in and actually try it. When you reach this stage and start doing it yourself, my role is to encourage you, gently correct you, and redirect you as needed.

YOU DO IT. As soon as you have the fundamentals down, I step back and give you some room so that you can master it and start to develop your own style and methods.

YOU DO IT AND SOMEONE ELSE WATCHES. The last thing I need to do in the development process is help you find someone to develop and encourage you to get started. You never really know something until you teach it to someone else. Besides, the process isn't really complete until you pass on what you've received to someone else.

If you dedicate yourself to the development of people and commit to it as a long-term process, you will notice a change in your relationships with the people who work with you. They will develop a strong loyalty to you because they know that you have their best interests at heart and you have proven it with your actions. And the longer you develop them, the longer they are likely to stay with you.

You never really know something until you teach it to someone else.

Knowing this, don't hold on to your people too tightly. Sometimes the best thing you can do for people is to let them spread their wings and fly. But if you have been diligent in the development process—and helped them to pass on what they've learned—someone else will step up and take their place. When you continually develop people, there is never a shortage of leaders to build the organization and help you carry the load.

Lead-Down Principle #4

Place People in Their Strength Zones

Most leaders agree that having the right people on the team and putting those people in the right places are important. But how much of a difference does it make, really? Are we talking about a small difference or a big one? That's what the people at the Gallup Organization asked themselves while doing research for *Now, Discover Your Strengths*. Here is what the book's authors learned:

> In our latest meta-analysis The Gallup Organization asked this question of 198,000 employees working in 7,939 business units within 36 companies: At work do you have the opportunity to do what you do best every day? We then compared the responses to the performance of the business units and discovered the following: When employees answered "strongly agree" to this question, they were 50 percent more likely to work in business units with lower employee turnover, 38 percent more likely to work in more productive business units, and 44 percent more likely to work in business units with higher customer satisfaction scores.[1]

That is a highly significant difference. What percentage of workers do you think are working in their areas of strength? According to the authors, the answer is only 20 percent.[2]

The number one reason people don't like their jobs is that they are not working in the area of their strengths. When employees are continually asked to perform in an area of weakness, they become demoralized, they are less productive, and they eventually burn out. Whose fault is that? Usually, it is their leaders' fault!

The number one reason people don't like their jobs is that they are not working in the area of their strengths.

Successful people find their own strength zones. Successful leaders find the strength zones of the people they lead. Individuals may seek a job with a particular organization, but they generally don't place themselves in their positions at work. For the most part, their leaders are the ones who do that.

When you place individuals in their strength zones, a couple of things happen. First, you change people's lives for the better. In an earlier chapter, I mentioned that people's personal lives color every aspect of their existence, including work. The reverse is also true. People's work lives color the other aspects of their lives. When you put people in their strength zones, their jobs become rewarding and fulfilling. It often makes the difference between someone who hates going to work and someone who loves it. The other benefit is that you help the organization and you.

Steps for Placing People in Their Strength Zones

The ability to help people find their best place in their careers is an awesome power and a great responsibility, one that we should not take lightly as leaders. As you think about the people who work for you, try to do the following for each individual:

1. Discover Their True Strengths

Most people do not discover their strengths on their own. They often get drawn into the routine of day-to-day living and simply get busy. They rarely explore their strengths or reflect on their successes or failures. That's why it is so valuable for them to have a leader who is genuinely interested in them help them to recognize their strengths.

There are many helpful tools available that you can use to aid people in the process of self-discovery. I've already mentioned the work of Buckingham and Clifton. Their book, *Now, Discover Your Strengths*, and the Strengths Finder material on their Web site can be helpful. So can personality tests such as DISC or Myers-Briggs. And there are many vocational tests as well. Whatever works in the context of your organization can be helpful. But don't limit yourself to tests. Often the most valuable help you can give will be based on your personal observations.

Successful people find their own strength zones. Successful leaders find the strength zones of the people they lead.

2. Give Them the Right Job

Moving someone from a job they hate to the right job can be life changing. One executive I interviewed said he moved a person on his staff to four different places in the organization, trying to find the right fit. Because he'd placed her wrong so many times, he was almost ready to give up on her. But he knew she had great potential, and she was right for the organization. Finally, after he found the right job for her, she was a star!

Because this executive knows how important it is to have every person working in the right job, he asks his staff once a year, "If you could be doing anything, what would it be?" From their answers, he gets clues about any people who may have been miscast in their roles.

Trying to get the right person in the right job can take a lot of time and energy. Let's face it. Isn't it easier for a leader to just put people where it is most convenient and get on with the work? Once again, this is an area where leaders' desire for action works against them. Fight against your natural tendency to make a decision and move on. Don't be afraid to move people around if they're not shining the way you think they could.

3. Identify the Skills They'll Need and Provide World-Class Training

Every job requires a particular set of skills that employees must possess in order to be really successful. Even someone with great personal strengths and a great "fit" will not truly be working in his strength zone if he doesn't have these skills. As the leader, it is your job to make sure your people acquire what they need to win.

Two of the most important questions to ask are:

> *What am I doing to develop myself?*
> *What am I doing to develop my staff?*

The first question determines your personal potential and ongoing capacity to lead. The second determines the potential of your team. If they aren't growing, then they will not be any better tomorrow than they are today.

In *The 17 Indisputable Laws of Teamwork*, the Law of the Niche says, "All players have a place where they add the most value." Whatever that niche is determines the best role that person should assume on your team. And it really does make a difference. When leaders really get this, the teams they lead perform at an incredible level. And it reflects positively on those leaders. I don't think it is an exaggeration to say that the success of a leader is determined more by putting people into their strength zones than by anything else.

> *The Law of the Niche: "All players have a place where they add the most value."*

When I was in high school, I was fortunate to have a coach who understood this. During one of our varsity basketball practices, our coach, Don Neff, decided he wanted to teach us a very important lesson about basketball. He got the first- and second-string teams out on the floor to scrimmage. That wasn't unusual—we scrimmaged all the time. Our second team had some good players, but clearly the first team was much better. This time he had us do something very different from the norm. He let the second-string players take their normal positions, but he assigned each of us starters to a different role from our usual one. I was normally a shooting guard, but for this scrimmage I was asked to play center. And as I recall, our center was put in the point-guard position.

> *"Having the best players on the floor isn't enough. You have to have the best players in the right positions."*
>
> —Don Neff

We were instructed to play to twenty, but the game didn't take long. The second team trounced us in no time. When the scrimmage was over, Coach Neff called us over to the bench and said, "Having the best players on the floor isn't enough. You have to have the best players in the right positions."

I never forgot that lesson. And as I've led people over the last thirty years, I've applied it to much more than basketball. It doesn't matter what kind of a team you're leading. If you don't place people in their strength zones, you're making it almost impossible for them—and you—to win.

Lead-Down Principle #5

Model the Behavior You Desire

One of my favorite leadership books is *Learning to Lead* (Word, 1986), by Fred Smith. I remember very vividly where I was when I first read it. I was on a plane flying back to San Diego. It stands out in my memory because when I read his ideas on "incarnational leadership," I pulled out a legal pad to begin brainstorming. In the book Fred said that when a leader's identity and actions are consistent, the results he gets are consistent. When they are inconsistent, then so are the results.

On my legal pad, I created three columns. At the top of the first, I wrote, "What I Am." There I intended to write down the qualities I desired to embrace as a leader. At the top of the second column, I wrote, "What I Do," the actions that would be consistent with each character trait. The third column contained the results of consistent character and behavior.

What I Am	What I Do	Results
Character driven	Do right	Credibility
Relational	Care	Community
Encourager	Believe in people	High morale

What I Am	What I Do	Results
Visionary	Set goals	Direction
Student	Learn	Growth
Inspiring	Motivate	Action
Selfless	Focus on others	Reaching out
Confident	Make decisions	Security

A list like this can be a real eye-opener, because when we don't get the results we want, we are often tempted to try to place the blame outside of ourselves.

The Leader's Impact

Just as consistency can create power in your personal life, it can also create power in your leadership. Leaders set the tone and the pace for all the people working for them. Therefore, they need to be what they want to see. Let me explain how this works.

Leaders need to be what they want to see.

Your Behavior Determines the Culture

One of the easiest places to see distinct cultures is in sports. For example, think about the NFL's Oakland Raiders. For years they have prided themselves on their bad-boy image. Their owner, Al Davis, is a renegade. Their players are tough guys. Even their fans follow suit. During a game, just look at the area in their stadium that they call "the black hole." Your culture determines whom you attract. The behavior of that team for decades has created its culture.

Think about another team in the NFL, the Dallas Cowboys. For a long time, the team was a perennial winner, and for years the Cowboys were called "America's Team." Tom Landry, the team's coach at that time, helped to create that culture. After Landry left the team, the behavior of the coaches and players began to change—and so did the culture. Nobody—except maybe an occasional Texan—calls the Cowboys "America's Team" anymore.

If you desire to instill a particular value into your organization's culture, then you need to ask yourself whether it is an identifiable behavior among the people of your organization—starting with yourself. And the only way to change the culture is to change your behavior.

Your Attitude Determines the Atmosphere

Have you ever worked for someone who had a glass-is-half-empty kind of attitude? No matter what the circumstances, the outlook was gloomy. It is night and day different from working for someone whose attitude is upbeat and optimistic. The happiest people don't necessarily have the best of everything. They just make the best of everything.

The leader's attitude is like a thermostat for the place she works. If her attitude is good, the atmosphere is pleasant, and the environment is easy to work in. But if her attitude is bad, the temperature is insufferable. Nobody wants to work in an environment that is overheated or icy cold.

Your Values Determine the Decisions

Roy Disney, brother and partner of Walt Disney, said, "It's not hard to make decisions when you know what your values are." Not only is that true, but I'd add that it's also not hard to stay with the decisions you make when they are based on your values. Decisions that are not consistent with our values are always short-lived.

Decisions that are not consistent with our values are always short-lived.

Whatever you embrace will come out in the decisions of your people. If you value shortcuts, then your employees will make decisions that value speed over quality. If you are insensitive to others' feelings, then your staff will make decisions that don't take people's feelings into account. If you exhibit even the slightest tolerance for dishonesty, then you can bet that someone on the team will think it is okay to make decisions that violate the standards of integrity.

YOUR INVESTMENT DETERMINES THE RETURN

Just like in the world of finance, the only way you get a return with people is to make an investment in them. The seeds you sow determine the harvest you reap. Our problem is that we often focus on the reaping rather than the sowing.

What's worse than training your people and losing them? Not training them and keeping them.

I've already written about the importance of developing and equipping employees, so I don't need to say a lot more here. I'll give you just one thought: What's worse than training your people and losing them? Not training them and keeping them.

YOUR CHARACTER DETERMINES THE TRUST

Do people trust you? Are the people who work for you quick to believe that you have their best interests at heart? Or do they question your intentions and weigh your motives when you introduce them to a new idea? The answers to those questions can be traced back to your character.

Trust is not given nor can it be assumed simply because you have a leadership position with others. Trust has to be earned, and it usually comes when you are tested. Whether you pass or fail the test is almost always determined by your character. And here's the really tough thing. When you went to school, 60 percent was probably a passing grade; or if your school had particularly high standards, maybe 70 percent. When it comes to trust, the only passing grade is 100 percent. If people can't trust you all of the time, then they will consider you untrustworthy.

YOUR WORK ETHIC DETERMINES THE PRODUCTIVITY

I love the story of the crusty old Scotsman who worked hard and expected the people he led to do the same. His workers would tease, "Hey Scotty, don't you know that Rome wasn't built in a day?"

"Aye, I know that," he would answer. "But I wasn't the foreman on that job."

Leaders truly do set the tone on the job when it comes to productivity. Employees soon feel very uncomfortable if they are lax in their work ethic but they can see their boss working diligently. Employees who possess strong character quickly feel prompted to pick up the pace.

Thomas Jefferson said, "It's wonderful how much can be done if we are always working." If you want your people to always be working, you had better be too.

Your Growth Determines the Potential

The most important leadership lesson I teach is the Law of the Lid: "Leadership ability determines a person's level of effectiveness." If your leadership is a 5 (on a scale from 1 to 10), then your effectiveness will be no greater than a 5. Leadership is the glass ceiling of personal achievement.

The same is true of the people you lead. Your leadership, if it is not continually growing, can be a lid to the potential of your people. Why? Because you teach what you know, but you reproduce what you are. You can't give people what you do not have. If you want to increase the potential of your team, you need to keep growing yourself.

One of my favorite examples of leadership modeling can be found in the story of David, king of ancient Israel. Most people are familiar with the story of David and Goliath. During a war between the Hebrew and Philistine peoples, Goliath, a warrior-giant, challenged any individual who would fight him to a winner-take-all battle. Saul, Israel's king, cowered in his tent—and so did his army. But David, a shepherd boy whose older brothers stood among the cowards, challenged Goliath and defeated him in combat. The incident is often recounted as a children's story.

Most people familiar with the Bible know that David became king.

What many don't know is that in the years before he ascended the throne, David drew warriors to him and created a strong private army. And those warriors became like David, to the point where several of them also became giant killers.

Though the results are not always that dramatic, it is always true that followers become like their leaders. They are influenced by their leaders' values. They adopt their working methods. They even emulate many of their quirks and habits. That's why we must always be aware of our own conduct before criticizing the people who work for us. If you don't like what your people are doing, first take a look at yourself.

Lead-Down Principle #6

Transfer the Vision

Let's say that you're doing a good job as a 360-Degree Leader, and you're leading down effectively. You're modeling the way. You're developing relationships with your people and building them up. You've trained them. You're developing them and plan to continue doing so. Now what? It's like you've taken the time to build a fine weapon and load it. So what do you do? You aim at the bull's-eye and pull the trigger! In the area of leadership, that means transferring the vision.

If you were the leader at the top of the organization, you would be transferring your own vision. As a leader in the middle of the organization, you will be transferring what is primarily the vision of others (as we discussed in Section II, Lead-Up Principle #6: "The Vision Challenge"). Leaders in the middle are the crucial link in that process. The vision may be cast by the top leaders, but it rarely gets transferred to the people without the wholehearted participation of the leaders lower in the organization who are closer to them. Though leaders in the middle may not always be the inventors of the vision, they are almost always its interpreters.

Though leaders in the middle may not always be the inventors of the vision, they are almost always its interpreters.

So how do 360-Degree Leaders interpret the vision in a way that fires up the people and sets them off in the right direction? If you include the following seven elements, you will be well on your way to hitting the target.

1. CLARITY

When I lived in San Diego, I used to go to a lot of Padres baseball games. I had great seats right behind the dugout. Back then, the team wasn't very good, and the organization would do a number of promotions, games, and activities to try to keep the crowd engaged. One of the regular things they would do between two of the innings was a fan game where they would put a player's picture on the big-screen in the stadium. But they didn't put the picture up all at once. They had divided it into about a dozen sections, and they would put up one piece at a time until finally the whole picture was complete.

> *When preparing to cast vision, ask:* What do I want them to know, and what do I want them to do?

I know that's not very exciting. What was really interesting to me was the crowd's reaction. You could tell by the sound of their reactions when people would get it. Early on, there was anticipation, but you could tell that nobody knew whose picture it was because it was just too disjointed and incomplete. Then you'd start to hear a murmur—that was the sound of the really quick people getting it. Then it would get a little louder as more got it, and suddenly, it got very noisy. That was when most of the people in the stadium had the picture.

The casting of vision is very similar. If the vision isn't clear, the people aren't clear. They just can't figure it out. You have to put all the pieces together for them to help them "get" it. When preparing to cast vision, ask yourself: *What do I want them to know, and what do I want them to do?* And once you know the answer, keep communicating and filling in the blanks until you can sense that most of your people get it—not just the quick ones.

2. Connection of Past, Present, and Future

I've noticed that most people who cast vision focus almost entirely on the future. On one level that makes sense. After all, vision is by its very nature focused on the future. But any leader who casts vision and neglects to tie in the past and present is really missing an opportunity.

Talking only about the past gives no hope for the future, so you certainly don't want to put your focus there. But if you ignore the past, you fail to connect people to the organization's history. If you show that you value what has gone before and honor the people who laid the foundation to get you where you are today, you validate those people who have worked hard and sacrificed to build what already exists. You also give the people who are new to the process the added security of knowing they are part of something bigger.

When people are able to touch the past, they will be more inclined to reach for the future. Anytime you can show that the past, present, and future are unified, you bring power and continuity to your vision casting.

3. Purpose

Although vision tells people where they need to go, purpose tells them why they should go. Not only does that help people to make sense of what they are being asked to do, but it also helps them to stay on target. It helps them to make adjustments, improvise, and innovate as they encounter obstacles or experience other difficulties.

Although vision tells people where they need to go, purpose tells them why they should go.

4. Goals

In *Leadership*, historian and political scientist James MacGregor Burns writes, "Leadership is leaders inducing followers to act for certain goals that present the values and the motivations—the wants and needs, the aspirations and expectations—of both leaders and followers"

(Harper Perennial, 1978). Without goals and a strategy to achieve them, vision isn't measurable or attainable.

I've met many leaders over the years who had a pie-in-the-sky idea, but little more than hope when it came to figuring out how to get there. Hope is not a strategy. When you give people a process, they realize that the vision is realistic. And that increases their confidence in you and the vision.

5. A Challenge

Just because you make the vision realistic doesn't mean you can't make it challenging. In fact, if vision doesn't require people to stretch, they may wonder if it is worthy of their dedication.

Some leaders seem to be afraid to challenge their teams, but a challenge makes good people want to spread their wings and fly. It fires up the committed people—and fries the uncommitted ones. You will accurately define your people if you ask them to stretch.

6. Stories

If you want to put a human face on a challenging vision, then include stories. They make the vision relational and warm. Think about people who have been involved in the advancement of the organization so far. Tell about their struggles and victories. Praise their contributions. Make it personal. When you do that, you make the vision and the process identifiable to the average people who are wondering, *Should I be a part of this? Can I be a part of this? Can I make a difference?* A story helps them to see that even though they may have to reach to help achieve the vision, it is within their grasp.

7. Passion

The final piece of the vision puzzle is passion. If there is no passion in the picture, then your vision isn't transferable; it is just a pleasant snapshot. Who's going to work hard, put in long hours, fight through obstacles, and go the extra mile for that? The wonderful thing about passion is that it is contagious. If you are fired up, then they will get fired up, and they will need that fire to keep them going.

There is definitely a link between ownership and success. You don't get the latter without the former, and 360-Degree Leaders cultivate the ownership. They take the vision "from me to we." The best person I've ever had on my staff when it came to the transfer of the vision was Dan Reiland. When I was at Skyline Church, Dan was my executive pastor. He did a great job of transferring the vision with the staff, but what impressed me most was the way he did it with the laypeople in the congregation.

If there is no passion in the picture, then your vision isn't transferable.

For more than a decade, Dan led a class here of young professional couples called Joint Venture. The people he attracted were really the up-and-coming leaders of the organization. During the last five years I was at Skyline, I think every new board member emerged from the ranks of Dan's leadership.

Every year at Christmas, Dan invited me to speak at Joint Venture's big Christmas party. It was always a first-class affair. It was usually hosted at a nice hotel or conference center, the food was great, and everybody was dressed to the nines—the ladies were in evening wear, many of the men in tuxes. It became a tradition that they were the first group of people in the congregation to whom I would cast vision for the coming year.

There were two reasons I did that. First, there were many influencers in that group. The second reason was that they always got it. They were right there tracking with me. Why? Because they were like their leader, Dan, who was continually transferring my vision to them the other fifty-one weeks of the year. I feel certain that the church would not have moved as quickly as it did if Dan hadn't been such a good leader in the middle of the organization.

People say that the bigger a ship is, the harder it is to turn. That may be true of ships, but it's really different in organizations. An organization is one big entity that has many small ones in it. If every leader in the middle of the organization is a 360-Degree Leader who excels at transferring the vision to the crew in their area, then even a huge organization would be able to turn very quickly. It is not the size of the organization that matters; it is the size of leaders within it.

Lead-Down Principle #7

Reward for Results

A man was enjoying an afternoon in a small fishing boat on a peaceful lake. He fished as he munched on a chocolate bar. The weather was perfect, his cell phone was turned off, and all he could think about was how happy he was.

Just then he spotted a snake in the water with a frog in its mouth. He felt sorry for the frog, so he scooped up the snake with his landing net, took the frog out of its mouth, and tossed it to safety. Then he felt sorry for the snake. He broke off a piece of his chocolate bar, gave it to the snake, and placed it back in the water, where it swam away.

There, he thought. *The frog is happy, the snake is happy, and now I'm happy again. This is great.* He cast his line back into the water and then settled back again.

A few minutes later, he heard a bump on the side of the boat. He looked over the side, and there was the snake again. This time it had two frogs in his mouth!

The moral of the story is this: Be careful what you reward, because whatever gets rewarded gets done.

I'm guessing that as a leader you are probably strongly aware of this truth. And it doesn't matter if the thing that gets rewarded is positive or negative. Whatever actions leaders reward will be repeated. That's why it's very important to reward results—and to do it the right way. When you use every tool at your disposal to reward your people, you not only inspire them to do the things that are right for the organization but also to work harder and to feel better about the job they're doing. Rewarding for results makes you a more effective—and more influential—360-Degree Leader.

Whatever actions leaders reward will be repeated.

To reward results most effectively, follow these seven principles:

1. Give Praise Publicly and Privately

The place to start when it comes to rewarding others is with your praise. You cannot praise too much. Billy Hornsby, EQUIP's European coordinator, advised, "It's okay to let those you lead outshine you, for if they shine brightly enough, they reflect positively on you."

In *25 Ways to Win with People*, Les Parrott and I explain the importance of praising people in front of other people. The more important the "audience" hearing the praise to the people receiving it, the more valuable it is. But I want to suggest that before you praise people publicly, first praise them privately. Doing that gives what you say integrity; people know you're not just trying to manipulate them by saying something kind. Besides, most of the time when people are praised privately, inside they wish others were there to hear it. If you praise privately first and then do it publicly, it is doubly important because it fulfills the longing they had for others to hear it.

"It's okay to let those you lead outshine you, for if they shine brightly enough, they reflect positively on you."
—Billy Hornsby

2. Give More Than Just Praise

Now that I've encouraged you to praise people, I need to tell you that you have to give them more than just praise.

If you praise them but don't raise them, it won't pay their bills.
If you raise them but don't praise them, it won't cure their ills.

Talk is cheap—unless you back it up with money. Good leaders take good care of their people. If you really think about it, the people who cost the organization the most aren't the ones who get paid the most. The ones that cost the most are the people whose work doesn't rise to the level of their pay.

When the pay that people receive doesn't match the results they achieve, then they become highly discouraged. If that happens under your watch as a leader, it will not only take a toll on your people's effort, but it will also take a toll on your leadership. One leader I interviewed said he once relocated to the northwestern United States to take a job running a dwindling department in an organization. In nine months' time, he doubled the impact of his department.

When he went for his annual review, his performance was totally ignored. He was told the staff was getting a blanket 5-percent increase in salary. That was hard to swallow, because he was to be rewarded the same as the other departmental leaders, even the ones who hadn't made any kind of significant improvement in their areas. But he became even more demoralized that his increase would be prorated down to 3.75 percent because he hadn't been there the whole year. Talk about taking the wind out of a person's sails!

3. Don't Reward Everyone the Same

That brings me to my next point. If you want to be an effective leader, you cannot reward everyone the same way. This is a major pressure for most leaders. All but the top people in an organization want everyone to be treated the same way. They say that they want everything to be "fair." But is it fair for someone who produces twice the revenue of her counterpart to be paid the same? Should the person who carries the team be paid the same as the one he has to continually carry? I don't think so. Mick Delaney said, "Any business or industry that pays equal rewards to its goof-offs and its eager beavers sooner or later will find itself with more goof-offs than eager beavers."

So how do you go about addressing the pressure to be fair while still rewarding results? Praise effort, but reward only results. Since whatever gets rewarded gets done, if you continually praise effort and do it for everyone, people will continue to work hard. If they are working in their strength zones and keep working hard, they will eventually achieve good results. At that time, reward them financially.

"Any business or industry that pays equal rewards to its goof-offs and its eager beavers sooner or later will find itself with more goof-offs than eager beavers."

—Mick Delaney

4. Give Perks Beyond Pay

Let's face it. Leaders in the middle of an organization often have limitations on how they can reward people financially. So what is a 360-Degree Leader to do? Reward people with perks. What would it be like if you had a special reserved parking place but gave it to one of your employees for a week or a month? What kind of an impression would that make on the person who received it? Anything you get as a perk you can share with the people who work with you, whether it's a parking place, free tickets to an event, or use of the corporate suite.

Another area where you can share your wealth is in your relationships. It requires a secure leader to do so, but if you introduce your employees to friends, acquaintances, and professionals who might interest or benefit them, they will feel rewarded and grateful.

Finally, though this may seem a little odd, I want to recommend that you try to extend perks or acknowledgment to your employees' family members, when appropriate. They are often the ones who make great sacrifices for the work to get done, especially during a crisis. One leader I interviewed told me a story that affirmed the positive impact of such an acknowledgment. He said his organization's lighting system had crashed two weeks prior to a planned production. For the performance to go on, the entire system had to be replaced in a week's time, and he was set to oversee the job. To make matters worse, the whole thing happened in December, as Christmas approached.

This leader started preparations a week before the installation, and once the electrician arrived to start the job, he didn't leave his side. He knew that if he went home while the crew was working, progress would stall. He worked more than one hundred hours that week, ate every meal at work, and never saw his kids the entire week.

He completed the work on Sunday, and then reported to work the next morning. His boss had a surprise for him. Knowing that the leader had missed spending time with his five-year-old son, his boss arranged for his son to attend an important staff meeting that was planned for that morning. As the adults met, the boy sat on his father's lap and colored. The leader later told me, "Bonuses are wonderful. Gifts are great. But that moment, appreciating my sacrifice to my family, meant more than anything!"

5. Promote When Possible

If you have the choice to promote someone from within or bring in someone from outside—all other factors being equal—promote from within. Few things reward an employee the way a promotion does. A promotion says, "You've done a good job, we believe you can do even more, and here is a reward for your performance." And the best promotions are the ones that don't need to be explained because everyone who works with the ones being promoted have seen them grow into their new jobs.

6. Remember That You Get What You Pay For

Not long ago I invited a young leader to attend a roundtable discussion with leaders of large churches from my area. Forums like these are really beneficial because leaders on a similar level can talk about their struggles, share information, and learn things from each other. At one point in the discussion, the leaders talked about staffs and budgets. They went around the table, sharing the percentage of their budgets that were spent on staff. When it was this young leader's turn to talk, he quickly changed the subject.

Later when I talked to him, he told me that as they talked he realized that he was underpaying his staff, because the percentage of his budget was very low. He went home after that meeting, met with his church's board, and radically changed their pay scale. He says that his church now has the best team it's ever had, and it is worth every penny. He doesn't ever want to lose a valuable team member because of pay.

A leader may be able to hire people without paying them a lot of money. And occasionally, it may be possible to keep a few good people while not paying them very well. But in the long run, you get what you pay for. If you want to attract and keep good people, you need to pay them what they're worth. Otherwise, you will end up with people who are worth what you pay.

When you were a kid in science class, did you ever work with an old-fashioned balance? I mean the kind like the scales held in the hand of Blind Justice at courthouses. They're made up of two shallow dishes suspended from chains from a lever. If you put something that weighs an ounce in one dish, then you need to put something that weighs the same in the other dish for it to level out.

Leadership is like one of those scales. The rewards leaders give are counterbalanced by the results that their people give in return. In an organization, the scales are always moving, weighing more heavily on one side or the other. The scales naturally seek equilibrium where they are level, and they will not stay out of balance permanently.

Leaders always want greater results, because that is where the fulfillment of the vision comes from. The impact, profits, and success of an organization all come from this. As a leader, you have a choice. You can try to push your employees to give more, hoping to swing the balance in your favor. Or you can load up the rewards side—which is the only side you really have significant influence over—and wait for the balance to swing back to level as your employees respond by producing more. That's what 360-Degree Leaders do. They focus on what they can give, not what they can get. By giving more, they get more—and so do their people.

Section V Review
The Principles 360-Degree Leaders Need to Lead Down

Are you relying on influence to lead down as a 360-Degree Leader should? Review the seven principles you need to master in order to lead down:

1. Walk slowly through the halls.
2. See everyone as a "10."
3. Develop each team member as a person.
4. Place people in their strength zones.
5. Model the behavior you desire.
6. Transfer the vision.
7. Reward for results.

How well are you doing those seven things? If you're not sure, take the 360-Degree Leadership assessment, offered free of charge to people who have purchased this book. Visit 360DegreeLeader.com for more information.

SECTION VI

THE VALUE OF 360-DEGREE LEADERS

Becoming a 360-Degree Leader isn't easy. It takes a lot of work, and it doesn't happen overnight. But it is worth every bit of the effort. In all my years of leadership teaching and consulting, I've never had a leader come to me and say, "We have too many leaders in our organization." So no matter how many good leaders your organization has, it needs more 360-Degree Leaders—and it needs you!

As you seek to grow as a leader, you will not always succeed. You will not always be rewarded the way you should be. Your leaders may not listen to you at times. Your peers may ignore you. Your followers won't follow. And the battle may feel like it's uphill all the way.

Please don't let that discourage you—not for long, anyway. By becoming a better leader, you add tremendous value to your organization. Everything rises and falls on leadership. The better 360-Degree Leader you become, the greater impact you will be able to make.

As you near the conclusion of this book, I want to give you some encouragement to keep on growing and learning. And I want to do it by letting you know why you should keep working to become a 360-Degree

Leader. Keep reading. And on the days when the climb seems too steep, reflect on these observations to help you remember why you should keep climbing and keep leading from the middle!

Value #1

A Leadership Team Is More Effective Than Just One Leader

Leadership is a complicated and difficult skill, one that no single person ever masters. There are some things I do well as a leader and some I do poorly. I'm sure it is the same for you. Even the greatest leaders from history had blind spots and weak areas.

> *For teams to develop at every level, they need leaders at every level.*

So what's the solution? Organizations need to develop leadership teams at every level! A group of leaders working together is always more effective than one leader working alone. And for teams to develop at every level, they need leaders at every level.

Leaders Who Build Teams

As a leader in the middle, if you develop a team, you will be making your organization better and helping it to fulfill its vision. You will be adding value no matter where you serve in the organization. As you do that, keep the following ideas in mind:

1. Visionary Leaders Are Willing to Hire People Better Than Themselves

One leader I interviewed for this book said that a pivotal moment in his leadership journey occurred when someone asked him, "If you could hire someone who you knew would move the organization forward, but you would have to pay them more than your salary, would you hire them?" He said that question really arrested him. He thought about it long and hard, and when he finally concluded that he would, it changed the way he viewed his team and himself.

360-Degree Leaders are willing to hire people better than themselves. Why? Because their desire is to fulfill the vision. That is paramount. Anytime leaders find themselves being selfish or petty, they can be sure that they have wandered far from the vision. The way to get back on track is to put the vision first, and let everything else settle back to its rightful place.

2. Wise Leaders Shape Their People into a Team

Leaders begin to develop wisdom when they realize they can't do anything significant on their own. Once they realize that, leaders can also develop more humility and begin working to build a team.

Each of us needs others on the team to complete us. 360-Degree Leaders don't build teams so that others can take a menial role and serve them. They don't hire others to do the dirty work or to become errand runners. They look for the best people they can find so that the team is the best it can be.

Chris Hodges said that one of the ways he learned the value of teamwork was by observing congressmen doing their work in Washington, D.C. When representatives want to propose a bill, the first thing they do is find a cosponsor. If they can find someone across the aisle, all the better. Chris takes that practice to heart. He said that before he tries to accomplish anything, the first thing he does is build a team of people who believe in what they are doing. A team of people will always be more powerful than an individual working alone.

3. Secure Leaders Empower Their Teams

Wayne Schmidt says, "No amount of personal competency compensates for personal insecurity." That is so true. Insecure leaders always have to go first. They are consumed with themselves. And that self-focus often drives them to bring second-best people around them.

On the other hand, secure leaders focus on others, and they want others to do well. They are happy to let their teams get all the credit. Their desire to see others succeed drives them to equip, train, and empower their people well. Anytime you focus on others, empowerment naturally becomes the by-product.

> *"No amount of personal competency compensates for personal insecurity."*
> —WAYNE SCHMIDT

4. Experienced Leaders Listen to Their Teams

Experienced leaders listen before they lead. General Tommy Franks said:

> Generals are not infallible. The army doesn't issue wisdom when it pins on the stars. Leading soldiers as a general means more than creating tactics and giving orders. Officers commanding brigades and battalions, the company commanders and the platoon leaders—all of them know more about their unit strengths and weaknesses than the general who leads them. So a successful general must listen more than he talks.[1]

Immature leaders lead first, then listen afterward—if they listen at all. Anytime leaders don't listen, they don't know the heartbeat of their people. They don't know what their followers need or want. They don't know what's going on. Good leaders understand that the people closest to the work are the ones who are really in the know.

> *Immature leaders lead first, then listen afterward.*

If your people aren't following, you need to listen more. You don't need to be more forceful. You don't need to find more leverage. You don't need to come down on them. If you listen, they will be much more inclined to follow.

5. Productive Leaders Understand That One Is Too Small a Number to Achieve Greatness

Over the past twenty-five years, I've watched the trends in business and nonprofits, and the solutions that organizations use to improve and to solve problems. I've seen a definite pattern. Perhaps you've seen it too.

- In the 1980s, the word was *management*. The idea was that a manager was needed to create consistency. (The goal was to keep standards from slipping.)
- In the 1990s, the key concept was *leadership by an individual*. Organizations saw that leaders were needed because everything was changing so quickly.
- In the 2000s, the idea is *team leadership*. Because leading an organization has become so complex and multifaceted, the only way to make progress is to develop a team of leaders.

I think organizations are going to improve greatly as they develop teams, because leadership is so complex. You can't do just one thing well and be a good leader. You can't even lead in just one direction—you need the skills to lead up, across, and down! A leadership team will always be more effective than just one leader. And a team of 360-Degree Leaders will be more effective than other kinds of leadership teams.

Value #2

Leaders Are Needed at Every Level of the Organization

In 2004 I was invited to teach a session on leadership to NFL coaches and scouts at the Senior Bowl in Mobile, Alabama. It was quite an experience. One of the things I taught that day was the Law of the Edge: "The difference between two equally talented teams is leadership."

After my session, I talked to a general manager of one of the teams, and he confirmed my observation. He said that because of the parity of talent in the NFL, the edge comes from leadership—from the owner, the head coach, the assistants, and right on down to the players. Leadership is what makes the difference at every level of the organization.

What Happens Without a Leader

I know I say this so often that some people are tired of hearing it, but I believe it down to the core of my being. *Everything rises and falls on leadership*. It really does. If you don't believe it, just put together a group of people without a leader, and watch them. They will drift. When there is no good leader on a team, in a department, at the top of an organization, or heading a family, then the following results are inevitable.

Without a Leader, Vision Is Lost

If a team starts out with a vision but without a leader, it is in trouble. Why? Because vision leaks. And without a leader, the vision will dissipate and the team will drift until it has no sense of direction.

On the other hand, if a team starts with a leader but without a vision, it will do fine because it will eventually have a vision. I say that because if you had to define leaders with a single word, perhaps the best one would be *visionary*. Leaders are always headed somewhere. They have vision, and that vision gives not only *them* direction, but it gives their people direction.

Without a Leader, Decisions Are Delayed

I love a story that President Reagan told showing how he learned the need for decision making early in his life. When he was young, a kind aunt took him to have a pair of shoes custom made. The shoemaker asked him if he wanted his shoes to have square toes or round toes, but Reagan couldn't seem to make up his mind.

"Come back in a day or two and let me know what you decide," the shoemaker told him. But Reagan didn't go back. When the man saw him on the street and again asked him what kind of shoes he wanted, Reagan said, "I haven't made up my mind yet."

"Very well," the man responded. "Your shoes will be ready tomorrow."

When Reagan went to pick them up, he discovered that the toe of one shoe was round and the other was square. Reagan later said, "Looking at those shoes taught me a lesson. If you don't make your own decisions, somebody else makes them for you."

Not all good decision makers are leaders, but all good leaders are decision makers.

Not all good decision makers are leaders, but all good leaders are decision makers. Often it takes a leader to make decisions—and if not to make them, then to help others make them more quickly.

WITHOUT A LEADER, AGENDAS ARE MULTIPLIED

When a team of people come together and no one is clearly the leader, then individuals begin to follow their own agendas. And before long, all the people are doing their own thing. Teams need leadership to provide a unifying voice.

WITHOUT A LEADER, CONFLICTS ARE EXTENDED

One of the most important roles of a leader is conflict resolution. In the absence of clear leadership, conflicts always last longer and inflict more damage. Often it takes a leader to step up, step in, and bring everyone to the table to work things out. When you lead others, you should always be ready to do what it takes to help your people resolve their conflicts.

WITHOUT A LEADER, MORALE IS LOW

Napoleon said, "Leaders are dealers in hope." When leaders are not present, people often lose hope and morale plummets. Why is that? Because *morale* can be defined as "faith in the leader at top."

WITHOUT A LEADER, PRODUCTION IS REDUCED

The first quality of leaders is the ability to make things happen. One of my favorite stories that illustrates this truth comes from the life of Charles Schwab, who once ran U.S. Steel. Schwab said:

> I had a mill manager who was finely educated, thoroughly capable and master of every detail of the business. But he seemed unable to inspire his men to do their best.
>
> "How is it that a man as able as you," I asked him one day, "cannot make this mill turn out what it should?"
>
> "I don't know," he replied. "I have coaxed the men; I have pushed them; I have sworn at them. I have done everything in my power. Yet they will not produce."
>
> It was near the end of the day; in a few minutes the night force

> would come on duty. I turned to a workman who was standing beside one of the red-mouthed furnaces and asked him for a piece of chalk.
>
> "How many heats has your shift made today?" I queried.
>
> "Six," he replied.
>
> I chalked a big "6" on the floor, and then passed along without another word. When the night shift came in they saw the "6" and asked about it.
>
> "The big boss was in here today," said the day men. "He asked us how many heats we had made, and we told him six. He chalked it down."
>
> The next morning I passed through the same mill. I saw that the "6" had been rubbed out and a big "7" written instead. The night shift had announced itself. That night I went back. The "7" had been erased, and a "10" swaggered in its place. The day force recognized no superiors. Thus a fine competition was started, and it went on until this mill, formerly the poorest producer, was turning out more than any other mill in the plant.[1]

Leaders are creative in finding ways to help others become productive. Sometimes it means laying out a challenge. Sometimes it means giving people training. Sometimes it means encouraging or putting up incentives. If the same thing worked for every person in every situation, then there would be no need for leaders. Because every person is different and circumstances are constantly changing, it takes a leader to figure out what's needed and to put that solution into action.

WITHOUT A LEADER, SUCCESS IS DIFFICULT

I believe many people want to dismiss the importance of leadership when it comes to organizational success. They don't see it—and in some cases they don't want to see it. That was the case for Jim Collins, author of *Good to Great*. I've met Collins, and I can tell you that he is an intelligent and perceptive guy. But he did not want to include leadership in the study that formed the foundation of the book. He wrote:

> I gave the research team explicit instructions to downplay the role of top executives so that we could avoid the simplistic "credit the leader" or "blame the leader" thinking common today . . . Every time we attribute everything to "Leadership," we're . . . simply admitting our ignorance . . . So, early in the project, I kept insisting, "Ignore the executives," but the research team kept pushing back . . . Finally—as should always be the case—the data won.[2]

Collins goes on to describe level five leaders—leaders who exhibit both a strong will and great humility—and how every great company they studied was led by one such leader.

Leadership comes into play, even when you don't want it to. Your organization will not function the same without strong leaders in every department or division. It needs 360-Degree Leaders at every level in order to be well led.

Value #3

Leading Successfully at One Level Is a Qualifier for Leading at the Next Level

Growing organizations are always looking for good people to step up to the next level and lead. How do they find out if a person is qualified to make that jump? By looking at that person's track record in his or her current position. The key to moving up as an emerging leader is to focus on leading well where you are, not on moving up the ladder. If you are a good 360-Degree Leader where you are, I believe you will be given an opportunity to lead at a higher level.

As you strive to become the best 360-Degree Leader you can be, keep the following things in mind:

1. Leadership Is a Journey That Starts Where You Are, Not Where You Want to Be

Recently while I was driving in my car, a vehicle to the left of me attempted to turn right from the middle lane and caused an accident. Fortunately, I was able to slow down quickly and lessen the impact; but still, my air bags deployed, and both cars were greatly damaged.

The first thing I noticed after I stopped and took stock of the situation was that the little computer screen in my car was showing my exact location according to the GPS system. I stared at it a moment, wondering why the car was telling me my exact latitude and longitude. And then I thought, *Of course!* If you're in real trouble and you call for help, the first thing emergency workers will want to know is your location. You can't get anywhere until you first know where you are.

Leadership is similar. To know how to get where you want to go, you need to know where you are. To get where you want to go, you need to focus on what you're doing now. Award-winning sportswriter Ken Rosenthals said, "Each time you decide to grow again, you realize you are starting at the bottom of another ladder." You need to have your eyes fixed on your current responsibilities, not the ones you wish to have someday. I've never known a person focused on yesterday to have a better tomorrow.

I've never known a person focused on yesterday to have a better tomorrow.

2. Leadership Skills Are the Same, but the "League of Play" Changes

If you get promoted, don't think that because your new office is just a few feet down the hall from your old place that the difference is just a few steps. When you get "called up" to another level of leadership, the quality of your game must rise quickly.

No matter what level you're working on, leadership skills are needed at that level. Each new level requires a higher degree of skill. The easiest place to see this is in sports. Some players can make the jump from recreational league to high school. Fewer can make it from high school to college. And only a handful can make it to the professional level.

Your best chance of making it into the next "league of play" is to grow on the current level so that you will be able to go to the next level.

3. Great Responsibilities Come Only After Handling Small Ones Well

When I teach at a conference or go to a book signing, people sometimes confide in me that they desire to write books too. "How do I get started?" they ask.

> *"The only conquests which are permanent and leave no regrets are our conquests over ourselves."*
>
> —Napoleon Bonaparte

"How much writing do you do now?" I ask in return.

Some tell me about articles and other pieces they are writing, and I simply encourage them; but most of the time they sheepishly respond, "Well, I haven't really written anything yet."

"Then you need to start writing," I explain. "You've got to start small and work up to it."

Leadership is the same. You've got to start small and work up to it. A person who has never led before needs to try to influence one other person. Someone who has some influence should try to build a team. Just start with what's necessary.

St. Francis of Assisi said, "Start doing what is necessary; then do what is possible; and suddenly you are doing the impossible." All good leadership begins where you are. It was Napoleon who said, "The only conquests which are permanent and leave no regrets are our conquests over ourselves." The small responsibilities you have before you now comprise the first great leadership conquest you must make. Don't try to conquer the world until you've taken care of things in your own backyard.

4. Leading at Your Current Level Creates Your Resumé for Going to the Next Level

When you go to see a doctor for the first time, you are usually asked a lot of questions about your family history. In fact, there are usually more questions about that than there are about your lifestyle. Why?

Because family history, more than anything else, seems to be what determines your health.

When it comes to leadership success, history is also similarly disproportionate. Your track record where you work now is what leaders will look at when trying to decide if you can do a job. I know that when I interview someone for a job, I put 90 percent of the emphasis on the track record.

If you want to get the chance to lead on another level, then your best chance for success is to lead well where you are now. Every day that you lead and succeed, you are building a resumé for your next job.

5. When You Can Lead Volunteers Well, You Can Lead Almost Anyone

At a recent President's Day conference where we were discussing leadership development, a CEO asked me, "How can I pick the best leader out of a small group of leaders? What do I look for?"

There are many things that indicate someone has leadership potential—the ability to make things happen, strong people skills, vision, desire, problem-solving skills, self-discipline, a strong work ethic. But there is one really great test of leadership that is almost foolproof, and that is what I suggested: "Ask them to lead a volunteer group."

If you want to test your own leadership, then try leading volunteers. Why is that so difficult? Because with volunteers, you have no leverage. It takes every bit of leadership skill you have to get people who don't have to do anything to do what you ask. If you're not challenging enough, they lose interest. If you push too hard, they drop out. If your people skills are weak, they won't spend any time with you. If you cannot communicate the vision, they won't know where to go or why.

If you lead others and your organization has any kind of community service focus, encourage the people on your team to volunteer. Then watch to see how they do. If they thrive in that environment, then you know that they possess many of the qualifications to go to another level in your organization.

Donald McGannon, former CEO of Westinghouse Broadcasting Corporation, stated, "Leadership is action, not position." Taking action—and helping others to do the same in a coordinated effort—is the essence of leadership. Do those things where you are, and you won't remain long there.

Value #4

Good Leaders in the Middle Make Better Leaders at the Top

In industrialized and free-market nations, we often take leadership for granted. A leadership culture has evolved to run the many organizations in such countries because commerce and industry are so strong. And because markets are so competitive, many of the leaders who emerge work hard to keep improving their leadership.

In developing countries, things are different. In the last five or six years, I've spent a lot of time teaching leadership around the world, and what I've found is that great leaders are few and far between in many of those countries—and 360-Degree Leaders are almost nonexistent. Most leaders in undeveloped countries are highly positional, and they try to keep as much distance as possible between their followers and themselves. It's one of the reasons there is such a difference between the haves and the have-nots. There are, of course, many exceptions to the broad generalization I'm making, but if you've traveled overseas a great deal, you have probably noticed it too.

In places where the top leaders try to keep everyone else down, the overall leadership is usually pretty poor. Why? Because when all the power is at the top and there are no leaders in the middle to help them, the top leaders cannot lead very effectively.

Just in case you think I'm being too critical of leaders in emerging nations, I can tell you that this is a problem any place where there is one leader at the top and no 360-Degree Leaders to help lead. I personally experienced it in my own life in my first leadership position because I didn't try to identify, develop, or empower anyone else to lead. As a result, my leadership was weak, the overall effectiveness of the organization was far below its potential, and within two years after I left the organization, it shrank to half its former size.

Good leaders anywhere in an organization make better leaders at the top.

It's hard to overestimate the value of 360-Degree Leaders in the middle of an organization. In fact, good leaders anywhere in an organization make better leaders at the top—and make for a much better organization overall.

Every Time You Add a Good Leader, You Get a Better Team

Good leaders maximize the performance of those on their team. They set direction. They inspire their people and help them work together. They get results. This is easy to see in sports where the only thing that changes on a team is the coach. When a better leader comes in, the same players often perform at a much higher level than they did before.

The same thing happens in any kind of organization. When a strong leader takes over a sales team, their performance goes up. When a good manager takes over at a restaurant, the operation runs more smoothly. When a better foreman runs the crew, the people get more done.

If you were to look at your entire organization (assuming it's not a mom-and-pop-sized operation), you would be able to locate the quality leaders even before you met them. All you would have to do is look for the teams with consistently high results. That is where the good leaders are.

Every Time You Add a Good Leader, All the Leaders in the Organization Get Better

I thought it was very interesting when Tiger Woods moved up from the amateur ranks to become a professional golfer. He was so good that the rest of the field looked weak. He won his first Master's Tournament at Augusta by a huge margin, and afterward he said he didn't even have his "A" game all the days he played. Many people feared that Woods would so dominate the game that nobody would ever be able to beat him.

But a funny thing happened after Woods had played for a few years. Everyone else's game went to another level. Why? Because strength brings out strength. The book of Proverbs says, "As iron sharpens iron, so one man sharpens another."[1]

When a good leader joins the team, it makes the other leaders take notice. Good leaders bring out the best, not only in their followers but also in other leaders. Good leaders raise the bar when it comes to performance and teamwork, and this often challenges other leaders in the organization to improve.

Good Leaders in the Middle Add Value to the Leaders Above Them

Leaders in the middle of an organization are closer to the people in the trenches than are the leaders on top. As a result, they know more about what's going on. They understand the people who are doing the work and the issues they face. They also have greater influence at those lower levels than the top leaders.

When there are no good leaders in the middle of an organization, then everyone and everything in the organization waits on the top leaders. On the other hand, when good leaders in the middle use their influence and commitment to assist the top leaders, they "stretch" the top leaders' influence beyond their reach. As a result, the top leaders are able to do more than they would ever be able to do on their own.

Good Leaders in the Middle Release Top Leaders to Focus on Their Priorities

The higher you climb in an organization as a leader, the more you will see but the less you will actually do. You can't move up and keep doing all the tasks that you do now. As you move up, you will have to hand off many of your old responsibilities to others. If the people who are supposed to do those tasks don't perform them well, then you will have to keep taking those things back. You probably will not be able to do your new responsibilities effectively if that happens.

Let's face it. There is no greater frustration for senior leaders than operating at a level below their own, because leaders in the middle need continual hand holding. If a leader has to do that, the organization ends up paying high-level dollars to solve low-end problems.

For this reason, the leaders at the top can only be as good as the middle leaders working for them. When you perform with excellence in the middle, you free up your leaders to perform with excellence above you.

Good Leaders in the Middle Motivate Leaders Above Them to Continue Growing

When a leader grows, it shows. Growing leaders continually improve in their personal effectiveness and their leadership. Most of the time that makes their leaders want to keep growing. Part of that comes from healthy competition. If you're in a race and someone is getting ready to pass you, it makes you want to pick up your pace and move faster.

There is also the contribution factor. When team members see others on the team making a significant contribution, it inspires them to step up. There is a natural joy that comes from being on a team that is functioning on an extremely high level.

Good Leaders in the Middle Give the Organization a Future

No organization keeps moving forward and growing using yesterday's ideas and ways of doing things. Future success requires innovation and growth. And it requires the continual emergence of new leaders. In *The Bible on Leadership* (Amacon, 2002), Lorin Woolfe writes, "The ultimate test for a leader is not whether he or she makes smart decisions and takes decisive action, but whether he or she teaches others to be leaders and builds an organization that can sustain its success even when he or she is not around."

Today's workers are tomorrow's leaders in the middle of the organization. And today's leaders in the middle will be tomorrow's leaders at the top. While you function as a 360-Degree Leader in the middle of the organization, if you keep growing you will probably get your opportunity to become a top leader. But at the same time, you need to be looking at the people working for you and thinking about how you can prepare them to join you and eventually take your place in the middle. You will be able to spot potential leadership candidates because they will be more than just good workers.

Today's Workers	Tomorrow's Leaders
Implement current ideas	Generate new ideas
Identify and define problems	Solve problems
Get along with the people they have	Attract sharp people
Work within the current framework	Take risks
Value consistency	Value and spot opportunities

Leadership expert Max DePree said, "Succession is one of the key responsibilities of leadership." That is true. There is no success without a successor. Being a 360-Degree Leader is about more than just doing a good job now and making things easier today for the people working above and below you. It is about making sure the organization has a chance to be good tomorrow too. As you teach others to perform 360-Degree Leadership, you will be giving the organization greater depth as well as strength. You will be helping to raise the bar in such a way that everybody wins.

Value #5

360-Degree Leaders Possess Qualities Every Organization Needs

When I was outlining this book, I talked to a friend about the whole concept of 360-Degree Leadership, and he asked, "What makes a 360-Degree Leader different from any other kind of a leader?" When I started to explain the concept of leading up, across, and down, he said, "Okay, but why are they able to lead in every direction? What makes them tick?"

I chewed on his question for a while as we talked about it, and I finally landed this answer: "360-Degree Leaders have certain qualities that enable them to lead in every direction, and that is what makes them valuable to an organization."

"You need to put that in the book," he advised, "because people can try to do all the right actions, but if they don't embrace those qualities internally, they may never get it."

I don't know if you've ever thought about it before, but what adds greater value to the people around you: what you *say* or what you *are*? You may not be aware of it, but you can actually add value to others simply by possessing the right qualities. The higher you go in an organization, the more that applies.

360-Degree Leaders, as I envision them, possess qualities that every organization wants to see in all of its employees, but especially in its leaders. Those qualities are adaptability, discernment, perspective, communication, security, servanthood, resourcefulness, maturity, endurance, and countability.

Adaptability—Quickly Adjusts to Change

People from the middle down are never the first to know anything in an organization. They are usually not the decision makers or policy writers. As a result, they must learn to adapt quickly.

When it comes to leading in the middle, the more quickly you can adapt to change, the better it will be for the organization. Here's why. All organizations contain early, middle, and late adapters. The early adapters are won over by new ideas quickly, and they are ready to run with them. Middle adapters take more time. And then the late adapters slowly (and sometimes reluctantly) accept the change.

Since you, as a leader in the middle, are going to be asked to help the people who follow you to accept the change, you need to process change quickly—the quicker the better. That may mean there will be times when you must embrace a change before you are even ready to do so emotionally. In such cases, the key is your ability to trust your leaders. If you can trust them, you will be able to do it. Just keep reminding yourself, *Blessed are the flexible, for they will not be bent out of shape*.

Blessed are the flexible, for they will not be bent out of shape.

Discernment—Understands the Real Issues

The president of the United States, an old priest, a young mountain climber, and the world's smartest man were riding together on a private plane when it suddenly suffered engine trouble. The pilot scrambled from the cockpit saying, "We're going down; save yourselves!" He then jumped out of the plane and activated his parachute.

The four passengers looked around but found only three parachutes.

The president took one and—as he jumped—said, "I must save myself for the sake of national security."

The world's smartest man grabbed one and jumped, saying, "I am an invaluable resource to the world and must save my intellect."

The old priest looked at the mountain climber and said, "Save yourself, my son. I've been in the Lord's service for forty years, and I'm not afraid to meet my Maker."

"No sweat, Padre," answered the young man. "The world's smartest man just jumped with my backpack!"

Good leaders cut through the clutter to see the real issues. They know what really matters. There's an old saying that a smart person believes only half of what he hears, but a really smart person knows which half to believe. 360-Degree Leaders cultivate that ability.

PERSPECTIVE—SEES BEYOND THEIR OWN VANTAGE POINT

Jack Welch said, "Leadership is seeing opportunity in tough times." That ability is a function of perspective. One of the advantages of being a leader in the middle of the organization is that you can see more than others do. Most people have the ability to see things on their own level and one level removed from their own.

> *"Leadership is seeing opportunity in tough times."*
>
> —JACK WELCH

The people at the bottom can see and understand things on their own level and, if they're perceptive, also on yours. The people at the top can see and understand things on their own level and on one below theirs, which would be yours. But as a leader in the middle, you should be able to see and understand not only things on your own level but also one level up and one level down. That gives you a really unique advantage—and opportunity.

Communication—Links to All Levels of the Organization

Because you have a unique perspective and understanding of the organization that others above and below you may not have, you should strive to use your knowledge not only for your own advantage but also to communicate both up and down the chain of command. We often think of communication in organizations as being primarily top-down. Leaders at the top cast vision, set direction, reward progress, and so forth. Good communication, however, is a 360-Degree proposition. In fact, sometimes the most critical communication is from the bottom up.

In *Leading Up* (Crown, 2001), Michael Useem gives examples of important messages that were sent "up the chain of command." Some messages were heeded and acted upon with positive effect. For example, when trade deputy Charlene Barshefsky came to the table to negotiate a trade deal between the U.S. and China, allowing China to enter the World Trade Organization, Barshefsky had previously listened to concerns of business and labor leaders, and she represented those interests at the table. The result was a successful negotiation.

Other messages that were sent "up" were ignored. Useem says that when General Roméo Dallaire, commander of the United Nations' troops in Rwanda, tried to persuade his superiors to let him take aggressive action to head off what he saw as the impending threat of genocide, his request was denied. The result was disastrous—the death of more than 800,000 people as the Hutus slaughtered the Tutsis.

> *"The biggest job in getting any movement off the ground is to keep together the people who form it."*
>
> —Martin Luther King Jr.

Martin Luther King Jr. said, "The biggest job in getting any movement off the ground is to keep together the people who form it. This task requires more than a common aim; it demands a philosophy that wins and holds the people's allegiance; and it depends upon open channels of communication between the people and their leaders."

SECURITY—FINDS IDENTITY IN SELF, NOT POSITION

I love the story of Karl, who enjoyed a good laugh at his office after he attached a small sign to his door—"I'm the Boss!" The laughter was even louder when he returned from lunch and saw that someone had made an addition to his sign. Next to it was a yellow Post-it note on which someone had scribbled, "Your wife called and said she wants her sign back."[1]

It takes a secure person to be a good leader in the middle of an organization. In our culture, people ask, "What do you do?" not, "Who are you?" or, "How are you making a difference?" Most people place too much emphasis on titles and position instead of on impact.

But if you have been effective as a leader in the middle for any length of time, you understand that your role is important. Organizations don't succeed without leaders who do their job well in the middle. 360-Degree Leaders must try to be secure enough in who they are *not* to worry about where they *are*.

The true measure of leaders is not the number of people who serve them but the number of people they serve.

If you are ever tempted to spend too much time and energy on getting out of the middle, then change your focus. Instead, put your effort toward reaching your potential and doing the most good you can where you are. Anytime you focus on developing your position instead of yourself, you are in effect asking, *Am I becoming the person others want me to be?* But if you focus on developing yourself instead of your title or position, then the question you will repeatedly ask is, *Am I becoming all I can be?*

SERVANTHOOD—DOES WHATEVER IT TAKES

I believe the true measure of leaders is not the number of people who serve them but the number of people they serve. 360-Degree Leaders adopt an attitude of servant first, leader second. Everything they do is measured in light of the value it can add. They serve the mission of the organization and lead by serving those on the mission with them.

Robert Greenleaf, founder of Greenleaf Center for Servant Leadership, gave an excellent perspective on this: "The servant-leader is a servant first. It all begins with the natural feeling that one wants to serve, to serve first. Then conscious choice brings one to aspire to lead. The difference manifests itself in the care taken by the servant—first to make sure that the other people's highest priority needs are served."

How do you know whether you are motivated by the desire to serve as a leader? It's actually very simple. You have the heart of a servant if it doesn't bother you to serve others. If you lack a servant's attitude, then it grates on you when you do have to serve.

Resourcefulness—Finds Creative Ways to Make Things Happen

With presses set to run three million copies of Theodore Roosevelt's 1912 convention speech, the speech's publisher discovered that permission had not been obtained to use photos of Roosevelt and his running mate, Governor Hiram Johnson of California. And that was a problem because copyright law put the penalty for such an oversight at one dollar per copy.

The quick-thinking chairman of the campaign committee was a resourceful leader. He dictated a telegram to the Chicago studio that had taken the pictures: "Planning to issue three million copies of Roosevelt speech with pictures of Roosevelt and Johnson on cover. Great publicity opportunity for photographers. What will you pay us to use your photographs?"

The reply: "Appreciate opportunity, but can pay only $250." The deal was done, the presses ran, and a potential disaster was averted.

Leaders in the middle of an organization need to be especially resourceful, because they have less authority and fewer resources. If you desire to be an effective 360-Degree Leader, then get used to doing more with less.

Maturity—Puts the Team Before Self

How do you define *maturity*? In the context of leadership, I define it as "putting the team before oneself." Nobody who possesses an unrelenting me-first attitude is able to develop much influence with others. To lead others, you need to put the team first.

I recently read a story about a group of principals in the Nashville school system who realized that for their students to succeed, they needed to employ a bilingual specialist. The only problem was that there was no money in their budgets to do it. What was their solution? They set aside the money that would have been used for their own raises to hire the person they needed. The team and the children they support were more important to them than personal gain. That's mature leadership!

In leadership, maturity is putting the team before oneself.

ENDURANCE—REMAINS CONSISTENT IN CHARACTER AND COMPETENCE OVER THE LONG HAUL

A couple of years ago when I was in Africa teaching on leadership, I had the opportunity to go on a photo safari. It was an incredible experience. One of the things we did while out in the bush was follow, for about an hour, a pair of cheetahs that were hunting. Cheetahs are amazing animals. They are the fastest land animals on the planet, with the ability to run at an amazing seventy miles per hour. But cheetahs are pure sprinters. If they don't run down their prey with their first burst, then they go hungry. The reason they can't run long is that they have small hearts.

360-Degree Leaders can't afford to have small hearts. With all the challenges that come to leaders—especially leaders in the middle—leadership is an endurance race. To succeed, 360-Degree Leaders need to respond well to challenges and keep responding well.

COUNTABILITY—CAN BE COUNTED ON WHEN IT COUNTS

In *The 17 Indisputable Laws of Teamwork*, one of my favorite laws is the Law of Countability: "Teammates must be able to count on each other when it counts." I love that law not only because it is true and very important for team building, but also because it gave me the opportunity to make up a word. I think *countability* really captures the idea of people being able to depend on one another no matter what.

When you trust a leader, when he or she possesses countability, it has greater value than just knowing you can count on that leader. It means you really do count on them. You depend on them for your success. You're in it together, and you will fail or succeed as a team. That kind of character really makes a difference in a culture where most people have an every-man-for-himself attitude.

I believe most leaders in the middle of organizations don't get enough credit, because the middle is where most organizations succeed or fail. The leaders at the top can make only so big an impact on any organization, and the workers in the trenches can do only so much. They are often more limited by the leaders above them than they are by resources or their own talent. Everything truly does rise and fall on leadership. If you want your organization to succeed, then you need to succeed as a 360-Degree Leader.

One of the finest examples I've ever encountered that shows the value and impact of a leader in the middle can be found in the life of General George C. Marshall. When most people think of the leadership that won World War II for the Allies, they think of leaders like Winston Churchill and Franklin D. Roosevelt. And while I acknowledge that the war would not have been won without those two great leaders, I also believe it would not have been won without the effective 360-Degree Leadership of Marshall.

Marshall was always a good soldier, and everywhere he served, he led well—up, across, and down. He attended the Virginia Military Institute, where he graduated as first captain. He went on to serve in the infantry in the U.S. Army. Marshall was such a good student and influenced his superiors so much that after finishing first in his class at the School of the Line at Fort Leavenworth, Kansas, and then taking a more advanced course, he was kept as an instructor.

Marshall never failed to add value wherever he served—in the Philippines (two tours); in France during World War I; as a senior aide to General Pershing during a tour in China; as the chief of instruction at the Infantry School at Fort Benning, Georgia; as well as at other posts. It's been said that Marshall "rose through the ranks of the military with a record of achievement rarely equaled by any other."[2]

Marshall's career was stellar, but you can really see him making a significant impact as the appointed U.S. Army chief of staff. From that position, he led up to the president, he led across to the other Allied commanders, and he led down with his own senior officers.

When he entered that office, the United States' military forces were anemic and ill equipped. All the branches of service combined comprised fewer than 200,000 people. With war breaking out in Europe, Marshall knew what he needed to do—build a large, well-prepared, and powerfully equipped army. And he set about the task immediately. In four years' time, Marshall expanded the military to a well-trained and well-equipped force of 8,300,000.[3] Winston Churchill called Marshall "the organizer of victory."

That alone would make Marshall a hero of World War II, but that wasn't his only contribution. He worked tirelessly throughout the war and continually showed an ability to lead up, across, and down. President Roosevelt found his advice invaluable and said that he could not sleep unless he knew Marshall was in the country. And Roosevelt requested Marshall's presence at every major war conference, from Argentia, Newfoundland, in 1941, to Potsdam in 1945.[4]

Marshall continually had to lead across in the area of military strategy. He is credited by some for ensuring cooperation between the Allied forces during the war. He went head-to-head against other generals when it came to strategy too. MacArthur wanted the United States to shift its primary focus to the Pacific theater of operations before defeating Germany. The British wanted to employ what was called the Mediterranean strategy against Hitler's forces. But Marshall was convinced that to win the war, the Allies had to cross the English Channel and engage the Germans in France.[5]

Marshall won everyone over, and for a year he and his general planned the invasion of Normandy. After the war, Churchill said of Marshall: "Hitherto I had thought of Marshall as a rugged soldier and a magnificent organizer and builder of armies—the American Carnot [a man known as the "organizer of victory" for the French Revolution]. But now I saw that he was a statesman with a penetrating and commanding view of the whole scene."[6]

Marshall was also as effective leading down as he was leading up and across. The people who served under him held a deep respect for him. After the war, General Dwight D. Eisenhower said to Marshall, "In every problem and in every test I have faced during the war years, your example has been an inspiration and your support has been my greatest strength. My sense of obligation to you is equaled only by the depth of pride and satisfaction as I salute you as the greatest soldier of your time and a true leader of democracy."[7]

Even after the war, Marshall continued his influence as a 360-Degree Leader. He was asked to serve as secretary of state by President Truman. And when a plan was needed to rebuild the countries of Europe in the wake of such a devastating war, Marshall gave his support in a speech at Harvard University to what he called the European Recovery Plan. I've read that when President Truman's aides wanted to call it the Truman Plan, the president wouldn't hear of it. He valued and respected his secretary of state's leadership so much that he called it the Marshall Plan.

There are not a lot of people about whom you can say that if he or she had not lived, the face of the world would look very different. Yet that is true for George Marshall. Europe, Asia, and the United States are different from what they would have been without his influence. There are few better examples of 360-Degree Leadership. In the end, Marshall's influence was so great and his service so selfless that he was awarded the Nobel Peace Prize. He is the only professional soldier in history to whom it has been given.

We can't all hope to make a global impact as Marshall did. But that isn't important. What matters is that we are willing to do what it takes to make a positive impact wherever we find ourselves in life—to add value in any way we can to others. I believe there is no better way to increase your influence and improve your chances of doing something significant than to become a 360-Degree Leader. As a 360-Degree Leader you can influence others no matter where you are in the organization, no matter what title or position you have, no matter what kind of people you work with. I hope you will keep working at it, and keep making a positive impact.

Section VI Review
The Value of 360-Degree Leaders

On those days when you wonder whether it's worth it to develop as a 360-Degree Leader and try to lead from the middle of the organization, remind yourself of the great value 360-Degree Leaders add:

1. A leadership team is more effective than just one leader.
2. Leaders are needed at every level of the organization.
3. Leading successfully at one level is a qualifier for leading at the next level.
4. Good leaders in the middle make better leaders at the top.
5. 360-Degree leaders possess qualities every organization needs.

If you still haven't taken the 360-Degree Leadership assessment, don't forget that it is offered free of charge to people who have purchased this book. Visit 360DegreeLeader.com for more information.

SPECIAL SECTION

Create an Environment That Unleashes 360-Degree Leaders

If you are the top leader in your organization, then I want to spend a few moments with you in this special section. Many leaders in the middle of organizations are highly frustrated. They have great desire to lead and succeed; yet their leaders are often a greater hindrance than help to them. More than two-thirds of the people who leave their jobs do so because of an ineffective or incompetent leader. People don't leave their company—they leave their leader.

As a top leader, you have the power the way nobody else does to create a positive leadership culture where potential leaders flourish. If you create that environment, then people with leadership potential will learn, gain experience, and come into their own. They will become the kind of 360-Degree Leaders who make an organization great.

If you're willing to work at making your organization a place where leaders lead and do it well, you'll need to shift your focus from

leading the people and the organization, to . . .

leading the people, finding leaders, and leading the organization, to . . .

leading the people, developing the leaders, and leading the organization, to . . .
leading and empowering the leaders while they lead the organization, to . . .
serving the leaders as they lead the organization.

Depending on where you're starting from, that process may take several years, and it may be a tough climb. But think of the alternative. Where will your organization be in five years if you don't raise up leaders in an environment that unleashes 360-Degree Leaders?

THE LEADER'S DAILY DOZEN

If you're ready to revolutionize your organization, then I want to encourage you to start the process by adopting what I call the "Leader's Daily Dozen." Every morning when you get up and get ready to lead your organization, make a commitment to these twelve power-unleashing activities.

1. PLACE A HIGH VALUE ON PEOPLE

The first shift for turning your organization into a leader-friendly environment must occur inside of you. You only commit yourself to things you value. And fundamentally, if you don't value people, you will never create a culture that develops leaders.

Most top leaders focus on two things: the vision and the bottom line. The vision is what usually excites us most, and taking care of the bottom line keeps us in business. But between the vision and the bottom line are all the people in your organization. What's ironic is that if you ignore the people and only pay attention to these other two things, you will lose the people and the vision (and probably the bottom line). But if you focus on the people, you have the potential to win the people, the vision, and the bottom line.

When Jim Collins studied great companies and came to discover and define what he called level five leaders, he noticed that these excellent leaders didn't take the credit for their organization's accomplishments. In fact, they were incredibly humble and gave the credit to their people. Without a doubt, level five leaders place a high value on people.

Many companies say they value their people and their customers. Those are trendy things to say, but talk is cheap. If you want to know whether this is a value in your organization, then talk to people who know your organization well but don't work for it. What would they say? Their answers would probably give you the most accurate picture.

But you know your own heart better than anyone else. It all starts with you. You need to ask yourself: *Do I place a high value on people?*

2. Commit Resources to Develop People

Once when I was flying to Dallas with Zig Ziglar, he asked if I ever received letters from people thanking me. When I acknowledged that I did, he asked, "When you get those letters, what do people thank you for?" I had never really thought about that before, but the answer was clear. People almost always said thanks for a book I had written or some other resource I had produced.

"It's the same for me," Zig said. "Isn't that interesting? You and I are known for our speaking, but that's not what prompts people to write."

I've done a lot of speaking over the past thirty-five years. I love doing it, and I do think it has value. Events are great for creating lots of energy and enthusiasm, but if you want to facilitate growth, you need resources. They are better for development because they are process oriented. You can take them with you. You can refer back to them. You can dig into the meat and skip the fluff—and you can go at your own pace.

Once when I was teaching leaders at a large corporation, one of the event's organizers stated from the platform that people were their organization's most appreciable asset. I applauded his sentiment, but I also expanded on it for the leaders in the room. His statement is true only if you develop those people.

It takes a lot of effort to develop leaders. The first question a top leader usually asks is, "What is it going to cost?" My answer is, "Whatever amount it costs, it won't be as high as the cost of not developing your people."

Once again, I have a question for you. Ask yourself, *Am I committed to providing resources for leadership development?*

3. Place a High Value on Leadership

People who run a one-person business may not have to worry about leadership. But for people who lead organizations, leadership is always an issue. Anytime you have two or more people working together, leadership comes into play. In some organizations, all the emphasis is placed on effort, and leadership isn't even on people's radar. What a mistake.

All good leaders recognize the importance of leadership and place a high value on it. I love what General Tommy Franks said about the ultimate leaders in the middle of the military—the sergeants:

> The months in the desert had reinforced my longstanding conviction that sergeants really were the backbone of the Army. The average trooper depends on NCOs for leadership by personal example. I thought of Sam Long and Scag, of Staff Sergeant Kittle—they had been examples of what a sergeant should be. If a noncommissioned officer is dedicated to his troops, the squad or section will have hard, realistic training, hot food when it's available, and the chance to take an occasional shower. If a sergeant is indifferent to the needs of his soldiers, their performance will suffer, and their lives might be wasted. A smart officer works hard to develop good NCOs.[1]

The American military understands the value of leadership and always places a high value on it. If you value leadership, leaders will emerge to add value to the organization.

This time the question to ask yourself is very simple: *Do I place a high value on leadership in my organization?*

4. Look for Potential Leaders

If leadership is on your radar and you value it, you will continually be on the lookout for potential leaders. Several years ago I did a lesson for one of my leadership development tape clubs that taught leaders what to look for in potential leaders. It was called "Searching for Eagles," and for many years it was our most requested lesson. These are the top ten characteristics of "eagles":

- They make things happen.
- They see opportunities.
- They influence the opinions and actions of others.
- They add value to you.
- They draw winners to them.
- They equip other eagles to lead.
- They provide ideas that help the organization.
- They possess an uncommonly great attitude.
- They live up to their commitments.
- They show fierce loyalty to the organization and the leader.

As you begin to search for potential leaders, look for people who possess these qualities. Meanwhile, ask yourself: *Am I continually looking for potential leaders?*

5. Know and Respect Your People

As you find leaders and develop them, you will get to know them better as individuals. I want to encourage you to use the guidelines in the "Walk Slowly Through the Halls" chapter to enhance that process. But there are also other characteristics that are common to all leaders that you should keep in mind as you take them through the development process.

- People want to see results.
- People want to be effective—they want to do what they do well.
- People want to be in the picture.
- People want to be appreciated.
- People want to be a part of the celebration.

As you select people to develop, work to strike a balance between these universal desires and the individual needs of your people. Try to tailor the development process for each individual as much as you can. To do that, continually ask yourself, *Do I know and respect my people?*

6. Provide Your People with Leadership Experiences

It is impossible to learn leadership without actually leading. After all, leadership is action. One of the places where many top leaders miss developmental opportunities comes in what we delegate. Our natural tendency is to give others tasks to perform rather than leadership functions to fulfill. We need to make a shift. If we don't delegate leadership—with authority as well as accountability—our people will never gain the experience they need to lead well.

It is impossible to learn leadership without actually leading.

The question you must ask yourself is, *Am I providing my people with leadership experiences?*

7. Reward Leadership Initiative

Taking initiative is such an important part of leadership. The best leaders are proactive. They make things happen. Most top leaders are initiators, but that doesn't mean that every top leader feels comfortable when others use their initiative. Just because they trust their own instincts doesn't mean they trust the instincts of their people.

It's true that emerging leaders often want to take the lead before they are really ready to. But potential leaders can only become full-fledged leaders if they are allowed to develop and use their initiative. So what's the solution? Good timing! If you rush the timing, you short-circuit the growth process. If you hold leaders back when they're ready to move, you stunt their growth.

One of the things that can help you navigate the timing issue is recognizing whether your mind-set is one of scarcity or abundance. If you believe that the world has only a limited amount of resources, a finite number of opportunities, and so forth, then you may be reluctant to let your leaders take risks—because you may think that the organization will not be able to recover from mistakes. On the other hand, if you believe opportunities are unlimited, that resources are renewable and unlimited, you will be more willing to take risks. You will not doubt your ability to recover.

How are you doing in this area? Ask yourself, *Do I reward leadership initiative?*

8. Provide a Safe Environment Where People Ask Questions, Share Ideas, and Take Risks

Pulitzer prize-winning historian Garry Wills said, "Leaders have a say in what they are being led to. A leader who neglects that soon finds himself without followers." It takes secure leaders at the top to let the leaders working for them be full participants in the organization's leadership process. If leaders in the middle question them, they don't take it personally. When they share ideas, the top leaders cannot afford to feel threatened. When people lower than they are in the organization want to take risks, they need to be willing to give them room to succeed or fail.

Leadership by its very nature challenges. It challenges out-of-date ideas. It challenges old ways of doing things. It challenges the status quo. Never forget that what gets rewarded gets done. If you reward complacency, you will get complacency from your leaders in the middle. But if you can remain secure and let them find new ways of doing things—ways that are better than yours—the organization will move forward more quickly.

> *"Leaders have a say in what they are being led to. A leader who neglects that soon finds himself without followers."*
>
> —GARRY WILLS

Instead of trying to be Mr. Answerman or Ms. Fix-it, when your leaders start coming into their own, move more into the background. Try taking on the role of wise counselor and chief encourager. Welcome the desire of your best leaders to innovate and improve the organization. After all, I think you'll agree that a win for the organization is a win for you.

So what role are you playing in your organization? Are you "the expert," or are you more of an advisor and advocate? Ask yourself, *Am I providing an environment where people can ask questions, share ideas, and take risks?*

9. GROW WITH YOUR PEOPLE

I've talked to a lot of top leaders during my career, and I've detected a number of different attitudes toward growth. Here's how I would summarize them:

- I have already grown.
- I want my people to grow.
- I'm dedicated to helping my people grow.
- I want to grow along with my people.

Guess which attitude fosters an organization where people are growing?

When people in an organization see the top leader growing, it changes the culture of the organization. It immediately removes many barriers between the top leader and the rest of the people, putting you on the same level with them, which makes the top leader much more human and accessible. It also sends a clear message to everyone: make growth a priority.

So the question I want you to ask yourself is very simple: *Am I growing with my people?*

10. Draw People with High Potential into Your Inner Circle

When Mark Sanborn, author of *The Fred Factor*, spoke at one of our leadership events, he made a remark that really stuck with me: "It's better to have a group of deer led by a lion than a group of lions led by a deer." Why? Because even if you have a group of deer, if they are led by a lion, they will act like a pride of lions. Isn't that a great analogy? It's really true. When people spend time with someone and are directed by them, they learn to think the way that person thinks and do what that person does. Their performance starts to rise according to the capability of their leader.

When I was working on *Developing the Leaders Around You*, I often took an informal poll at conferences to find out how people came to be leaders. I asked if they became leaders (a) because they were given a position; (b) because there was a crisis in the organization; or (c) because they had been mentored. More than 80 percent indicated that they were leaders because someone had mentored them in leadership—had taken them through the process.

The best way to develop high-caliber leaders is to have them mentored by a high-caliber leader. If you lead your organization, you are probably the best (or at least one of the best) leader in the organization. If you are not already doing so, you need to handpick the people with the greatest potential, invite them into your inner circle, and mentor them. It doesn't matter if you do it with one or with a dozen, whether you work one-on-one or in a group setting. The main thing is that you need to be giving your best to your best people.

Are you doing that? What is your answer to the question, *Am I drawing people with potential into my inner circle?*

11. Commit Yourself to Developing a Leadership Team

When I started out as a leader, I tried to do everything myself. Until I was about age forty, I thought I could do it all. After my fortieth birthday, I finally realized that if I didn't develop other leaders, my potential was only a fraction of what it could be. So for the next decade, developing people into good leaders was my focus. But even that has its limitations. I realize now that to reach the highest level of leadership, I must continually develop leadership teams.

Let's face it. No one does everything well. I can't do it all—can you? I wrote the *The 21 Irrefutable Laws of Leadership*, which contains every leadership principle I know based on a lifetime of learning and leading. I can't do all of the twenty-one laws well. So I need help.

You do too. If you want your organization to reach its potential, if you want it to go from good to great (or even average to good), you need to develop a team of leaders, people who can fill in each others' gaps, people who challenge and sharpen each other. If we try to do it all ourselves, we will never get beyond the glass ceiling of our own leadership limitations.

How are you in this area? Ask yourself, *Am I committed to developing a leadership team?*

12. Unleash Your Leaders to Lead

As leaders, if we feel any uncertainty or insecurity about the leadership development process, it is usually not related to the training we give. The uncertainty we feel comes when we contemplate releasing our leaders to lead. It is not dissimilar to what parents feel with their kids. My children are grown and have families of their own, but when they were teenagers, the hardest thing for my wife and me was releasing them to go their own way and make their own decisions. It is scary, but if you don't let them try out their wings, they will never learn to fly.

As I have grown older, I have come to think of myself as a lid lifter. That is my main function as an organizational leader. If I can lift the leadership lids for the members of my team, then I am doing my job. The more barriers I remove for my people, the more likely they are to rise up to their potential. And what's really great is that when the top leaders are lid lifters for the leaders in the middle, then those leaders become load lifters for the ones at the top.

When the top leaders are lid lifters for the leaders in the middle, then those leaders become load lifters for the ones at the top.

So here is the last question. Ask yourself, *Am I unleashing my leaders to lead?*

If you become dedicated to developing and releasing 360-Degree Leaders, your organization will change—and so will your life. I've found that leaders who go from leading alone to successfully developing 360-Degree Leaders go through three stages:

Stage 1: The Loneliness of Leading—"I am the only leader." When you are the one leader, you really have to personally lead everything.

Stage 2: The Lifting of a Leader—"I'm one of only a few leaders." When you begin leading and developing other leaders, then you lead only some of the more important things.

Stage 3: The Legacy of a Leader—"I'm only one of many leaders." When you develop 360-Degree Leaders, then you lead only a very few strategic things.

That's the situation Tom Mullins finds himself in at this point in his career. Tom is the senior pastor of Christ Fellowship, a very large congregation in West Palm Beach, Florida. Tom was the founding pastor of his church, so when he first started, he did everything. If a task was to be accomplished, if a goal was to be met, if a program was to be started, Tom had to lead it personally.

But Tom is an outstanding leader. He had no desire to go it alone, to be Mr. Answerman. As the organization grew, Tom dedicated himself not only to helping people but also to developing leaders. The more leaders he developed, the less time he needed to be on the front lines. For years, Tom has been developing and empowering 360-Degree Leaders to lead.

Today, more than ten thousand people attend his church every weekend. There are hundreds of programs and activities going on every week. The church is highly active in the community, building houses for the poor and feeding people. They are constantly reaching out to others. And where is Tom? He's in the middle of it all, coaching, advising, and encouraging. That's where he now leads from most of the time. Rarely is he the top leader in any endeavor anymore. Tom said he is more fulfilled by seeing others succeed—whether it's teaching on the platform or leading the team—than he is by taking the point position. The organization is succeeding beyond his wildest dreams as a result.

Isn't that what we all want as leaders—for our people and our organizations to succeed? Legendary Chinese philosopher Lao-Tzu said, "A leader is best when the people barely know he exists." That's what the best leaders do—help others succeed. They lead, empower, and then get out of the way. If you create an environment that develops 360-Degree Leaders, that is what you will someday be able to do.

Notes

Section I

Myth #4

1. Andy Stanley, "Challenging the Process," Catalyst Conference lecture, Atlanta, Georgia, 2 Nov. 2001.
2. Carol J. Loomis, "Why Carly's Big Bet is Failing," *Fortune*, 7 February 2005, 52.
3. Carol J. Loomis, "How the HP Board KO'd Carly," *Fortune*, 7 March 2005, 100.

Myth #6

1. James Carney, "7 Clues to Understanding Dick Cheney," *Time*, 30 December 2002, www.time.com/time/archive.

Myth #7

1. Cora Daniels, "Pioneers," *Fortune*, 22 August 2005, 74.
2. Ibid., 76.
3. Ibid., 83.

Section II

Challenge #1

1. D. Michael Abrashoff, *It's Your Ship: Management Techniques from the Best Damn Ship in the Navy* (New York: Warner Business, 2002), 29–30.

Challenge #2

1. Proverbs 29:18 KJV.
2. Tom Peters, *The Circle of Innovation* (New York: Knopf, 1997), 86–87.

Challenge #5

1. "Mix and Match: from Playmakers like Terrell Owens to the Thugs in the Trenches, Our All-star Squad Has a Bit of Everything—All-pro Team," *Football Digest,* April, 2002, www.findarticles.com.
2. Becky Weber, "Athletes In Action Breakfast: Second Annual Frank Reich Call to Courage Award Given," buffalobills.com, 16 April 2003, www.buffalobills.com.
3. "Clement Attlee," http://en.wikipedia.org/wiki/Clement_Attlee.

Challenge #7

1. David Seamands, *Healing Grace* (Wheaton, IL:Victor Books, 1988).

Introduction to Section III

1. Rosamund Stone Zander and Benjamin Zander, *The Art of Possibility* (New York: Penguin, 2000) 71–72.
2. Ibid.

Lead-Up Principle #1

1. Tommy Franks and Malcolm McConnell, *American Soldier* (New York: Regan Books, 2004), 99.
2. Jim Collins, *Good to Great* (New York: Harper Business, 2001), 139.

Lead-Up Principle #2

1. "'The Buck Stops Here' Desk Sign," Truman Presidential Museum and Library, http://www.trumanlibrary.org/buckstop.htm.

Lead-Up Principle #3

1. John C. Maxwell, *Developing the Leader Within You* (Nashville: Thomas Nelson, 1993), 75–76.

Lead-Up Principle #4

1. Franks and McConnell, *American Soldier*, 142.

2. Charles Garfield, *Peak Performers: The New Heroes of American Business* (New York: Avon, 1986), 289.

LEAD-UP PRINCIPLE #6

1. Lev Grossman, "Out of the Xbox: How Bill Gates Built His New Game Machine—and Change Your Living Room Forever," *Time*, 23 May 2005, 44.
2. Proverbs 18:16 NIV.
3. "The Champ," *Reader's Digest*, January 1972, 109.

LEAD-UP PRINCIPLE #9

1. Warren Bennis and Bert Nanus, *Leaders: The Strategies for Taking Charge* (New York: Harperbusiness), 2003, 56.
2. Longfellow, http://www.blupete.com/Literature/Poetry/Psalm.htm.
3. Jack Welch with Suzy Welch, *Winning* (New York: Harper Business, 2005), 61.

SECTION IV

LEAD-ACROSS PRINCIPLE #1

1. Dennis W. Bakke, *Joy at Work: A Revolutionary Approach to Fun on the Job* (Seattle, WA: PVG, 2005), 72.

LEAD-ACROSS PRINCIPLE #4

1. Matthew 7:12.
2. "Politician," *Webster's New Universal Unabridged Dictionary* (New York: Barnes and Noble Books, 1996), 1497.

LEAD-ACROSS PRINCIPLE #5

1. Tim Sanders, *Love is the Killer App: How to Win Business and Influence Friends* (New York: Three Rivers Press, 2002), 15–16.

LEAD-DOWN PRINCIPLE #2

1. Bennet Cerf, *The Sound of Laughter* (Garden City, NY: Doubleday and Company, 1970), 54.

2. Morton Hunt, "Are You Mistrustful?" *Parade*, 6 March 1988.

SECTION V

LEAD-DOWN PRINCIPLE #3

1. Del Jones, "Employers Learning that 'B Players' Hold the Cards," *USA Today*, 9 September 2003, 1A.

LEAD-DOWN PRINCIPLE #4

1. Marcus Buckingham and Donald O. Clifton, *Now, Discover Your Strengths* (New York: The Free Press, 2001), 5.
2. Ibid., 6.

SECTION VI

VALUE #1

1. Franks and McConnell, *American Soldier*, 164.

VALUE #2

1. Charles M. Schwab, *Succeeding with What You Have* (New York: Century Co., 1917), 39–41.
2. Jim Collins, *Good to Great* (New York: Harperbusiness, 2001), 21–22.

VALUE #4

1. Proverbs 27:17 NIV.

VALUE #5

1. *Reader's Digest*, January 2000, 171.
2. Robert C. Baron, Samuel Scinta, and Pat Staten, *20th Century America: 100 Influential People* (Golden, CO: Fulcrum Publishing, 1995), 73.
3. "Marshall, George C.," Britannica Online, http://search.eb.com/normandy/articles/Marshall_George_C.html.
4. Forrest C. Pogue, "George C. Marshall," Grolier Online, http://gi.grolier.com/wwii/wwii_marshall.html.

5. Baron, *20th Century America*, 73–74.
6. "George C. Marshall: A Life of Service," George C. Marshall Foundation, http://20thcenturyrolemodels.org/marshall/quotesabout.html.
7. Ibid.

SPECIAL SECTION

1. Franks and McConnell, *American Soldier*, 163–164.

About the Author

John C. Maxwell, known as America's expert on leadership, speaks in person to hundreds of thousands of people each year. He has communicated his leadership principles to Fortune 500 companies, the United States Military Academy at West Point, and sports organizations such as the NCAA, the NBA, and the NFL.

Maxwell is the founder of Injoy Stewardship Services, as well as several other organizations dedicated to helping people reach their leadership potential. He dedicates much of his time to training leaders worldwide through EQUIP, a nonprofit organization. The *New York Times* best-selling author has written more than forty books, including *Winning with People*, *Thinking for a Change*, and the two million-sellers, *Developing the Leader Within You* and *The 21 Irrefutable Laws of Leadership*.

25 WAYS TO WIN WITH PEOPLE

HOW TO MAKE OTHERS FEEL LIKE A MILLION BUCKS

AND LES PARROTT, PH.D.

To Tom Mullins,

You are like the Pied Piper. When you walk into a room, people instantly want to follow you. More than anyone I know, you embody the 25 ways to win with people. You make everyone around you feel like a million bucks—including me!

—JOHN C. MAXWELL

To Mike Ingram and Monty Ortman,

Few people build a better business team, win more respect, and achieve bigger results than you two. You both have a winsome way of relating to everyone you meet. Your generous spirits and your investment in people will pay dividends for decades. I'm a better person for having known you both.

—LES PARROTT

CONTENTS

ACKNOWLEDGMENT

Thank you to Charlie Wetzel
for his help in writing this book.

LIFE'S GREATEST JOY

BY JOHN C. MAXWELL

In the spring of 2004, soon after turning in the finished manuscript of *Winning with People*, the publisher sent out a number of advance copies of the book, as they often do, to get feedback and endorsements. One of the people who received a copy was Les Parrott.

Now, you may know Dr. Les Parrott from any one of a number of his successes: he is a professor of psychology at Seattle Pacific University, the founder of the Center for Relationship Development, a nationally successful speaker to Fortune 500 companies, and a best-selling author of books such as *High-Maintenance Relationships* and *Love the Life You Live*. He has been a guest on CNN, *The NBC Nightly News*, *Oprah*, and other programs. But I know Les as a friend. In fact, when I first met Les, he was only a kid. He was just beginning his Ph.D. studies in psychology. And the instant I met him, I could see he was sharp. I knew he would soon be a rising star.

In the summer of 2004, I got a phone call from Les. "John," he said, "I loved *Winning with People*. I think it's going to help a lot of folks. It's going to prompt them to change their attitudes and see their relationships with people in a whole new light. And by the way, I wrote a nice endorsement for it. But I have an idea for you. I think you should write a sequel."

I had put my whole heart and a lifetime of relational learning into *Winning with People*, so I was a bit skeptical. But I have a lot of respect for Les, and he always has great ideas, so I was all ears.

"What's your idea?" I asked.

"I've watched you with people for years," Les continued. "When you spend time with people, you make them feel like a million bucks. You've made *me* feel like a million bucks. I bet you could sit down and come up with a couple of dozen specific things that you've mastered that you could teach others to do." That got my juices flowing. "And John, I think you should call the book *How to Make Others Feel Like a Million Bucks*."

Then Les started to rattle off some of the things he thought I should teach, such as giving others a reputation to uphold, mining the gold of good intentions, telling good stories, and helping people win. The more I thought, the more I liked the idea. *Winning with People* had been written to change the fundamental way people approached relationships. Doing what it suggests would take a period of time to accomplish. On the other hand, the book Les was suggesting would be able to help people learn specific skills that could be mastered in a matter of days.

"You know," I said after a long pause, "it's a great idea. Why don't you write it with me?"

Les was surprised.

"I think we'd make a great team," I told him. "You said yourself that you've watched me for years. You're a trained psychologist. Together we'll figure out what skills to write about. I'll teach how I work with people, and you can help people understand the psychology behind the practices."

And that's how *25 Ways to Win with People* came to be written. Les and I had a great time comparing notes, talking about relationships, and telling stories. My one reservation is that Les insisted on telling so many stories about me. I'm not anywhere near as good as Les makes me out to be. Like everyone, I've done stupid things, stepped on toes, and hurt people's feelings. But I've always tried to do my best. And I'm still working daily to improve my skills with others.

And I can tell you this: these skills really do work! Les and I believe that if you practice the skills in this book, your life will change. Why? Because will be able to help others see themselves in a positive light. You will often make them feel like a million bucks.

I believe there is no greater joy in life than seeing others blossom, grow, and reach their potential. This book can help you have a part in making that happen for the people in your life.

BETTER FOR HAVING KNOWN YOU

BY LES PARROTT

Some people possess an invisible quality that draws others to them like a magnet. They're more than just likable. Their charisma defines everything they do and every encounter they have. Accordingly they build better teams, win more respect, and achieve bigger results. Are they merely lucky in life, blessed with personality traits that spell success without effort? Not on your life!

This alluring and invisible trait is not inherited as much as it is honed. It's a captivating spirit that can be taught and caught. For too long people haven't tried to cultivate these qualities because of the false impression that you either have "it" or you don't. This book will help change that misinformed notion. For here you will find twenty-five of the most compelling keys to unlocking a charismatic spirit—a spirit that will help you win with almost everyone you encounter.

WHY WE'RE WRITING THIS BOOK TOGETHER

No one who has ever come in close contact with John Maxwell has walked away unaffected. That's certainly true for me. As a mentor, John has left a permanent imprint on nearly every aspect of my personal and professional life. More than twenty years ago, before I launched into my graduate training to become a clinical psychologist, I flew from my home in Chicago to spend a week with John in San Diego for the sole purpose of soaking up his wisdom. Some years later, it was John who encouraged me to write books and begin a speaking career. And these days, a dozen books later, when we happen to share the same platform, John is always my biggest fan. It's no exaggeration to say that John believes in me more than I could ever have the right to ask.

I'm a better person because John Maxwell is in my life. John taught me how to summon my courage; how to find my purpose and tap into my passion; how to hone my vision and strive toward my goals. He taught me how to "fail forward," how to make each day count, and how to cultivate a can-do attitude. Interaction with a people person like John can have that kind of an impact on you. Directly and indirectly, John has taught me multiple and invaluable life lessons. But more than anything, John has taught me how to win with people. He has a winsome way of relating to nearly everyone—whether it's a server at a restaurant or the chairman of a major corporation.

The Secrets of Interpersonal Magic

Down through the decades, I've studied John as he lifts people up. And as a friend, I wanted to know how I could personally cultivate more of his interpersonal magic. Anyone who has spent even a short period of time with John knows that he puts you at ease and makes you feel good. Not the kind of "good" that comes from a flippant compliment or insincere affirmation—and certainly not from a smarmy or manipulative slap on the back. I'm talking about the kind of goodness that comes from knowing he genuinely wants the best for you. He's pulling for you and wants you to win.

I've kept my eyes focused on even the most minute of interactions. Time and again, John displays an almost uncanny ability to disarm, entertain, and engage whomever he meets. In other words, he has the ability to make others feel like a million bucks. So as he already told you, one day I approached him with the idea of his sharing the secrets of his magnetic personality to help you learn to do what he does. When John invited me to write this book with him, I spent hours with him to draw out the things he does reflexively on a daily basis. And I also talked extensively to John's friends and staff. I heard story after story about the ways John has won with them and added value to their lives. I tell many of these stories in the book so that you can "see" the practices in action.

Within Your Reach

The twenty-five secrets we include in this book have the potential to change your life. They can help you to become the kind of magnetic person who lights up the room when you arrive. These skills are readily learnable. They are not just for a lucky few who seem to be hardwired with exclusive qualities. They are within reach of anyone who wants them. And they are crucial for anyone wanting to win with people.

1

START WITH YOURSELF

Your relationships can only be as healthy as you are.
—NEIL CLARK WARREN

LES . . . ON STARTING WITH YOURSELF

If you want to win with people, you've got to be a winner yourself—or at the very least be on your way to becoming one. There's no avoiding this simple fact.

As a psychologist specializing in relationships, I've seen hundreds of people in therapy. I've spoken to hundreds of thousands in seminars. I've written more than a dozen books on the subject. People close to me understand that I'm passionate about helping others win with people. But if there is one thing I know, it's that a new tip or technique to win with others will fall flat if you don't start with yourself.

Let me say it straight. If you try to practice the "ways" of winning with people that you are about to learn in the following chapters before you give serious attention to how you can be a winner yourself, you'll be sorely disappointed. However, if you will first take the time to focus on yourself, you'll soon be ready to focus on others.

You've Got to Start with Yourself

William James, the first American psychologist, said, "The hell to be endured hereafter, of which theology tells, is no worse than the hell we make for ourselves in this world by habitually fashioning our characters in the wrong way." If we do not form a winning character, we are sure to lose with other people. That's why this first step is so significant. In fact, there are at least two compelling reasons why winning with people hinges on starting with yourself.

You Can't Be Happy Without Being Healthy

Psychology used to think it was critical to focus on—and then eliminate—negative emotions. We now know there is a better way. A new generation of research has shifted psychology's primary analysis from that of misery to an understanding of wellness.

The new research reveals that you can't be happy simply by being unencumbered by depression, stress, or anxiety. No—you can't be happy unless you are healthy. And there's a lot more to health than not being sick. Emotional health is more than the absence of dysfunctional emotions. Emotional health is at the center of winning with people.

You Can't Give What You Don't Have

One of the oldest psychological truisms in the world is that you cannot give what you do not have. In fact, like every other psychologist-in-training, when I first began my graduate education, I was urged to get into psychotherapy myself. "Les," my advisor said, "as a psychologist, you will only be able to take a person as far as you have gone yourself." Why? Because you cannot give what you do not have. You cannot enjoy others until you enjoy yourself.

Harry Firestone said, "You get the best out of others when you give the best of yourself." So true. But if the best you have isn't any better than what those "others" already possess, you'll never take them any higher than they already are.

The bottom line? If you are not becoming a winner, you'll find it almost impossible to win with others. But here's the good news: your desire and attempts to win with others help to make you a winner. It's what American essayist Charles Warner was getting at when he said, "No one can sincerely try to help another without helping himself."

How to Be a Winner

"There's a period of life when we swallow a knowledge of ourselves," said Pearl Bailey, "and it becomes either good or sour inside." Everyone has little anxieties and insecurities. If I were to ask you to describe a winning person, a person who is whole and healthy, you might say something about this person being confident, warm, kind, stable, giving, and so on. And you'd be right, in a sense. But there's more to becoming a winner than having a list of enviable attributes. Being a winner comes down to one thing: your value.

Winners are valuable. Ask any star athlete or gold medalist who has just signed a multimillion-dollar endorsement deal. But truth be told, being a winner, in the purest sense of the word, has nothing to do with your performance, your salary, or your earning potential. It has to do with your value and whether or not you have *owned* it. When you embrace your own personal value, when you are secure in who you are, then you have become a winner.

Here are a few ways of doing just that:

RECOGNIZE YOUR VALUE. On more than one occasion, I've told the story of being on a speaking platform with my friend Gary Smalley when he did something that captivated the crowd. Before an audience of nearly ten thousand people, Gary held out a crisp fifty-dollar bill and asked them, "Who would like this fifty-dollar bill?" Hands started going up everywhere.

"I am going to give this fifty dollars to one of you," he said, "but first let me do this." He proceeded to crumple up the bill. Then he asked, "Who still wants it?" The same hands went up in the air.

"Well," he continued, "what if I do this?" He dropped it on the ground and started to grind it into the floor with his shoe. He picked it up, all crumpled and dirty. "Now, who still wants it?" Again, hands went into the air.

"You have all learned a valuable lesson," Gary said. "No matter what I do to the money, you still want it because it doesn't decrease in value. It is still worth fifty dollars."

Gary's simple illustration underscores a profound point. Many times in our lives we are dropped, crumpled, and ground into the dirt by the decisions we make or the circumstances that come our way. We may feel as though we are worthless, insignificant in our own eyes and in the eyes of others. But no matter what has happened or what will happen, we *never* lose our value as human beings. Nothing can take that away. Never forget that.

ACCEPT YOUR VALUE. How many times have you heard people say, "He has issues"? What they mean is that the person is stuck. The person is not healthy. He's got a hang-up. He's uncomfortable in his own skin. It's what we psychologists are getting at when we talk about self-acceptance.

Let's face it. All of us walking around on this planet have insecurities and issues that we wish we could change about ourselves. But certain things we can't. Some things about us just *are*. Maybe you weren't born with the kind of looks you would like. Or you aren't as tall as you desire. Your genes dealt you a hand that you've eventually got to accept—either that or you reject your personal value and spend your days trying to compensate for your insecurities. You become hung up, stuck on not being dealt a better hand.

The term *acceptance* comes from the Latin *ad capere* that means "to take to oneself." In other words, inherent in the process of accepting others is the act of self-acceptance. I'll say it again: you will never win with people until *you* become a winner.

INCREASE YOUR VALUE. Perhaps you already recognize and accept your value. Maybe you know at the center of your being, deep in your soul, that you are loved by God and are of inestimable value. Congratulations! The next step is to increase your value to others by solving as many of your problems as you can. In other words, you need to maximize who you are by overcoming or fixing those things that are within your power to change.

You may struggle with a hair-trigger temper, for example. Maybe you have difficulty setting boundaries or taking responsibility. Maybe you have some bad habits, or perhaps your attitude needs an overhaul. All of us have hurdles we can overcome. Forty-five percent of Americans report that they would change a bad habit if they could.[1] The truth is, they can change. Each of us can improve ourselves whenever we decide to.

In his book *Teaching the Elephant to Dance* (Crown, 1990), James Belasco described how trainers shackle young elephants with heavy chains to deeply embedded stakes. In that way the elephant learns to stay in its place. Older, more powerful elephants that have been trained in this way never try to leave—even though they have the strength to pull up the stake and walk away. Their conditioning limits their movements. Eventually, with only a small, unattached metal bracelet on their legs, they stand in place—even though the stakes are actually gone!

It's a story you've probably heard before, but like the powerful elephants, many people are bound by the restraints of previous conditioning. Just as the unattached chain around the elephant's leg keeps it from moving, some people impose needless limits on their personal progress. Don't let this happen to you. Don't mindlessly accept restraints on your abilities. Challenge them and keep growing.

BELIEVE IN YOUR VALUE. Once you've recognized your value, accepted it, and increased it, you've eventually got to believe it. You've got to believe it with such conviction that you'd be willing to bank on it.

Chuck Wepner never learned this lesson. As a boxer, he earned the nickname "The Bayonne Bleeder" because of the punishment he took even while winning. In the boxing world he was what's called "a catcher," a fighter who often uses his head to block the other guy's punches. Wepner continually pressured his opponent until he either won or got knocked out. He never cared how many shots he had to absorb before landing a knockout blow. Trainer Al Braverman called him "the gutsiest fighter I ever met. He was in a league of his own. He didn't care about pain. If he got cut or elbowed, he never looked at me or the referee for help. He was a fighter in the purest sense of the word."

When Wepner knocked out Terry Henke in the eleventh round in Salt Lake City, boxing promoter Don King offered Wepner a title shot against then–heavyweight champion George Foreman. But when Ali defeated Foreman, Wepner found himself scheduled to fight "The Greatest"—Muhammad Ali. On the morning of the fight, Wepner gave his wife a pink negligee and told her she would "soon be sleeping with the heavyweight champion of the world."

Ali scored a technical knockout with just nineteen seconds remaining in the fight. But there was a moment—one glorious moment in the ninth round—when a hamlike paw to Ali's chest knocked the reigning champion off his feet.

Wepner recalled, "When Ali was down, I remember saying to my ringman, Al Braverman, 'Start the car, we're going to the bank, we're millionaires.' And Al said to me, 'You'd better turn around. Because he's getting up.'" After the fight,

Wepner's wife pulled the negligee out of her purse and asked, "Do I go to Ali's room or does he come to mine?" (see www.wepnerhomestead.com)

That story would be nothing more than an odd boxing footnote except for one thing. A struggling writer was watching the fight. And then it suddenly struck him: *There it is*, he said to himself. "So I went home and I started writing. And I wrote for three days straight." That's how writer and actor Sylvester Stallone described the birth of the Academy Award–winning movie *Rocky* to James Lipton on *Inside the Actor's Studio*.

The movie studio offered the struggling writer an unprecedented $400,000 for his script, but Stallone refused the money, choosing instead just $20,000 and the right to play the part of Rocky for actor's minimum wage, a paltry $340 a week. The studio also made an offer to Wepner since the movie was based on his life. He could receive a flat fee of $70,000 or 1 percent of the movie's gross profits. Wanting the guaranteed payday, Wepner took the $70,000, a decision that ultimately cost him $8 million. Today Chuck Wepner lives in Bayonne and works as a liquor salesman.

The same thing happens whenever you sell yourself short. If you don't believe that you have something of great value to offer another person—namely yourself—you'll never truly win with people. Who you are is the greatest asset you'll ever possess. And as long as you recognize this valuable asset, accept it, increase it, and believe it with deep conviction, the ways of winning with people in this book can become a part of your character. And when they come from the heart, they work like a charm.

JOHN . . . WITH A MAXWELL MENTORING MOMENT

If I could meet you in person, one of the first things I would tell you is that I believe in you. You may find that hard to swallow because I don't even know you. But I do know this: everyone has value and something of value to offer others. One of my missions in life is to see that value in others, help them discover it, and encourage them to reach their potential. You can become a winner and help others do the same.

That's why I want to mentor you. I may not be able to sit down with you in person, but I've written this book with Les because I want to help you. In each chapter ahead, I will come alongside you for a mentoring moment and teach you a specific way to make others feel like a million bucks. It's my way of helping you win with people. And when we're done, I want to suggest that you seek out a face-to-face mentor, a winner who can add value to you and walk you through many of life's additional lessons.

LES . . . ON BRINGING IT HOME

Each of the chapters in this book closes with a piece on bringing it home. It's designed to help you put the chapter's "winning way" into action. This little outline has served me well, so I pass it along to you.

To apply John's teaching to your own life . . .

Forget about:

Whatever makes you feel insecure.

Ask:

How can I increase my value in order to benefit others, rather than just myself?

Do it:

List the things you can improve about yourself (bad habits to break, etc.), along with specific steps to take to make the improvements.

Remember:

Your relationships can only be as healthy as you are.

2

PRACTICE THE 30-SECOND RULE

He who waits to do a great deal of good at once,
will never do anything.
—SAMUEL JOHNSON

LES . . . ON SEEING THE PRACTICE IN ACTION

One of the most valuable lessons in winning with people that I have ever learned from John is the 30-Second Rule: within the first thirty seconds of a conversation, say something encouraging to a person.

John is a master at it. While I was sitting in a meeting at one of his companies a short time ago, John entered the room and within just a few minutes said something encouraging to each person around the table.

"David, I heard you hit it out of the park this morning on that conference call."

"Larry, you are making me look so good with that consultation in Denver. Thank you."

"Kevin, I just saw the numbers for April. Nobody else in the world sees and seizes an opportunity the way you do."

"Les, I'm so glad you made the trip out here to be with us today. I know you're going to add tremendous value to our discussion."

Very early on, John had genuinely encouraged each one of us. And it seemed almost effortless. Since I was trying to learn more about John's winning ways with people, after the meeting I asked John to tell me about what he did. That's when I first heard the term "the 30-Second Rule."

"I learned this from my father," John said. "Years ago, he was the president of a college, and I would often walk across the campus with him. He continually stopped to say encouraging things to the students. When I was tempted to complain, I would look at the students' faces and realize Dad had deposited good words inside of them.

"People never forget that kind of encouragement," John continued. "Yesterday I talked to my dad on the phone, and he excitedly told me about his many former students who keep coming to Florida from all over the United States to see him. He was surprised that they would go out of their way to see him, but I wasn't. The 30-Second Rule that Dad had practiced with everyone every day was returning to him big time."

"I've seen you do this for years," I told John, "but I never knew it was something you picked up from your dad."

"I've learned a lot of great lessons from my dad. He's an incredible leader," John replied. "I practice this rule every day with everyone I meet. You see, someone once said to me, 'Be kind . . . everyone you meet is fighting a hard battle.' People everywhere need a good word, an uplifting compliment to fire their hopes and dreams. It takes very little effort to do, but it really lifts people up."

JOHN . . . WITH A MAXWELL MENTORING MOMENT

When most people meet others, they search for ways to make themselves look good. The key to the 30-Second Rule is reversing this practice. When you make contact with people, instead of focusing on yourself, search for ways to make *them* look good.

Every day before I meet with people, I pause to think about something encouraging I can tell them. What I say can be one of many things: I might thank them for something they've done for me or for a friend. I might tell others about one of their accomplishments. I might praise them for a personal quality they exhibit. Or I might simply compliment their appearance. The practice isn't complicated, but it does take some time, effort, and discipline. The reward for practicing it is huge, because it really makes a positive impact on people.

If you desire to encourage others by practicing the 30-Second Rule, then remember these things the next time you meet people:

THE 30-SECOND RULE GIVES PEOPLE THE TRIPLE-A TREATMENT

All people feel better and do better when you give them *attention*, *affirmation*, and *appreciation*. The next time you make contact with people, begin by giving them your undivided attention during the first thirty seconds. Affirm them and show your appreciation for them in some way. Then watch what happens. You will be surprised by how positively they respond. And if you have trouble remembering to keep your focus on them instead of on yourself, then perhaps the words of William King will help you. He said, "A gossip is one who talks to you about other people. A bore is one who talks to you about himself. And a brilliant conversationalist is one who talks to you about yourself."

"A gossip is one who talks to you about other people. A bore is one who talks to you about himself. And a brilliant conversationalist is one who talks to you about yourself."

—William King

THE 30-SECOND RULE GIVES PEOPLE ENERGY

Psychologist Henry H. Goddard conducted a study on energy levels in children using an instrument he called the "ergograph." His findings are fascinating. He discovered that when tired children were given a word of praise or commendation, the ergograph showed an immediate upward surge of energy in the children. When the children were criticized or discouraged, the ergograph showed that their physical energy took a sudden nosedive.

You may have already discovered this intuitively. When someone praises you, doesn't your energy level go up? And when you are criticized, doesn't that comment drag you down? Words have great power.

What kind of environment do you think you could create if you continually affirmed people when you first came into contact with them? Not only would you encourage them, but you would also become an energy carrier. Whenever you walked into a room, the people would light up! You would help to create the kind of environment everyone loves. Just your presence alone would brighten people's days.

THE 30-SECOND RULE INSTILLS MOTIVATION

Vince Lombardi, the famed Green Bay Packers football coach, was a feared disciplinarian. But he was also a great motivator. One day he chewed out a player who had missed several blocking assignments. After practice, Lombardi stormed into the locker room and saw that the player was sitting at his locker, head down, dejected. Lombardi mussed his hair, patted him on the shoulder, and said, "One of these days, you're going to be the best guard in the NFL."

That player was Jerry Kramer, and Kramer says he carried that positive image of himself for the rest of his career. "Lombardi's encouragement had a tremendous impact on my whole life," Kramer said. He went on to become a member of the Green Bay Packers Hall of Fame and a member of the NFL's All-50-Year Team.

Everybody needs motivation from time to time. Using the 30-Second Rule helps encourage people to be and do their best. Never underestimate the power of motivation:

- Motivation helps people who know what they should do . . . to do it!

- Motivation helps people who know what commitment they should make . . . to make it!
- Motivation helps people who know what habit they should break . . . to break it!
- Motivation helps people who know what path they should take . . . to take it!

Motivation makes it possible to accomplish what you should accomplish.

One of the great side benefits of the 30-Second Rule is that it also helps you. You can't help others without also helping yourself. Benjamin Franklin realized this truth, and he encouraged others with it. In a letter to John Paul Jones, Franklin wrote:

> Hereafter, if you should observe an occasion to give your officers and friends a little more praise than is their due, and confess more fault than you can justly be charged with, you will only become the sooner for it, a great captain. Criticizing and censuring almost everyone you have to do with, will diminish friends, increase enemies, and thereby hurt your affairs.

If you want others to feel good about themselves and to feel glad every time they see you, then practice the 30-Second Rule. Remember this: those who add to us, draw us to them. Those who subtract, cause us to withdraw.

Those who add to us, draw us to them. Those who subtract, cause us to withdraw.

LES . . . ON BRINGING IT HOME

Social psychologists have studied "first impressions" for decades. If you want to make an impression that is lasting and positive, we now know what works and what doesn't. And John's 30-Second Rule is one of the most effective means for finding success in this area. In research it's called the "primacy effect," and its initial impact goes a long way in making others feel connected with you.[1]

To apply John's teaching to your own life . . .

Forget about:

Searching for ways to make yourself look good.
Instead, search for ways to make others look good.

Ask:

What positive, encouraging thing can I say to each person I will see today?

Do it:

Give everyone you meet the Triple-A Treatment—attention, affirmation, and appreciation.

Remember:

Within the first thirty seconds of a conversation, say something encouraging.

3

Let People Know You Need Them

The greatest compliment that was ever paid me was when someone asked me what I thought, and attended to my answer.

—Henry David Thoreau

LES . . . ON SEEING THE PRACTICE IN ACTION

One day I asked John the secret to getting people to join a team, and he told me it could be found in a single sentence: "I can't do it without you." He went on to say that great leaders stumble when they believe people need *them* instead of recognizing that the very opposite is true. "Leaders can become great," said John, "only when they realize that *they* are the ones who need people."

As we talked, John pulled a laminated card from his desk drawer and told me he had developed a tool years ago for asking people for help. "Les, I wrote this back in 1974," he said. "I was facing a major building project and I needed to raise more than a million dollars. It was the first time I understood how far over my head I truly was in leadership.

"That's when I realized that if I was ever to achieve something great," John continued, "it would be the result of turning the dream from *me* to *we*." I scribbled down that phrase, intending to "borrow" it for an upcoming lecture. John went on, "I also realized that any dream I could achieve without the help of other people was too small."

Then John handed me the laminated card. On it were these words:

> I Have a Dream
>
> History tells us that in every age there comes a time when leaders must come forth to meet the needs of the hour. Therefore, there is no potential leader who does not have an opportunity to better mankind. Those around him also have the same privilege. Fortunately, I believe that God has surrounded me with those who will accept the challenge of this hour.
>
> My dream allows me to . . .
>
> - Give up at any moment all that I am in order to receive all that I can become.
> - Sense the invisible so I can do the impossible.
> - Trust God's resources since the dream is bigger than all my abilities and acquaintances.

- Continue when discouraged, for where there is no faith in the future, there is no power in the present.
- Attract winners, because big dreams draw big people.
- See my people and myself in the future. Our dream is the promise of what we shall one day be.

> Yes, I have a dream. It is greater than any of my gifts. It is as large as the world, but it begins with one. Won't you join me?
>
> —John Maxwell

"Les," he said, "I've given these cards out by the hundreds, and I have seen people time and again join up to help me accomplish my dream for one primary reason—because I let them know I needed them."

JOHN . . . WITH A MAXWELL MENTORING MOMENT

The day that I realized I could no longer do everything myself was a major step in my development as a person and a leader. I've always had vision, plenty of ideas, and vast amounts of energy. But when the vision gets bigger than you, you really only have two choices: give up on the vision or get help. I chose the latter.

> When the vision gets bigger than you, you really only have two choices: give up on the vision or get help.

No matter how successful you are, no matter how important or accomplished, you *do* need people. That's why you need to let them know that you cannot win without them. President Woodrow Wilson said, "We should not only use all the brains we have—but all that we can borrow." Why stop with just their brains? Enlist people's hands and hearts, too! Another president, Lyndon Johnson, was right when he said, "There are no problems we cannot solve together, and very few that we can solve by ourselves."

Asking others for help is a great way to make them feel like a million bucks. Why?

People Need to Be Needed

Have you ever stopped to ask someone for directions? You roll down your car window and ask a passerby, "Can you tell me how to find Larry's Market?" Nearly every time, people stop whatever they are doing and help if they can—even if it means crossing the street or standing in traffic. They may even repeat the directions a couple of times to make sure you get it. Why? Because whenever a person feels that he or she knows something you don't, it gives that person an ego boost. Everyone likes to be an expert, even if it's for a moment. It gives them a great sense of superiority and of accomplishment when they help. That translates into an increased sense of self-worth. And it all stems from the universal need to be needed.

People Need to Know They Need People.

"It marks a big step in your development when you come to realize that other people can help you do a better job than you could do alone," said steel magnate and philanthropist Andrew Carnegie. Sadly, many people never achieve that level of maturity or insight. Some people still want to believe that they can achieve greatness alone.

Every individual's fate is tied to that of many others. We cannot be like the shipwrecked man who sits at one end of a lifeboat doing nothing while everyone at the other end bails furiously, and says, "Thank God that hole isn't in *my* end of the boat!" We all need people, and if we don't know it, we're in trouble.

PEOPLE NEED TO KNOW THEY ARE NEEDED.

Cartoonist Charles Schulz often captured the longings of the human heart in his comic strip *Peanuts*. He really understood the needs of people. In one of his creations, Lucy asks Charlie Brown to help with her homework. "I'll be eternally grateful," she promises.

"Fair enough. I've never had anyone be eternally grateful before," replies Charlie. "Just subtract 4 from 10 to get how many apples the farmer had left."

Lucy says, "That's it? That's it? I have to be eternally grateful for that? I was robbed! I can't be eternally grateful for this—it was too easy!"

With a blank look of discouragement, Charlie replies, "Well, whatever you think is fair."

"How about if I just say 'thanks, bro'?" replies Lucy.

As Charlie leaves to go outside, he meets Linus, who asks, "Where've you been, Charlie Brown?"

"Helping Lucy with her homework."

"Did she appreciate it?" Linus asks.

Charlie responds, "At greatly reduced prices."

Ever felt like Charlie Brown? You're not alone. Every

human being longs for a life of significance. We all need to know we are needed and that what we offer to others is of value.

PEOPLE NEED TO KNOW THAT THEY HELPED.

Whenever someone tells me how valuable the people on my team are to them, I encourage him to tell the individuals who were so helpful. Why? Because people need to know that they helped someone. "Good leaders make people feel that they're at the very heart of things, not at the periphery," says author and leadership expert Warren Bennis. "Everyone feels that he or she makes a difference to the success of the organization. When that happens people feel centered and that gives their work meaning."

> "Good leaders make people feel that they're at the very heart of things, not at the periphery."
>
> —WARREN BENNIS

Walter Shipley of Citibank says, "We have 68,000 employees. With a company this size, I'm not 'running the business' . . . My job is to create the environment that enables people to leverage each other beyond their own individual capabilities . . . I get credit for providing the leadership that got us there. But our people did it." Shipley understands what successful leaders know: people need to know that they made an important contribution to reaching the goal.

It's not a sign of weakness to let others know you value them. It's a sign of security and strength. When you're honest about your need for help, specific with others about the value they add, and inclusive of others as you build a team to do something bigger than you are, everybody wins.

LES . . . ON BRINGING IT HOME

Research proved long ago that when people feel needed, they are far more likely to be productive and creative. In fact, studies of twins with similar IQ scores show that each performs quite differently when they are in differing environments, one supportive (where they know they are needed and appreciated) and the other not. The person who feels needed consistently performs better.[1]

To apply John's teaching to your own life . . .

Forget about:

A prideful attitude that causes you to prove how capable you are without the help of others.

Ask:

Who specifically can help me do a better job than I can do alone? Who is just waiting to be asked to join in what I am doing?

Do it:

Sincerely ask others for input or help and attend carefully to what they have to say.

Remember:

Individuals who win with people make others feel that they are at the very heart of things, not at the periphery.

4

Create a Memory and Visit It Often

Memory is the treasury and guardian of all things.
—Cicero

LES . . . ON SEEING THE PRACTICE IN ACTION

People who spend quality time with John know that they are going to walk away with a memory. It's inevitable. John just has a knack for making memories; it's one of the things that makes him a winner with people.

John also enjoys it when others create a memory for him. One day when we were talking about creating memories, told me this story: he was scheduled to speak to three thousand young leaders in Phoenix at an event, but as he stepped onto the platform that day, he realized his host had something different in mind. "He didn't want me to speak at all," John explained. The group that was gathered had been reading his books and listening to his tapes through the years and had planned a surprise. Instead of having John speak to them, they wanted to speak to John, so they had him sit on the platform and simply listen as they honored him. One after another, twelve preselected leaders from the audience came up to the podium to tell the group about how John's teaching had made an impact on his or her life.

"It was completely unexpected," John said. "And not only did they shower me with kind words, but each speaker presented me with a memento—a tangible remembrance of something they said they had learned from me. I was completely overwhelmed by the experience."

One person gave John a beautiful painting with two images: one of a child reading one of John's books and another of the child as a grown man coaching others.

"Les," John said, tears in his eyes and his voice cracking, "I don't know how many times I've reminisced about that day. I keep the mementos around my office to relive it. That experience meant so much to me. And it renewed my desire to create memories for others."

JOHN . . . WITH A MAXWELL MENTORING MOMENT

Few things bond people together like a shared memory. Soldiers who battle together, teammates who win a championship, and work teams that hit their goals share a connection that never goes away. Married couples who experience rough times can often look back on their earlier experiences together to keep them going. Families bond when they rough it on camping trips or share adventures on vacation and then love recounting their experience years later.

Some memories come as the result of circumstance, but many can be proactively created. Author Lewis Carroll wrote, "It's a poor sort of memory that only works backward." What does that mean to you and me? The richest memories are often those we plan and intentionally create. Here are some hints for creating memories that will help you win with people:

Initiative—Make Something Happen

Memories don't find us—we find them. Even better, if we are intentional, we can *make* memories. If you mention the word *chariot* to friends Dan and Patti Reiland or Tim and Pam Elmore, I can tell you exactly what will come to mind—a crisp autumn day in New York City when we did something that still makes us laugh. After lunch at Tavern on the Green, I hired three "bicycle chariots" with peddling drivers to take each couple on a race through Manhattan to Macy's. It was up to each couple to motivate their driver to win (using whatever financial incentives they wanted). The race was neck-and-neck the entire way, and we laughed the whole time.

We still laugh when we think about it or look at the photos we took that day. But it never would have happened if we hadn't initiated it.

Time—Set Aside Time to Make Something Happen

For years parents have debated the issue of quality time versus quantity of time. As a father and grandfather, I have discovered that it takes quantity time to find quality time. If you don't carve out the time, you can't create the memory.

Haven't you found that most memories you have are with the people you spend the most time with? I know that's true for me. If you want to make memories with your family, spend more time with them. If you want to create memories with your employees, you won't do it behind the door of your office. You simply can't make memories with people if you don't take time to be with them.

Planning—Plan for Something to Happen

Most people don't lead their lives—they accept their lives. They wait for memorable experiences to happen, never giving a thought to planning an experience that will make a memory. One of the most extravagant memories I ever planned was with Margaret, my wife, for our twenty-fifth wedding anniversary. We decided to share it with thirty of our closest friends. We chartered a yacht and picked everyone up in San Diego Bay. Once on board, we had a delectable meal and then surprised the group by having Frankie Valens entertain us with some of his trademark songs like "Sixteen Candles." Our friends loved it. But the most memorable highlight of the evening was created when Margaret and I said a few words about each person and why that person held such a special place in our hearts. That night is not only a great memory for Margaret and me, but it is a great memory for the people who attended, too.

Most people don't lead their lives—they accept their lives.

CREATIVITY—FIND A WAY TO MAKE SOMETHING HAPPEN

What do you do when you find yourself at an event where you expect to share a memory but nothing seems to happen? You get creative. I've been asked over and over to tell the story of the Holiday Bowl I attended in San Diego with friends about fifteen years ago. The game was so dull that I ended up buying newspapers for everyone in my section so that we would have something to do. Another guy nearby, not to be outdone, bought one hundred bags of peanuts and distributed them to everybody in the section. The two of us got a standing ovation, and soon the news crews were more focused on us than the game. I don't remember the score or much about the game, but it's a night I'll never forget. Neither will the buddies who went with me.

SHARED EXPERIENCES—MAKE SOMETHING HAPPEN TOGETHER

Memories compound when they are experienced with someone you love. Years ago our family went to Jasper Park in Canada for a vacation. While we were there, I took my children, Elizabeth and Joel Porter, fishing. On our way back to our cabin, we called Margaret to let her know we were coming home, and she asked the kids how they did.

"We caught eight trout," Joel said. He was acting low-key about it, but I could tell he was proud. As we drove back, we talked about how great it was going to be to have a dinner of trout we had just pulled from a cold mountain stream. When we arrived, we carried the trout into the kitchen, and there on the counter we saw four steaks ready to be cooked.

"What gives?" Joel asked his mother. "We caught eight trout! And we're looking forward to a trout dinner."

Margaret started to laugh. "I thought you said *a* trout, so I went out and bought steaks." Then I started laughing, and Elizabeth did too. Finally, with a gleam in his eye, Joel said, "Mom's not too good with numbers, is she?"

That happened with our kids when they were eleven and thirteen years old. Every time we've had a cookout since then, the kids have told the trout story. Even now that both of them are married and have kids of their own, they still love to say, "Mom's not too good with numbers," and make us laugh.

Mementos—Show That Something Happened

"Almost anything you do today will be forgotten in just a few weeks," says author and research scientist John McCrone. "The ability to retrieve a memory decreases exponentially unless boosted by artificial aids such as diaries and photographs."

Don't you find that to be true? Do you keep pictures or souvenirs on your desk where you can see them? Do you carry photos of people you love in your wallet? Do you have a trophy, plaque, game ball, or other award on a shelf where you and others can see it? We all have things we love—not because they have any material value but because they remind us of places we've been or things we've done. When you help someone else create a memory, give that person something to remember it by.

Relive the Memory—Talk About What Happened

The most important part of creating a memory is reliving it. It's the payoff! Many times when I travel with others, at the end of our trip I ask them to share a favorite memory. It often leads to rich conversations. Or I write a note to someone soon afterward to share my own favorite memory. It creates a connection that bonds us together and makes both of us feel great.

LES . . . ON BRINGING IT HOME

There isn't a person in the world who doesn't understand the value of positive memories. They can sustain people during the worst of times and inspire them during the best of times. And best of all, anyone can create a memory and visit it often!

To apply John's teaching to your own life . . .

Forget about:

Trying to have quality time to make a memory if you aren't willing to invest the quantity of time it requires.

Ask:

What memories have I already created with people in my life that we need to relive together?

Do it:

Plan an experience that will commemorate an achievement or milestone that people will talk about years from now. And don't forget to create a memento of it.

Remember:

We shouldn't wait for memories to happen to us. We need to make memories happen.

5

Compliment People in Front of Other People

Admonish thy friends in secret, praise them openly.
—Publilius Syrus

LES . . . ON SEEING THE PRACTICE IN ACTION

Complimenting people in front of other people is a John Maxwell trademark. He's known for doing this far and wide. So when I asked a few people around his company to tell me how John does this, I didn't have to look far for stories. Instead, I had to decide which of numerous ones to choose. Many of these stories contained sentiments similar to the ones I heard from Charlie Wetzel, who has worked with John on his books for more than a decade:

For almost twenty years, John has written and recorded leadership lessons, which he used to mentor tens of thousands of people every month, first for the Injoy Life Club and now for Maximum Impact. In 1995, he did a lesson that was designed to teach leaders how to find people with great potential and how to create an environment for them to flourish and emerge as full-fledged leaders. He called it "Searching for Eagles."

John now often records such lessons on-site at corporations and other organizations around the country. But at that time he delivered the teaching to his own church staff and a few people from Injoy, the leadership development company he founded. It was his way of continually developing his people so that they would grow and learn. I sat in the audience that day and took notes as I learned the ten marks of an eagle:

1. Eagles make things happen.
2. Eagles see and seize opportunities.
3. Eagles influence the opinions and actions of others.
4. Eagles add value to you.
5. Eagles draw winners to them.
6. Eagles equip other eagles to lead.
7. Eagles provide ideas that help the organization.
8. Eagles possess an uncommonly great attitude.
9. Eagles live up to their commitments and responsibilities.
10. Eagles show fierce loyalty to the organization and the leader.

> It was an inspiring and instructive message. As John wrapped up the lesson, he named some of the eagles that had come into his life through the years. And then John said, "But I want to finish this lesson by telling you about another eagle who has come on board recently. His name is Charlie Wetzel. He's only been working with us a short time, but he makes things happen."
>
> John went on to tell how a connection I made on my own initiative with the editor of a national publication led to the acceptance of a Maxwell article that would be read by over three million subscribers. John then said so many kind and complimentary things about me that it brought tears to my eyes.
>
> John had always said positive things about me in front of my wife and my visiting parents, but this time he was speaking to the entire staff of my church and the president of his company—not to mention the thousands of people who would be listening to the message on tape. It was overwhelming. Before that moment, I'd never thought of myself as an "eagle." Even to this day, it touches my heart when I think about it.

It's been a decade since John paid Charlie that compliment, yet its impact hasn't lessened. That's the power of complimenting people in front of other people.

JOHN . . . WITH A MAXWELL MENTORING MOMENT

The most fundamental and straightforward way of winning with people is to give them a compliment—a sincere and meaningful word of affirmation. If you want to make others feel like a million bucks, you've got to master this elementary skill. And it's essential that you learn to give your compliments in front of others as well as one-on-one. Why? Because that private compliment turned public, instantly and dramatically increases in value. Here are reasons why that's so important:

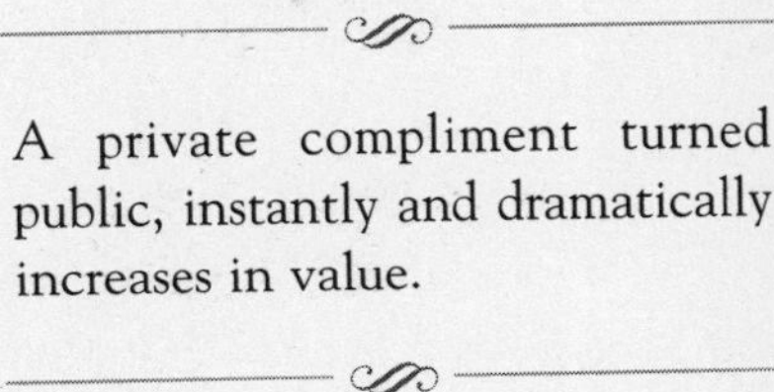

PEOPLE WANT TO FEEL WORTHWHILE IN LIFE

"Everyone has an invisible sign hanging from his neck," says Mary Kay Ash. "It says, 'Make Me Feel Important!'" Mary Kay drilled this principle into her sales team. She told them again and again, "Never forget this message when working with people." She knew compliments and affirmation were critical to enjoying success with others.

And by the way, it's one of the reasons she was so successful. With her life savings of $5,000 and the help of her then twenty-year-old son, she launched Mary Kay Cosmetics in 1963. The company now has more than 500,000 independent beauty consultants in twenty-nine markets worldwide, and Mary Kay Inc., is ranked as one of the 100 best companies to work for in America.

Mary Kay, like every other person who wins with people, knew that people want to feel worthwhile. When you continually keep this in mind, you can't help but give compliments freely.

Compliments Increase in Value When We Value the Person Who Gives Them

Willard Scott, the former longtime weatherman on NBC's *Today Show,* remembers his radio days when he received his all-time favorite letter from a fan:

> Dear Mr. Scott, I think you're the best disc jockey in Washington. You play the best music and have the nicest voice of anyone on the air. Please excuse the crayon—they won't let us have anything sharp in here.

Not all compliments are created equal. Who gives the compliment has a lot to do with how much we prize it. A nice remark from someone who's not allowed to have sharp objects doesn't carry the same weight as a compliment given by your boss in front of people you respect.

Compliments Affirm People and Make Them Strong

To affirm is to make firm. An affirmation is a statement of truth you make firm in a person's heart when you utter it. As a result, it cultivates conviction. For example, when you compliment a person's attitude, you reinforce it and make it more consistent. Because you notice it in a positive way, he will be more likely to demonstrate that same attitude again.

Likewise, when you affirm people's dreams, you help their dreams become more real than their doubts. Like the repetition of a weight-lifting regimen, routine compliments build up people's qualities and strengthen their personalities.

"There are high spots in all of our lives," wrote author George Matthew Adams, "and most of them have come about through encouragement from someone else. I don't care how great, how famous or successful a man or woman may be, each hungers for applause. Encouragement is oxygen to the soul. Good work can never be expected from a worker without encouragement. No one can ever have lived without it."

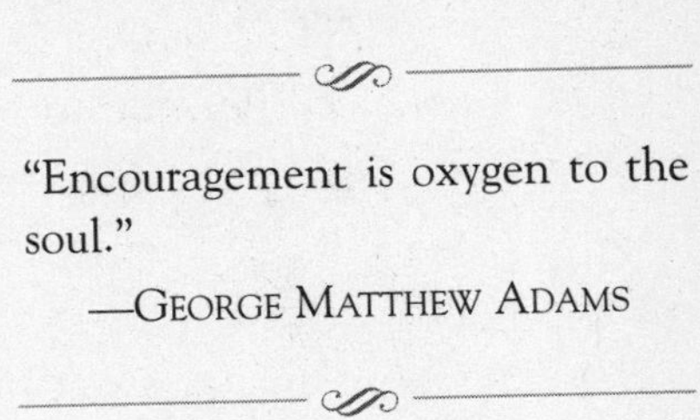
"Encouragement is oxygen to the soul."
—George Matthew Adams

Compliments in Front of Others Are the Most Effective Ones You Can Give

As commander of a $1 billion warship and a crew of 310, Mike Abrashoff used grassroots leadership to increase retention rates from 28 percent to 100 percent, reduce operating expenditures, and improve readiness. How did he do it? Among other things, he placed supreme importance on public compliments.

"The commanding officer of a ship is authorized to hand out 15 medals a year," he wrote. "I wanted to err on the side of excess, so I passed out 115." Nearly every time a sailor left his ship for another assignment, Captain Abrashoff gave him or her a medal. "Even if they hadn't been star players, they got medals in a public ceremony as long as they had done their best every day. I delivered a short speech describing how much we cherished the recipient's friendship, camaraderie, and hard work." Sometimes the departing sailor's shipmates told funny stories, recalling his or her foibles, trials, and triumphs. But the bottom line was that Abrashoff wanted to make them feel good by complimenting them in front of others.

"There is absolutely no downside to this symbolic gesture," said Abrashoff, "provided it is done sincerely without hype." He knew how to make his sailors feel like a million bucks.

You can do the same thing for the people around you. Whenever you have the opportunity to publicly praise another person, don't let it slip by. Of course, you can create these opportunities, as Captain Abrashoff did, but you can also find countless opportunities if you just look for them.

LES . . . ON BRINGING IT HOME

Think about the last time you received a compliment in the presence of people who mattered to you. How did it make you feel? Few things can lift a person up the way a sincere compliment does.

To apply John's teaching to your own life . . .

Forget about:

Giving compliments only in private. Instead, give public praise whenever you can.

Ask:

Who can I spotlight in front of others?

Do it:

Compliment someone around you in front of other people today.

Remember:

When you give someone a public compliment, you give him or her wings like an eagle.

6

Give Others a Reputation to Uphold

Treat a man as he appears to be and you make him worse. But treat a man as if he already were what he potentially could be, and you make him what he should be.

—Goethe

LES . . . ON SEEING THE PRACTICE IN ACTION

A few years ago, John and Margaret went to London with friends Dan and Patti Reiland, Tim and Pam Elmore, and Andy Stimer. While there, each person had his own must-see destination. For Tim, it was the bunker and war room that Winston Churchill and his advisors used during World War II.

John told me about his experience there. It was not an impressive place: it was basically a basement about twelve feet beneath a building containing a big map room with a large table, a communication room, and some smaller rooms where people could rest. But what had occurred there during the war was impressive. It was from there that Churchill had strategized and rallied the British people.

As we talked, I could tell that John loves history. He talked about Churchill—one of his leadership heroes—and how the prime minister helped to uplift millions of his countrymen in the wake of Britain's June 1940 defeat at the battle of Dunkirk. John quoted part of the speech Churchill used to address the House of Commons upon that occasion:

> We shall not flag or fail . . . We shall fight in France, we shall fight in the seas and oceans, we shall fight with growing confidence and growing strength in the air, we shall defend our island, whatever the cost may be, we shall fight on the beaches, we shall fight on the landing grounds, we shall fight in the fields and in the streets, we shall fight in the hills; we shall never surrender . . .[1]

John explained, "Churchill did a lot of remarkable things during the war, but one of the greatest was his continual ability to give the English people a reputation to uphold. He inspired them; he motivated them; he challenged them. And in response they rose to the occasion. They loved him for it."

John has tried to embody this quality. He says that as he interacts with others, he constantly asks himself, *What is special, unique, and wonderful about this individual?* Then he shares it with others. I've seen John do this time after time. About Linda Eggers, his assistant, he says, "She always represents me well." He calls John Hull, the president of EQUIP,

"Mr. Relationship." He tells everyone that Kirk Nowery, the president of ISS, is "the pastor's best friend."And he points out how Doug Carter, the vice president of EQUIP, "never misses an opportunity to tell the EQUIP story." John thinks the best of people and speaks about the fine qualities he sees in them.

JOHN . . . WITH A MAXWELL MENTORING MOMENT

One of the best ways to inspire others and make them feel good about themselves is to show them who they could be. Years ago, a manager for the New York Yankees wanted rookie players to know what a privilege it was to play for the team. He used to tell them, "Boys, it's an honor just to put on the New York pinstripes. So when you put them on, play like world champions. Play like Yankees. Play proud."

When you give someone a reputation to uphold, you give him something good to shoot for. It's putting something that was beyond his reach within his grasp. By speaking to their potential, you help the people around you to "play proud," as the Yankees do. Why is that important? Because people will go farther than they thought they could when someone they respect tells them they can.

If you desire to give others a reputation to uphold, here are suggestions on how to get started:

Have a High Opinion of People

The opinions you have of people in your life affect them profoundly. Dr. J. Sterling Livingston, formerly of the

Harvard Business School and founder of the Sterling Institute management consulting firm, observed, "People perform consistently as they perceive you expect them to perform."

A reputation is something that many people spend their entire lives trying to live down or live up to. So why not help others up instead of pushing them down? All people possess both value and potential. You can find those things if you try.

Back Up Your High Opinion of Others with Action

When you back up your belief in people with action, their self-doubt begins to evaporate. It's one thing to tell your teenager that you believe he's a good driver; it's another to let him have the keys to your car for the evening. Likewise, if you want a new manager to rise to the high opinion you've expressed about her, then give her significant responsibility. Nothing gives people confidence like seeing someone they respect put his money where his mouth is. Not only does it empower them emotionally, but it also resources their drive toward success.

Look Past Their Pasts and Give Them Reputations for Their Futures

Old negative names, labels, or nicknames can block a person's growth and progress. Perhaps that's why the rites of passage in many cultures include giving a new title or name to the person being honored. A new name gives someone a hope for a new future.

A fun example of this can be found in the movie and play *The Man of La Mancha*, based on Cervantes's classic work *Don Quixote*. The protagonist, Don Alonzo, pursues a life of chivalry and seeks to become a knight-errant long after that age of history has passed. He sees giants where others see windmills and quests where others see rabbit trails. Comically, he "rescues" a common prostitute named Aldonza, whom he sees as a beautiful lady. He calls her Dulcinea and makes her the object of his knightly exploits.

At first she resents him. She thinks he is mocking her, because she hates herself and her life. But with time, his vision of her replaces her own and gives her hope. And as the old man lies on his deathbed, she thanks him for seeing in her what she could not see in herself.

Of course, the most dramatic examples of someone overlooking the pasts of others and giving them reputations for the future can be found in the Bible. The book of Genesis recounts how God changed the life of Abram, an old man with no offspring. God renamed him Abraham,[2] which means "father of many," and made it possible for Abraham to become a father in his old age. And God took Jacob, a trickster who cheated his brother, lied to his father, and constantly schemed to get ahead; and renamed him Israel—his future becoming the inception of the nation of Israel.[3]

Give People a New Name or Nickname That Speaks to Their Potential

Harry Hopman, one of the finest tennis captains and coaches in Australia's history and a member of the International Tennis Hall of Fame, at one time built the Australian team to the point that it dominated the tennis world. How did he do it? By emphasizing what he called "coaching by affirmation." For example, he had a slow player whom he nicknamed "Rocket." Another player, who was not known for his strength or constitution, he called "Muscles." And it certainly gave them a boost. "Rocket" Rod Laver and Ken "Muscles" Rosewall became champions in the tennis world.

I love giving people nicknames that speak to their potential and their greatest strengths. In fact, it's something I'm known for in my family. My own children, Elizabeth and Joel Porter, I call "Apple of My Eye" and "Number One Son." I call my nieces Rachael and Jennifer "Angel" and "Sweet Pea." Grandchildren Madeline, Hannah, John Porter, and Ella are "Sunshine," "Hannah Banana," "JP," and "Peanut."

Each time a child is born in our extended family, the kids want to know what I'm going to call the newest member. It's a tradition we all love. Why? Because everyone enjoys the encouragement that comes from someone seeing—and speaking to—their potential.

LES . . . ON BRINGING IT HOME

I sometimes encounter leaders who believe you shouldn't stroke people's egos by giving them reputations they haven't quite earned. And I always point these folks to the "ten-year rule." It's derived from research showing that elite performers, those whose reputations precede them, usually needed at least ten years of dedicated and consistent practice before they obtained any *recognizable* level of excellence. The research also shows that the process can be cut dramatically when individuals see signs that they are already beginning to achieve a recognizable reputation.[4]

To apply John's teaching to your own life . . .

Forget about:

A person's failures in the past and focus on his or her potential in the future.

Ask:

What is special, unique, and wonderful about this person? How can I show it to others?

Do it:

Back up your high opinion of a person with action that reinforces that opinion.

Remember:

Many people go farther than they thought they could go because someone else believed they could and told them so.

7

SAY THE RIGHT WORDS AT THE RIGHT TIME

No man has a prosperity so high or firm, but that two or three words can dishearten it; and there is no calamity which right words will not begin to redress.

—RALPH WALDO EMERSON

LES . . . ON SEEING THE PRACTICE IN ACTION

Ask nearly anyone who knows John well, and he will tell you a story of a specific time when John said the right words to him at the right time. One of the most touching I heard while working on this book came from Dan Reiland, John's close friend and former right-hand man. "John has done this so often in my life," explained Dan. "But the time that stands out above all the others is when my mother died."

Her death was sudden and unexpected. Dan promptly got word to John, who was out of town at the time. John and

Margaret quickly changed their plans and flew back home to San Diego. Dan recalled, "John and Margaret came in the door of our house in Rancho San Diego, walked right up to me, gave me a big hug, and said, 'I love you.' That was it. There's nothing anyone could have done that would have been better." Dan told me that John also said many wise things to his brother, Lan, and greatly encouraged his sister, Jean. I could tell that Dan was still touched by it even though it had occurred nearly a decade ago.

"And John gave a beautiful memorial service," remembered Dan. "He gave me his notes afterward, which I cherish. I value everything John did during that time, but nothing quite holds the power of those three words at that very moment when he walked through that door."

People who have not been around John "up close and personal" are sometimes surprised to find out how good he is at saying the right words at the right time. They're used to his public persona as a speaker, where he also excels at communication and timing. But what they may not realize is that John is a genuine encourager who loves to help people and who really understands them, both on- and offstage.

I remember hearing John speak to an audience of managers about the value of what we say and when we say it. He said . . .

- The *wrong words* said at the *wrong time* discourage me.
- The *wrong words* said at the *right time* frustrate me.
- The *right words* said at the *wrong time* confuse me.
- The *right words* said at the *right time* encourage me.

I've certainly found that to be true in my own life. Haven't you? The right words at the right time are like a soothing breeze of encouragement.

JOHN . . . WITH A MAXWELL MENTORING MOMENT

Most people recognize that words have incredible power. Editor and theologian Tyron Edwards observed, "Words are both better and worse than thoughts; they express them, and add to them; they give them power for good or evil; they start them on an endless flight, for instruction and comfort and blessing, or for injury, sorrow and ruin." But saying the right words is not enough. Timing is crucial.

Sometimes, the best thing we can do for someone else is to hold our tongue. When tempted to give advice that's not wanted, to show off, to say "I told you so," or to point out another's error, the best policy is to say nothing. As nineteenth-century British journalist George Sala advised, we should strive "not only to say the right thing in the right place, but far more difficult, to leave unsaid the wrong thing at the tempting moment."

When it is time to speak up, how can you best encourage others using the right words at the right time? Keep these thoughts in mind:

Be Sensitive to Time and Place

It's said that during one of the last major offensives of World War II, General Dwight Eisenhower was walking near the Rhine and came upon a GI who seemed depressed.

"How are you feeling, son?" he asked.

"General," the young man replied, "I'm awful nervous."

"Well," Eisenhower said, "you and I are a good pair then, because I'm nervous too. Maybe if we just walk along together, we'll be good for each other."

The first key to saying the right thing at the right time is paying attention to the context. That is one of the secrets of successful communication to a large audience, and it is just as important when talking with someone one-on-one. King Solomon of ancient Israel was speaking to this truth when he wrote, "Like apples of gold in settings of silver is a word spoken in right circumstances."[1] If you can learn to be sensitive to your setting, you've won half the battle in saying the right words at the right time.

> "Like apples of gold in settings of silver is a word spoken in right circumstances."
>
> —KING SOLOMON OF ISRAEL

SAY IT FROM THE HEART

It's not just what you say and when you say it: it's also *how* you say it. A *Peanuts* comic strip shows Lucy saying to pianist Schroeder, "Do you think I'm the most beautiful girl in the world?" Naturally, she has to ask several times in different ways, until Schroeder, to be finally rid of her, says, "Yes."

Lucy mopes disconsolately and comments, "Even when he says it, he doesn't say it."

People can tell the difference between hollow words and something that is said from the heart. Idaho businessman Don

Bennett was the first amputee to climb to the summit of Mount Rainier. That's 14,410 feet, on one leg and two crutches! During an especially difficult portion of the climb, Bennett and his team had to cross an ice field. To get across the ice, the climbers had to put crampons on their boots, which would give them traction. Unfortunately, one boot didn't help Bennett much. The only way he could get across the ice field was to fall face forward onto the ice, pull himself as far forward as he could, stand up, and then fall forward again.

Bennett's teenage daughter, Kathy, was with him on the climb. She stayed by his side through the entire four-hour struggle. She kept cheering him on, saying, "You can do it, Dad. You're the best dad in the world. You can do it!"[2] His daughter's words, spoken from the heart, helped him to keep going.

Recognize the Power of the Right Words at the Right Time

Saying the right words at the right time can do more than just make a person feel good in the moment. It can have an impact that is positive and lasting.

Painter Benjamin West said that he loved to paint as a youngster. When his mother left the house, he would get out the oils and try to paint. One day when he pulled out paints, brushes, paper, and various other implements, he made quite a mess. When he realized his mother would be home soon, he tried desperately to get everything cleaned up, but he didn't make it. When she walked into the room, he expected the worst.

West said that what she did next completely surprised him. She picked up his painting, looked at it, and said, "My, what a beautiful painting of your sister." She gave him a kiss on the cheek and walked away. With that kiss, West said, he became a painter.

I don't know what kind of experience you had growing up. Perhaps, like me, you had parents who understood the power of encouragement. If not, what would you have given to have someone speak into your life at the right time—a parent, teacher, coach, or pastor? Whether or not you received it then, you can give it now. Look for opportunities to uplift others with your words. It just might change their lives.

LES . . . ON BRINGING IT HOME

Numerous studies back up that when you say the right words at the right time, there are a number of positive outcomes. One of the most important outcomes is trust. When you can offer something to a person at the point of his or her need—even when that person is a stranger—you are very likely to become trusted and seen as honorable. You will be seen as someone who is dependable and considerate.[3] Isn't that encouraging?

To apply John's teaching in your own life . . .

Forget about:

What you want to say and focus on what the other person needs to hear.

Ask:

What would I want to hear if I was in this person's shoes?

Do it:

Change someone's day—or maybe even his entire life—by saying the right words at the right time, from the heart.

Remember:

"Like apples of gold in settings of silver is a word spoken in the right circumstances."

8

ENCOURAGE THE DREAMS OF OTHERS

Keep away from people who try to belittle your ambitions. Small people always do that, but the really great make you feel that you, too, can become great.

—MARK TWAIN

LES . . . ON SEEING THE PRACTICE IN ACTION

When I began talking to John's office staff, one of the things I found out is that he receives dozens of letters every week thanking him for the positive changes that have come as a result of his books, seminars, and lessons on CD. I asked Sue Caldwell if I could see some of the letters, and she handed me a thick folder that contained some that she had shared with the staff. As I flipped through the pages, I noticed how many times people had written about hopes and dreams being rekindled in them.

Two letters jumped out at me because they referred to

things that occurred at a conference for young Christian leaders at which John had spoken. The first, from Kevin, said:

> Thank you! Without being overly dramatic, I cannot begin to tell you how much value you have added to my life over the past six years. I was one of the 5,500 emerging leaders who attended "Catalyst" this past week . . . I feel like God answered my prayer as you poured out your heart to us during your session . . . You said, "I wish you believed in yourself as much as I believe in you." That is the first time I have heard that from anyone in your generation. It was tremendously empowering to hear.

The second one, written by Matt, said:

> Over the past few months, I had become very discouraged and resigned myself to the fact that the dream [I had previously pursued] was dying. Then I came to Catalyst '03. Totally unexpectedly to me, God moved in my heart and reassured me His plan was still alive. When you prayed over us during the session, I could not stop weeping. Your words were directly from God's heart to mine. I will never forget that moment . . . Thanks for impacting my life.

Matt went on to say that he had rededicated himself to his dream and would persevere during this preparation period of his life.

As I talked to John's employees and associates, I discovered that he had repeatedly encouraged their dreams, even when that meant he might lose someone he valued. Often when Tim Elmore—a pastor on John's staff in San Diego for more than ten years—was recruited by another organization, he would go to John and ask him to "take off his employer hat and put on his mentor hat" so that he could ask John's advice. Tim says that John could be remarkably objective, and several times he actually encouraged Tim to pursue it, saying, "This just might be a good fit for you. I don't want you to have regrets if you don't go and see about it. I think you should go."

One of those trips eventually took Tim away when he accepted a position as a vice president of a parachurch organization in Colorado. And John was nothing but encouraging. He truly wanted Tim to realize his dreams and fulfill his potential.

JOHN . . . WITH A MAXWELL MENTORING MOMENT

I consider it a great privilege when people share their dreams with me. It shows a great deal of courage and trust. And at that moment, I'm conscious that I have great power in their lives. That's no small matter. A wrong word can crush a person's dream; the right word can inspire him or her to pursue it.

If someone thinks enough of you to tell you about his or her dreams, take care. And keep these things in mind as you work to encourage that person:

Understand That Dreams Are Fragile

Actress Candice Bergen commented, "Dreams are, by definition, cursed with short life spans." I suspect she said that because there are people who don't like to see others pursuing their dreams. It reminds them of how far they are from living their own dreams. As a result, they try to knock down anyone who is shooting for the stars. By talking others out of their dreams, critical people excuse themselves for staying in their comfort zones.

> "Dreams are, by definition, cursed with short life spans."
>
> —Candice Bergen

Never allow yourself to become a dream killer. Instead, become a dream releaser. Even if you think another person's dream is far-fetched, that's no excuse for criticizing them.

To Lose a Dream Is a Great Loss

Have you given up on one of your dreams? Have you buried a hope that once looked bright and gave you energy? If so, what did it do to you? Norman Cousins, former editor of the *Saturday Review* and adjunct professor of psychiatry at UCLA, believed, "Death is not the greatest loss in life. The greatest loss is what dies inside of us while we live."

> "Death is not the greatest loss in life. The greatest loss is what dies inside of us while we live."
>
> —Norman Cousins

Our dreams keep us alive. Benjamin Franklin observed, "Most men die from the neck up at age twenty-five because they stop dreaming." That's why it's so important that you help keep others' dreams alive. By doing so, you can literally help them live. Encouraging another person's dream can nurture her soul.

Encouraging Others in Their Pursuit of a Dream Is to Give Them a Wonderful Gift

Because dreams are at the center of our souls, we must do everything in our power to help turn dreams into reality. That is one of the greatest gifts we can ever give. How can you do it? Follow these six steps:

1. *Ask them to share their dream with you.* Everyone has a dream, but few people are asked about it.
2. *Affirm the person as well as the dream.* Let the person know that you not only value his or her dream but that you also recognize traits in that individual that can help him or her achieve it.
3. *Ask about the challenges they must overcome to reach their dream.* Few people ask others about their dreams; even fewer try to find out what kinds of hurdles the person is up against to pursue them.
4. *Offer your assistance.* No one achieves a worthwhile dream alone. You'll be amazed by how people light up when you offer to help them achieve their dream.
5. *Revisit their dream with them on a consistent basis.* If you really want to help others with their dreams, don't make it a one-time activity you mark off your list. Check in with them to see how they're doing and to lend assistance.
6. *Determine daily to be a dream booster, not a dream buster.* Everyone has a dream, and everyone needs encouragement. Set your mental radar to pick up on others' dreams and help them along.

People Will Live Up to Their Dreams When They Have a Chance to Fulfill Them

Scott Adams, creator of the popular *Dilbert* cartoon, tells this story about his beginnings as a cartoonist:

> You don't have to be a "person of influence" to be influential. In fact, the most influential people in my life probably are not even aware of the things they've taught me. When I was trying to become a syndicated cartoonist, I sent my portfolio to one cartoon editor after another—and received one rejection after another. One editor even called and suggested that I take art classes. Then Sarah Gillespie, an editor at United Media and one of the real experts in the field, called to offer me a contract. At first, I didn't believe her. I asked if I'd have to change my style, get a partner—or learn how to draw. But she believed I was already good enough to be a nationally syndicated cartoonist. Her confidence in me completely changed my frame of reference and altered how I thought about my own abilities. This may sound bizarre, but from the minute I got off the phone with her, I could draw better.

Editor Sarah Gillespie gave Adams a chance to live out his dream, but because so many people had tried to discourage him, he was almost afraid to say yes. But because of her encouragement—and the opportunity she gave him—*Dilbert* has become one of the most popular cartoons in the nation.

There is no telling what might happen if you were to begin encouraging the dreams of the people around you. When you come to the end of your life, wouldn't you love to be the person about whom others say, "I succeeded because this person believed in me when nobody else did"? Start encouraging others. The more you do, the more they will share their dreams with you. And the greater the chance you will get to watch them bloom.

LES . . . ON BRINGING IT HOME

In case you fear that encouraging people's dreams will simply cause them to keep their heads in the clouds, research reveals that this practice does more than cause individuals to seek something positive in the future. It actually causes them to be more engaged in their present activities. Technically speaking, it's called the "resonance performance model," but whatever you call it, you can't go wrong by encouraging the dreams of others.

To apply John's teaching to your own life . . .

Forget about:

Critiquing another person's dream. Instead, affirm his lofty vision and his pursuit to realize it.

Ask:

Who can I encourage today in reaching their dreams?

Do it:

Offer specific help in bringing another person closer to making his or her dream a reality.

Remember:

When a person shares his or her dream with you, it is the center of that person's soul.

9

PASS THE CREDIT ON TO OTHERS

If each of us were to confess his most secret desire,
the one that inspires all his plans, all his actions,
he would say: "I want to be praised."

—E. M. CIORAN

LES . . . ON SEEING THE PRACTICE IN ACTION

One of my favorite topics of conversation with John is publishing. We've talked about it for nearly two decades now. Whether book ideas, titles, marketing campaigns, publishers, bookstore shelf space, or agents, we have bandied about nearly every conceivable aspect of the industry. And since John has been one of the most successful authors in the area of leadership and sold more than nine million books, I'm always intrigued to learn about the ins and outs of his publishing experiences.

Some time ago John and I were both speaking at a conference in Virginia, and between sessions I asked him to pinpoint a publishing highlight in his career.

"That's a tough one, Les," he told me. "I've been blessed in ways I could have never anticipated."

"Surely something stands out," I gently pressed.

"Well, when *The 21 Laws of Leadership* sold one million copies, Thomas Nelson, the publishing house, hosted a celebration banquet for about 120 people from their company and Injoy to mark the occasion. They gave me some beautiful gifts that night, including these." John pulled up the sleeve of his jacket and pointed to the gold cuff links he was wearing, each bearing the number "21." "What an honor that evening was."

Sometime later, I spoke to a few of the people who attended that banquet, including John's wife, Margaret. She said that when John got up to address everyone, he expressed his gratitude and quickly started crediting the people who had helped make it happen. He told how Victor Oliver had come up with the original concept for the book and had provided the title. He credited a group of key leaders at Injoy who had helped him hone the laws. He thanked Charlie Wetzel, his writer, for being the book's wordsmith. He thanked Ron Land of Thomas Nelson and Kevin Small and the Injoy team for putting together the book tour that helped put *The 21 Laws* on the *New York Times*'s best-seller list. He thanked publisher Mike Hyatt, the Nelson sales and marketing staff, the booksellers, and many other individuals, including his parents. Margaret said that by the time John finished, there wasn't a dry eye in the room.

Making a book successful and getting it into the hands of

people it can help is always a team effort, though not all authors see it that way. Everybody involved in the process has a part to play, and John did his best to pass along the credit by recognizing each person's contribution.

JOHN . . . WITH A MAXWELL MENTORING MOMENT

I'll never forget that night in Orlando. When I wrote my first book in 1979, I never dreamed that anything I wrote would sell a million copies. As Margaret and I went back to our hotel room, she asked me what I considered to be the highlight of the banquet. Without hesitation I replied that it was passing on the credit to the people who helped me so much. Rarely do we get an opportunity to say thank you enough to the people who help us, especially in such a public setting. I really wanted to make the most of it. Not only does it make me feel good to share any success I might have, but it uplifts others—and it makes them feel like a million bucks.

Passing the credit on to others is one of the easiest ways to win with people. If you'd like to practice it, here are a few suggestions to get you started:

Check Your Ego at the Door

The number one reason people don't pass along credit to others is that they think it will somehow hurt them or lessen their value. Many people are so insecure that they constantly feed their egos to compensate for it. But you simply cannot practice this method of winning with people if you can't set your ego aside.

Have you ever heard the saying "An egotist is not a person who thinks too much of himself; it's someone who thinks too little of other people"? If you want to give others credit, put your focus on others. What do they need? How will giving them credit make them feel? How will it enhance their performance? How will it motivate them to reach their potential? If you highlight their contributions, it makes them *and* you look good.

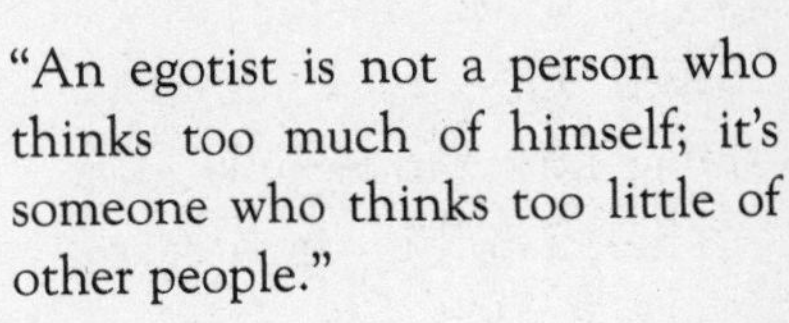
"An egotist is not a person who thinks too much of himself; it's someone who thinks too little of other people."

DON'T WAIT—PASS THE CREDIT ASAP

I love what H. Ross Perot once said about passing on credit: "Reward employees while the sweat's still on their brow." Isn't it true that one of the very best times to give credit to others is when the amount of work and sacrifice something took is still fresh in their minds? Why wait? You may have heard management expert Ken Blanchard's teaching that you should catch people while they're doing something good. What a great idea! The sooner you give credit to someone else, the bigger the payoff.

In 2003, when I interviewed UCLA basketball coach John Wooden, he told me how he would often teach his players who scored to give a smile, wink, or nod to the player who gave them a good pass. "What if he's not looking?" asked a team member. Wooden replied, "I guarantee he'll look." Everyone enjoys having his contribution acknowledged.

Say It in Front of Others

You've already read the chapter that encourages you to compliment people in front of other people, but it bears saying again. When you give credit to others in front of their peers and loved ones, the value of your compliment multiplies. Former New York Yankees player and manager Billy Martin observed, "There's nothing greater in the world than when somebody on the team does something good and everybody gathers around to pat him on the back." By giving credit in a crowd, you can help to create the kind of environment Martin described.

Put It in Print

When you give people credit verbally, you uplift them for a moment. When you take the time to put it in writing, you have the potential to uplift them for a lifetime. People put plaques on their walls as reminders of their achievements. They save and cherish letters containing recognition and praise for things they've done. Deep down, everyone wants to make a difference, and some days, everyone is in need of some encouragement.

I have a file in my office with letters and notes that have special significance for me. Every now and then, I'll pull out the file and read some of the things people I respect have told me. It allows me to relive that moment of encouragement. It's said that even President Abraham Lincoln used to carry in his pocket a newspaper clipping extolling his accomplishments as president. He was one of the finest leaders in our nation's history, yet he desired something to keep his spirits up.

Please don't underestimate the impact that an article, a public notice, or a personal note can make. What takes you only a few minutes to write may be something that inspires another person for decades.

Only Say It If You Mean It

I love this old joke: As an old man lay dying, his wife of many years sat close by his bed. He opened his eyes and saw her. "There you are, Agnes," he said, "at my side again."

"Yes, dear," she replied.

"Looking back," the old man said, "I remember all the times you were by my side. You were there when I got my draft notice and had to go off to fight in the war. You were with me when our first house burned to the ground. When I had the accident that destroyed our car, you were there. And you were at my side when my business went bankrupt and we lost every cent we had."

"Yes, dear," his wife said.

The old man sighed.

"I tell you, Agnes," he said, "you've been a real jinx."

It may seem obvious, but I want to go ahead and say it anyway so that I'm not misunderstood. You should never say something you don't believe just to uplift someone. If you're not sincere, you don't make people feel good; you make them feel they're being schmoozed. When you pass credit on to others, you need to do it from the heart.

LES . . . ON BRINGING IT HOME

Passing credit along to coworkers or colleagues is more than mere niceness. According to research, when you pass credit along to others, you actually change their biochemistry and create an "emotional stamp" that forever associates you in their minds with their success.

To apply John's teaching to your own life . . .

Forget about:

Your ego. Focus on the people around you and the credit they deserve.

Ask:

Who has made me more successful than I would have been on my own?

Do it:

Publicly pass along credit for a successful endeavor to as many people as you can.

Remember:

If each of us were to confess our most secret desire, we would say: "I want to be praised."

10

OFFER YOUR VERY BEST

I do the very best I know how—the very best I can; and I mean to keep on doing so until the end.

—ABRAHAM LINCOLN

LES . . . ON SEEING THE PRACTICE IN ACTION

For many years now I've received the leadership lessons on tape and CD that John does every month. After listening to one titled "Preparation: The Separation Between Winning and Losing," I had to ask John a question.

"I loved the teaching, and I pulled some nuggets from it that have really helped me," I said, "but I need to ask you a question. Do you really believe preparation is that important in a person's life?"

"Absolutely," John answered. "It really does make the difference between winners and losers. Preparation is more than just a discipline. It's an attitude, a way of life. My father used to quote the Bible verse that says, 'Whatever your hands find to do, do it with all your might.' In other words, in what you do, in what you have, offer your very best. I try to embrace that in everything I do."

I've watched John for years, and I believe that's true. Everything he does, he does with excellence. But it's also more than that. While we were working on this book, we had a meeting in San Diego where John was spending some time while awaiting the birth of his fourth grandchild. When we were done, John took us to dinner at his favorite restaurant in San Diego—Peohe's, which has excellent food and an even better view. It's on Coronado island and is situated on the bay across the water from San Diego's beautiful skyline.

The hostess seated us outside right by the water, and John and Margaret immediately took the two seats facing the restaurant so that everyone else in the party could enjoy the view of the bay. During our meeting earlier in the day in an ocean-view room, John had also sat with his back to the window, allowing others who were visiting from other parts of the country to enjoy the view. And neither time had it been by accident. I know John: he always thinks through what's going to be happening at a meeting and picks his seat carefully. He had taken the worst seat because he wanted to offer all of us the very best.

JOHN . . . WITH A MAXWELL MENTORING MOMENT

For years I've been invited to be the keynote speaker for organizations at their special events. It's something I really enjoy. Communicating to an audience energizes me. It would be easy for me to "wing it" or do a canned speech that I have done elsewhere before. But I never do that because I don't believe it would serve them well. Instead, I spend time researching the company. I find out as much as I can about the particular event they've planned and what they desire to accomplish. You may wonder why I would go to such trouble when I don't necessarily need to. I do it because I have a goal every time I speak. After I'm done communicating with the audience, I want the person who invited me to speak at the event to say, "You exceeded our expectations." I want to deliver for them . . . and then some.

Perhaps you are someone who already possesses an offer-your-best mind-set. If so, I commend you, and I want to encourage you to maintain that attitude. If not, I hope the following thoughts will help you develop that mind-set:

Anyone Can Be an Important Person to Me

We are most likely to give our best to those we love and respect. I think back to my days in school, and I remember loving some teachers and having others who left me cold. I know that I always did my best for the teachers I liked, and for the others I did only what was needed to get a grade. Later, I realized that my off-and-on efforts frequently hurt my relationships with others as well as my potential for success. But then I discovered the antidote: if I saw *everyone* as important—not just the people I liked the most—I would always offer my very best. That change in attitude prompted a change in my actions.

Anything We Do Can Be Made Important

Most moments in life become special only if we treat them that way. The average day is average only because we don't make it something more. The most excellent way to elevate an experience is to give it our best. That makes it special. An average conversation becomes something better when you listen with great interest. A common relationship transforms when you give it uncommon effort. An unremarkable event becomes something special when you spice it up with creativity. You can make anything more important by giving your best to it.

You Can Become Important to Anyone

Who are the most important people in your life? Are they the ones who never give you the time of day, who never seem to be there when you need them? Of course not. Usually the people who are important to you are the ones who treat *you* as important. We naturally value the people who value us. So if you want to be important to others, treat *them* as important. The most effective way to do that is to give them your very best.

Make the Most of Your Gifts and Opportunities

More than thirty years ago I memorized a quote that has shaped the way I live: "My potential is God's gift to me. What I do with my potential is my gift to Him." I believe I am accountable to God, others, and myself for every gift, talent, resource, and opportunity I have in life. If I give less than my best, then I am shirking my responsibility. I believe UCLA coach John Wooden was speaking to this idea when he said,

"Make every day your masterpiece." If we give our very best all the time, we can make our lives into something special. And that will overflow into the lives of others.

> "My potential is God's gift to me. What I do with my potential is my gift to Him."

There's a story I love about President Dwight Eisenhower. He once told the National Press Club that he regretted not having a better political background so that he would be a better orator. He said his lack of skill in that area reminded him of his boyhood days in Kansas when an old farmer had a cow for sale. The buyer asked the farmer about the cow's pedigree, butterfat production, and monthly production of milk. The farmer said, "I don't know what a pedigree is, and I don't have an idea about butterfat production, but she's a good cow, and she'll give you all the milk she has." That's all any of us can do—give all that we have. That's always enough.

LES . . . ON BRINGING IT HOME

A tremendous amount of recent psychological research has focused on the value of virtues. And experts are finding that when people strive toward excellence in character traits—for example, when they work to possess a giving spirit—they routinely benefit themselves while in the process of benefiting others. This is known in the field as cultivating "fulfillments."[1] One hardly needs a research study, however, to know that when you give your very best, you are bound to feel fulfilled.

To apply John's teaching to your own life . . .

Forget about:

Doing the minimum required to get by, and focus instead on your maximum effort.

Ask:

What can I do for someone who could never repay me?

Do it:

Voluntarily give beyond what is required.

Remember:

Everybody appreciates a person who gives his very best.

11

Share a Secret with Someone

Conceal not your secret from your friend,
or you deserve to lose him.
—Portuguese Proverb

LES . . . ON SEEING THE PRACTICE IN ACTION

In 1996 John made a major decision concerning his company, and for a time let only a few people in on it. Charlie Wetzel was one of them. Here's what Charlie has to say about what that did for him and his relationship with John:

> One day John asked me to come up to his home office so that we could work on our current book project. We had a very productive work session, and after we were done, John said, "Charlie, before you go, I want to talk to you about something."

When an employee hears those words from his boss, he takes notice. Sometimes the words that follow include the phrases "tough economy," "poor performance," or "you're fired!"

John continued, "In about twelve months, we're going to move the company out of San Diego. We're not going to announce it to all the staff yet, but I'm telling the people on the executive team—my inner circle—about the move so that they can begin processing the information. We're going to be moving to Atlanta."

John went on to explain that flying out of San Diego was taking its toll, not only on him, but also on the consultants who worked for the company. When John had asked his assistant, Linda Eggers, to calculate how many days he spent the previous year just making flight connections from San Diego to Dallas, Chicago, or Atlanta, Linda came back with a mind-boggling figure: thirty days! That's when John knew he had to make a move.

That was a lot of information, so I started processing it. Then John said, "Charlie, I sure hope you'll come with us."

John spoke to me for probably only two minutes, but what he communicated changed my life. At that time I had been working with John for about two years, and we had already written five or six books together. I had worked hard for him, and John had always been lavish with his praise. But I had no idea he valued me as much as he did. Once he shared this secret, my place in his estimation, in my career, and even in my own eyes changed.

John has done a lot of wonderful things for my family and me through the years. He is very generous, and many of those things have cost him a lot of time and money. Sharing the secret of our move cost him nothing, yet it made a huge impact on me. It made me feel like a million bucks.

It's not a secret how powerful sharing with another person can be. It's a surefire way to win with people.

JOHN . . . WITH A MAXWELL MENTORING MOMENT

A Sicilian proverb says, "Only the spoon knows what is stirring in the pot." When you allow another person to know what is stirring within you, giving him a "taste" of a plan or idea, you instantly make a meaningful connection with him. Who doesn't want to know what's going on in the mind of someone they care about?

Reading Charlie Wetzel's story might make you think that sharing a secret with someone always has to be a big deal with life-changing ramifications. It doesn't. Of course, when you let people in on something impacting, it makes quite an impression. But you can make sharing a secret part of your everyday life using everyday things. The first time you share something with others, aren't you sharing something that has been secret up to that moment? Why not let the person to whom you're talking know that you're revealing it for the first time? That makes him feel special.

Sharing a secret with someone is really a matter of two things: reading the context of a situation and desiring to build up the other person. If you do those two things, you can learn this skill. As you try it out, keep these three things in mind:

1. Sharing a Secret Means Giving Valuable Information.

When you share a secret, the information needs to be something that the people you're talking to care about. It plays to their interests or meets a felt need they possess. For example, two experienced deep-sea fishermen decided to go ice fishing. They each chopped holes in the ice, put worms on their hooks, dropped their lines into the water, and waited. After three hours, they had caught nothing.

As they sat, they watched a boy come along and cut a hole in the ice midway between them. He put a worm on his hook, dropped his line into the water, and almost instantly he caught a fish. The boy repeated the process and quickly had a catch of more than a dozen fish. The two other fishermen watched and were flabbergasted.

Finally, one of the men approached the boy and said, "Young man, we've been here for more than three hours and haven't caught a single fish. You've caught at least a dozen in just a few minutes. What's your secret?"

The boy mumbled an answer, but the man didn't catch a word of it. Then he noticed a large bulge in the boy's left cheek. "Please, could you take the bubble gum out of your mouth so I can understand what you're saying?" the man said.

The boy cupped his hands, spat it out, and said, "It's not bubble gum; it's my secret. You've got to keep the worms warm."

2. Sharing a Secret Makes People Feel Special.

Letting people in on something always boosts their egos. Charlie's comment says it all: "I had no idea he valued me as much as he did. My place in his estimation, in my career, and even in my own eyes changed." But as I said, the secret doesn't always have to be dramatic to have a positive effect. For example, when I play golf, I usually carry a laminated card with me that contains tips given to me by golf pro Scott Szymoniak. Occasionally if a friend in the group is not playing well, I'll pull him aside and say, "I want to share a secret with you that has really helped my golf game." Then I'll pull out the card and show him the six basic things a golfer must know and do. And I'll let him know that it's my personal golf plan and that I don't share it with everybody.

How does it make you feel when you know that you're the first person being told something? I know it makes me feel special. That's one of the reasons my wife, Margaret, and I have practiced telling each other first about many of the things that happen to us during the day. To help me do that, I carry a note card or small pad and jot down things I want to tell her. Anything I write down I "save" to tell her first. It leads to special times together every day.

3. Sharing a Secret Includes Others in Your Journey.

The bottom line on sharing a secret with others is that it is an act of inclusion. It invites others into your life, into your experience. It includes them in your success. When I speak to an audience—whether it's a roundtable of executives or an arena full of people—I intentionally use inclusive language. I let people in on my personal journey. And when I'm revealing something I've not previously

The bottom line on sharing a secret with others is that it is an act of inclusion.

said publicly, I let them know that I'm doing so. It communicates to people that I care about them and want to help them.

LES . . . ON BRINGING IT HOME

When people are "in the know," according to research, a slew of positive attributes are correlated with their lives. For example, they are far more likely to feel that their jobs fit their ambitions. They are more likely to be active in public service. They have patterns of rich friendships and happier marriages. Researchers call this an "adaptive mental mechanism."[1]

Whatever terminology you use, it turns out that when you share a secret with others, you are doing far more than imparting mere information. You are increasing the odds of a closer relationship.

To apply John's teaching to your own life . . .

Forget about:

Hoarding information for yourself.

Ask:

Whom can I benefit most by letting them in on some otherwise private information?

Do it:

Find someone to let in on a secret today.

Remember:

Sharing a secret with someone is bound to boost their self-esteem.

12

Mine the Gold of Good Intentions

To err is human; to forgive is not company policy.

—Unknown

LES . . . ON SEEING THE PRACTICE IN ACTION

Do you ever struggle to give people the benefit of the doubt—to mine the "gold" of their good intentions? I know I do. Especially when I think they've dropped the ball or tried to hurt me. But if you're like me, you also know that this tendency can be a costly interpersonal mistake if you want to win with people. So when I confessed this faux pas to John one day, he immediately identified with what I said. But he also told me how he had learned to give people the benefit of the doubt: he watched his mother.

"Mom knew my heart and she always evaluated my behavior in light of it," John explained. "Today when I say to someone, 'I didn't mean to do that,' I often wish that they would 'mine the gold of my good intentions' like my mom did. Her ability and willingness to do this in my life was a tremendous gift—and it's helped me to give the benefit of the doubt to others."

"Are you saying your mom looked past all your mistakes?" I asked.

John laughed. "Definitely not. Like every other kid, I got my fair share of reprimands. And trust me, I deserved them! But Mom never seemed to jump to conclusions with me. She never assumed the worst. Instead, she always assumed the best. And that's key to cultivating this quality.

"You see," John continued, "it did so many things for me." He counted them off: "It allowed me to draw close to her. It made her approachable. It brought out the best in me. And it taught me how to do this for others."

"Okay, John," I asked as I considered his words, "do you think that a person who wasn't raised in a home where this kind of quality was modeled is going to have a tougher time doing this for others?"

"Les, I don't really think so," he said. "Sure, a person whose home life wasn't positive won't have seen it modeled, so that person may not do it *naturally*. But when it comes right down to it, giving others the benefit of the doubt is a choice. And I've seen a lot of people who grew up with few advantages rise above that and become winners in every sense of the word."

That gives everyone hope.

JOHN . . . WITH A MAXWELL MENTORING MOMENT

Let's start by being honest. Not everyone has pure intentions. If you mine the gold of good intentions, occasionally people will take advantage of you. They have in my life. And they will in the future. But because I assume the best in others, so many people have done so many wonderful things for me I literally cannot count them all.

I've found that when I am suspicious of others, it causes me to display wrong behavior toward them. And it actually makes any interaction with them worse. In general, you get what you expect from others. So I have chosen to take the high road, expect the best, and be blessed most of the time. If you desire to do the same, do the following:

Believe the Best About People

The first thing you need to do is check your attitude. How do you see others? Do you believe that, deep down, every person desires to be good, to do his best? That matters, because if you don't believe the best in others, you will never believe that their intentions are good. And if you don't believe in their intentions, I imagine you will not exert the effort to "mine" the gold that is in them.

See Things from Their Perspective

The issue of perspective really has to do with maturity. Consider the story of two Cub Scouts whose younger brother had fallen into a lake. They rushed home to Mother with tears in their eyes. One of them sobbed, "We tried to give him CPR, but he kept getting up and walking away."

Without maturity, we lack perspective. The less mature one is, the more difficult it is to see things from another's point of view. Think about the biblical story of the woman caught in adultery where Jesus challenged the people without sin to cast the first stone. The *oldest* people in the crowd were the first to drop their stones and walk away. Why? Their maturity gave them better perspective.[1]

"Since we tend to see ourselves primarily in light of our *intentions*, which are invisible to others," said philosopher J. G. Bennett, "while we see others mainly in the light of their *actions*, which are all that's visible to us, we have a situation in which misunderstanding and injustice are the order of the day." And that's precisely why the ability to see things from another's perspective is essential to finding the gold of their good intentions.

Give People the Benefit of the Doubt

When you were a child, perhaps you were taught the Golden Rule: "Do unto others as you would have them do unto you." I've often found that when my intentions were right but my action turned out wrong, I wanted others to see me in light of the Golden Rule. In other words, I wanted others to give me the benefit of the doubt. Why shouldn't I try to extend the same courtesy to others?

Frank Clark commented, "What great accomplishments we would have in the world if everybody had done what they intended to do." While I'd agree that's true, I'd also add, "What great relationships we would have if everybody was appreciated for what they intended to do—in spite of what they may have done." When you give someone the benefit of the doubt, you are following the most effective interpersonal rule that has ever been written.

"Since nothing we intend is ever faultless, and nothing we achieve without some measure of finitude and fallibility we call humanness, we are saved by forgiveness."

—DAVID AUGSBURGER

REMEMBER THEIR GOOD DAYS, NOT THEIR BAD ONES

We all have good days and bad days. I don't know about you, but I'd like to be remembered for my good ones. And I can only ask to be forgiven for my bad ones. Fuller Theological Seminary Professor David Augsburger observes, "Since nothing we intend is ever faultless, and nothing we achieve without some measure of finitude and fallibility we call humanness, we are saved by forgiveness." If you desire to mine the gold of good intentions in others, then forgiveness is essential. And it's rarely a one-time thing. Civil rights leader Martin Luther King Jr. was right when he said, "Forgiveness is not an occasional act; it is a permanent attitude."

"Forgiveness is not an occasional act, it is a permanent attitude."

—MARTIN LUTHER KING JR.

And remember, it is with the attitude with which you judge others that you will also be judged. If you mine the gold of good intentions in your relationship with others, then people will more likely do the same for you.

LES . . . ON BRINGING IT HOME

If you grew up in an environment where the worst was assumed about you instead of the best, take heart. A research study that followed children for thirty years found that exceptional and caring adults often emerged from difficult childhoods. What made the difference? Two qualities stood out: (1) they found a nurturing relationship somewhere along the line—whether it was a mentor or other kind of role model, and (2) they had a desire to help other people.[2]

To apply John's teaching to your own life . . .

Forget about:
Justice; instead, focus on grace and forgiveness.

Ask:
How would I feel and what would I do if I were in this person's shoes?

Do it:
Practice the Golden Rule by appreciating what others intend, not only what they do—just as you would like for them to do with you.

Remember:
If I fail to believe the best in others, I will not give the effort to "mine" the gold contained in them.

13

KEEP YOUR EYES OFF THE MIRROR

I don't know what your destiny will be,
but one thing I know: the only ones among you who will be really happy are those who have sought and found how to serve.

—ALBERT SCHWEITZER

LES . . . ON SEEING THE PRACTICE IN ACTION

Soon after John relocated his companies from San Diego, California, to Atlanta, Georgia, in 1997, he hired researcher George Barna to fly to Atlanta and do some strategic planning with the executive team. Barna is the leading director of the Barna Group, a full-service marketing research company located in Ventura, California. Their expertise is in tracking cultural trends and collecting information on the Christian church.

The leaders and top thinkers from John's companies gathered together in the conference room for an all-day session where they could ask Barna anything they wanted to help them plan business and marketing strategies for the next several years. It took everyone no time at all to dive in and begin picking Barna's brain. He answered question after question. They brainstormed concepts and strategies. And they bounced ideas off of Barna to see if he thought they would fly.

Linda Eggers, John's longtime assistant, noticed that during the long sessions, John listened attentively but rarely chimed in. He seemed content to just listen. At the end of the day, when she and John sat down to attend to calendar items, correspondence, travel arrangements, and the like, Linda noticed that John had an entire legal pad of questions for George Barna that he had never asked.

Linda was surprised—especially since she had booked Barna and she knew exactly how much John had paid for the consultation.

"John, you just let everyone else talk today," she remarked. "Why didn't you ask him any of *your* questions?"

"You know what, Linda?" John said. "Everybody was obviously very excited about meeting with George, and it was so energizing to them, I didn't want to do anything to ruin the momentum. It doesn't matter that I didn't get my questions answered. Some other time."

Linda says that is one of the reasons she loves working for John. "I know that because he seems larger than life and has such charisma in front of an audience," Linda said, "there are people out there who think he has a big ego. They have no idea how much he thinks about others and puts them first."

If you focus on others, continually working to give them what they need, then you are able to keep your eyes off the mirror. And that's a wonderful way to win with people.

JOHN . . . WITH A MAXWELL MENTORING MOMENT

One of the key questions I ask in my book *Winning with People* is the Connection Question: Are we willing to focus on others? The foundational concept for that question is the Big Picture Principle, which states: "The entire population of the world—with one minor exception—is composed of other people." If you've never thought of life in those terms, then it's time to give it a try. If individuals think they are the center of the universe, not only are they in for a big disappointment when they discover it's not true, but they'll also alienate themselves from everyone around them. I've never met a person that truly wins with other people who has not mastered the ability to keep his eyes off the mirror and serve others with dignity.

Most people would readily admit that unselfishness is a positive quality, and even the most egocentric individual possesses the desire, deep down, to help others. The problem, sometimes, is changing our behavior so that we get in the habit of focusing on others instead of on ourselves. Here are a few thoughts to help you remember to keep your eyes off the mirror:

Focusing on Others Can Give You a Sense of Purpose

If you grew up in the 1950s and '60s, you may remember Danny Thomas, the entertainer who starred in the TV show *Make Room for Daddy*. Thomas observed, "All of us are born for a reason, but all of us don't discover why. Success in life has nothing to do with what you gain in life or accomplish for yourself. It's what you do for others."

Not only did Thomas believe that, but he also lived it. As a successful entertainer and television star, he could have done nothing but enjoy the benefits of his achievement. But he desired something more. He founded St. Jude's Hospital, a research facility that focuses on treating children who suffer from catastrophic diseases. And Thomas dedicated much of his life to supporting it. It helped him enjoy a greater purpose.

Focusing on Others Can Give You Energy

Continual focus on yourself can actually drain you of energy, while focusing on others can have the opposite effect. My friend Bill McCartney knew this back when he was head football coach for the University of Colorado Buffaloes. Coach Mac had heard that most people spend 86 percent of their time thinking about themselves, but only 14 percent of their time thinking about others. Yet he knew instinctively that if his players focused their attention on someone they cared about instead of just on themselves, a whole new source of energy would be available to them.

In 1991 Coach Mac decided to use this information when he was facing a great challenge. Colorado was scheduled to play its archrival, the Nebraska Cornhuskers, on Nebraska's home turf. The problem was that Colorado had not won a game there in twenty-three years. But Coach McCartney believed in his team and looked for a way to inspire them to achieve. In the end, he decided to appeal to their love of others.

He did it by challenging each player to call an individual he loved and tell that person he was dedicating the game to him or her. Coach Mac also encouraged the players to ask that person to watch every play, knowing that every hit, every tackle, every block, and every score was being dedicated to him or her.

Coach Mac also took one more step. He arranged to distribute sixty footballs with the game's final score written on them, so that each player could send a ball to the individual he had chosen.

The Colorado Buffaloes won the game. The final score written on the footballs was "27 to 12."

Focusing on Others Can Give You a Sense of Contentment

I'm told that psychological research shows that people are better adjusted and more likely to feel content if they serve others. Serving others actually cultivates health and brings about happiness. People have instinctively known that for centuries—even before the science of psychology was formally developed. For example, look at the wisdom (and humor) found in this Chinese proverb:

> If you want happiness for an hour—take a nap.
> If you want happiness for a day—go fishing.
> If you want happiness for a month—get married.
> If you want happiness for a year—inherit a fortune.
> If you want happiness for a lifetime—help others.

You can actually *help yourself* by helping others.

Remember that, and it will help you to take—and keep—your eyes off the mirror.

LES . . . ON BRINGING IT HOME

Some researchers call it the "ultraself" and consider it the hallmark of wisdom. It refers to a sense of serenity that allows one to focus on others from an emotionally secure place. It is free from petty jealousy and competitiveness. It takes genuine joy in another's success. And study after study shows it to be one of the most important ways to make meaningful connections with others.[1]

To apply John's teaching to your own life . . .

Forget about:

Trying to find happiness by tending to your own needs first.

Ask:

What can I do to forget myself and focus on others?

Do it:

Set your needs aside and do something specific, today, that will help you keep your eyes off the mirror.

Remember:

Success in life has everything to do with what you do for others.

14

Do for Others What They Can't Do for Themselves

You have not lived today until you have done something for someone who can never repay you.

—John Bunyan

LES . . . ON SEEING THE PRACTICE IN ACTION

Early on, John gave a boost to my speaking career when he opened doors I could have never opened myself. On his recommendation, I was standing on speaking platforms around the country, addressing audiences of several thousand at a time. The people who booked the events didn't know me; they knew John and trusted his endorsement of a young speaker who was just getting started.

That was fifteen years ago, and I'm just as grateful now for what John did for me in those early days as I was when it first happened. John gave me something that I could have never gotten without him—a launch to my professional speaking career.

Countless people could tell stories of how John extended himself in some way to help them along personally or professionally. When I talked to Tim Elmore, a longtime friend and employee who is now a vice president of EQUIP, he said, "It's hard for me to narrow it down. John has done so many things for me, and I owe him so much."

He thought for a moment and then told me this:

> Maybe something more personal will really show you John's heart. John and I were in Bangalore, India, to teach leadership—a trip, I might add, that I would not have gotten to take if John hadn't hired me at EQUIP. Before we left the country, my wife, Pam, asked John to keep an eye on me because I'm diabetic. If my blood sugar level drops suddenly, I get disoriented, I have no clue that I'm getting into trouble physically, and I usually need to go to a hospital for help. It can be scary—especially when you're overseas.
>
> When we got to India, John was received like a rock star! You wouldn't believe the way people treated him. Overseas, people wait in lines literally for hours to meet him and have him sign his books. Anyway, John taught a session in Bangalore, and the crowd was going nuts, and the people were all crowding around him, and what does he do? He pushes his way through the crowd, grabs the kit with my diabetic supplies, and checks up on me to make sure I'm not in trouble.
>
> That probably sounds like a small thing but it's hard to

> believe that anybody would not get caught up in that kind of moment and would instead focus on somebody else's needs. It really reveals John's heart and desire to do for others.

Tim got choked up as he told me the last part. I was touched by his story. But there's something that made an even greater impression on me. All the people I talked to about this quality in John said that they desired to do for others what John did for them. Because they have been helped to do things they otherwise couldn't do on their own, they're inspired to give others a boost.

JOHN . . . WITH A MAXWELL MENTORING MOMENT

Ambassador and poet Henry Van Dyke observed, "There is a loftier ambition than merely to stand high in the world. It is to stoop down and lift mankind a little higher." What a great perspective! Doing for others what they can't do for themselves is really a matter of attitude. I believe that whatever I've been given is to be shared with others. And because I have an abundance mind-set, I never worry about running out myself. The more I give away, the more I seem to get to give away.

> "There is a loftier ambition than merely to stand high in the world. It is to stoop down and lift mankind a little higher."
>
> —Henry Van Dyke

No matter how much or how little you think you have, you have the ability to do for others what they cannot do for themselves. Exactly how you do that will depend on your unique gifts, resources, and history. However, you can approach the task by thinking in terms of four areas:

1. Introduce Others to People They Can't Know on Their Own.

My dad, Melvin Maxwell, has done many incredible things for me during the course of my life. One of the things that impacted me most was his introducing me to great men. As a teenager, I met Norman Vincent Peale, E. Stanley Jones, and other exceptional men of the faith. And because I had declared my intention to go into the ministry, my father asked these preachers to pray for me. I can't express in words what that did for me.

Today, I am often in a position to do for others what my father did for me. I love introducing young people to my heroes. I love helping people make business contacts. There are often times when I meet someone, and as we talk, it just hits me: I need to introduce this person to so-and-so. That can mean walking somebody across the room, making a phone call on his or her behalf, or arranging a meeting. Several years ago, I was talking to Anne Beiler, the founder of Auntie Anne's, the pretzel company, and she mentioned in passing that Chick-fil-A's founder, Truett Cathy, was one of her heroes. Since I knew Truett, I offered to introduce them to each other. I hosted a dinner party for them at my house, and it was a great night.

Please don't get the impression that you have to know someone famous to help others in this area. Sometimes it's as simple as introducing one friend to another or one business associate to another. Just make connections. Be the bridge in people's relationships with others.

2. Take Others to Places Where They Can't Go on Their Own.

Early in our marriage, Margaret and I were dirt poor. Right out of college, I put in long hours for my career, and Margaret worked three jobs for us to make ends meet. And we did manage to get by, but there was no money left over for luxuries, such as vacations. Fortunately, I had an older brother who loved us and took care of us. The first five or six years of my professional life, any vacation we took was at the invitation of Larry and his wife, Anita. A wonderful trip to Acapulco, Mexico, especially stands out in my mind.

It seems that during the first half of my career, if I got to go anywhere of value to me, it was because someone invited me. Dozens of times I've had experiences that I could not have gained access to on my own: I've gone to ball games, played golf courses, seen churches, attended conferences, and visited countries that appeared to be beyond my reach.

You may have the power to give someone an experience that seems inaccessible to them. If you can't help a friend or colleague, then start with your family. Take your children places they could not go on their own. There's no telling what kind of positive impact it will make.

3. Offer Others Opportunities They Can't Reach on Their Own.

Les mentioned that I helped him to reach larger audiences early in his speaking career. The same thing was done for me. Nearly twenty-five years ago, Professor C. Peter Wagner of Fuller Seminary invited me to speak to audiences of pastors around the country about leadership. He put me on a national stage for the first time and gave me credibility that I didn't possess on my own.

Few things are of greater value to a prepared person than an opportunity. Why? Because opportunities increase our potential. Demosthenes, the great orator of ancient Greece, said, "Small opportunities are often the beginning of great enterprises." An opportunity seized is often a source of success. Help people win by giving them opportunities, and you will win with them.

"Small opportunities are often the beginning of great enterprises."
—DEMOSTHENES

4. SHARE IDEAS WITH OTHERS THAT THEY DON'T POSSESS ON THEIR OWN.

What is an idea worth? Every product begins with an idea. Every service begins with an idea. Every business, every book, every new invention begins with an idea. Ideas are what make the world move forward. So when you give people an idea, you give them a great gift.

One of the things I love about writing books is the process that it takes me through. It usually starts with a concept that I'm anxious to teach. I get a few ideas down on paper, and then I call together a group of good creative thinkers to help me test the concept, brainstorm ideas, and flesh out the outline. Every time we've done this, people have given me great ideas that I never would have come up with on my own. I have to say I'm very grateful.

One of the things I enjoy most about creative people is that they love ideas, and they always seem to have more coming.

The more they give away, the more new ideas they seem to have. Creativity and generosity feed each other. That's one of the reasons I'm never reluctant to share ideas with others. I'm convinced that I will run out of time long before I run out of ideas. It's better to give some away and contribute to another person's success than to have them lying dormant in me.

LES . . . ON BRINGING IT HOME

When you do something for others that they can't do for themselves, you are fostering relationships with those individuals that are sure to be meaningful. Studies on what researchers call the "self-determination theory" have shown that supporting other people's goals cements the relationship, since you are ultimately helping them to align their goals with themselves.[1]

To apply John's teaching to your own life . . .

Forget about:

Focusing on what you can get from others and focus instead on what you can do for others.

Ask:

What opportunity, idea, or experience could I provide that someone might never be able to have without my help?

Do it:

Consider specific things you might be able to do for others by making a list of your unique skills, resources, and connections.

Remember:

We all need others to do for us what we cannot do for ourselves.

15

Listen with Your Heart

The most important thing in communication is
to hear what isn't being said.
—Peter Drucker

LES . . . ON SEEING THE PRACTICE IN ACTION

As a psychologist, I've been trained to listen for people's feelings, not just their ideas. And I've observed that many leaders—especially strong ones with type-A personalities—are not particularly good at listening. When they do listen, their attitude is usually, *Never mind the delivery story, just show me the baby*.

I would consider John to be a pretty strong person. He can be a take-charge, take-no-prisoners kind of leader. But he is also an effective listener. And he's particularly adept at sensing how people feel. Since that characteristic is unusual for most people like him, I asked him how he came to be such a good listener.

"Failure," was his answer. "Repeated failure. I started out as a terrible listener. Early in my career, I thought I knew it all. The only reason I let people talk was that I knew my turn to talk was coming.

"In my marriage, I was a *little* bit better," John continued. "I very much *wanted* to listen to Margaret because of my love for her. However, that didn't stop me from being Mr. Answer Man. In *Winning with People*, I tell about how I used to win arguments but run over her emotionally. Finally, understanding how I was hurting her feelings caused me to stop what I was doing and learn how to listen—not just to the words, but to the feelings behind her words. I learned to listen with my heart."

"So how did you make the transfer from home to your career?" I asked.

"I saw the value in it from the way Margaret's and my relationship changed. But I also came to realize that it was good leadership too. President Woodrow Wilson said, 'The ear of the leader must ring with the voices of the people.' For a couple of years, whenever I was in a meeting, I wrote a large 'L' at the top of my legal pad to remind myself to listen. In time, it became a skill I mastered."

If you are already a good listener, you are ahead of the game. All you have to do is listen "between the lines" for cues that will tell you how others feel. If you're more like John, it may take you some time to learn the skill of listening with your heart. But anyone can do it—you don't need to be a trained psychologist!

JOHN . . . WITH A MAXWELL MENTORING MOMENT

If you are a poor listener, as I was, then do the following to transform yourself into someone who listens with the heart:

Focus on the Person

Herb Cohen, often called the world's best negotiator, says, "Effective listening requires more than hearing the words transmitted. It demands that you find meaning and understanding in what is being said. After all, meanings are not in words, but in people." Many people put their focus on the ideas being communicated, and they almost seem to forget about the person. You can't do that and listen with the heart.

I am naturally very impatient, so I continually have to fight against the tendency to put my agenda first. I think that is often the case with poor listeners. If that is true for you, slow down and put the person first. Focus on the individual, not just the ideas being expressed.

Unclog Your Ears

Even after you have begun to focus on the person with whom you are conversing, you may still experience many potential barriers to effective listening. Here are a few of them:

Distractions—Phone calls, TV, pagers, and things of that sort can make good listening nearly impossible.

Defensiveness—If you view complaints or criticism as a personal attack, you can become defensive. Once you begin to protect yourself, you will care little about what others think or how they feel.

Closed-mindedness—When you think you have all the answers, you close your mind. And when you close your mind, you close your ears.

Projection—Automatically attributing your own thoughts and feelings to others prevents you from perceiving how they feel.

Assumptions—When you jump to conclusions, you take away your own incentive to listen.

Pride—Thinking we have little to learn from others is, perhaps, the most deadly of distractions to listening. Being full of yourself leaves little room for input from others.

Obviously, your goal is to remove these barriers to good communication. Whenever possible, put yourself in a good physical environment for listening—away from noise and distractions. And also put yourself in a good mental environment for listening—set aside your defenses and preconceived notions so that you are *open* to communication.

Listen Aggressively

There's a difference between listening passively and listening aggressively. To listen with your heart, your listening has to be active. In his book *It's Your Ship* (Warner, 2002), Captain Michael Abrashoff explains that people are more likely to speak aggressively than to listen aggressively. When he decided to become an intentional listener, it made a huge difference in him and his crew. He wrote:

> It didn't take me long to realize that my young crew was smart, talented, and full of good ideas that frequently came to nothing because no one in charge had ever listened to them. Like most organizations, the Navy seemed to put managers in a transmitting mode, which minimized their receptivity. They were conditioned to promulgate orders from above, not to welcome suggestions from below.
>
> I decided that my job was to listen aggressively and to pick up every good idea the crew had for improving the ship's operation. Some traditionalists might consider this heresy, but it's actually just common sense. After all, the people who do the nuts-and-bolts work on a ship constantly see things that officers don't. It seemed to me only prudent for the captain to work hard at seeing the ship through the crew's eyes. Something happened in me as a result of those interviews. I came to respect my crew enormously. No longer were they nameless bodies at which I barked orders. I realized that they . . . had hopes, dreams, loved ones, and they wanted to believe that what they were doing was important. And they wanted to be treated with respect.

There's a difference between listening passively and listening aggressively. To listen with your heart, your listening has to be active.

As Abrashoff's attitude changed, his crew

transformed, his ship turned around, and the results were astounding.

Listen to Understand

The fundamental cause of nearly all communication problems is that people don't listen to understand; they listen to reply. David Burns, a medical doctor and professor of psychiatry at the University of Pennsylvania, says: "The biggest mistake you can make in trying to talk convincingly is to put your highest priority on expressing your ideas and feelings. What most people really want is to be listened to, respected, and understood." If you want to meet others' needs and make them feel like a million bucks, then you need to listen.

One of the ironies of becoming a good listener is that listening to others and making them feel understood also has a side benefit. According to Burns, "The moment people see that they are being understood, they become more motivated to understand your point of view." Listening with the heart produces a win-win situation in relationships.

LES . . . ON BRINGING IT HOME

Few relational topics have had more empirical support than the importance of active listening. Psychologists sometimes call it "listening with the third ear." And the bottom line of most studies shows exactly what John is teaching. When we listen for genuine understanding, we are no longer "playing the role" of listening, but we are fully in the moment, and the person knows it.[1]

To apply John's teaching to your own life . . .

Forget about:

Trying to get your own point across and put your energy into understanding the other person's point.

Ask:

How can I better understand what this person is feeling and thinking?

Do it:

Listen aggressively by eliminating distractions and focusing on the other person's point of view.

Remember:

The best way to persuade is with your ears.

16

Find the Keys to Their Hearts

Coaches who can outline plays on a blackboard are a dime a dozen. The ones who succeed are those who get inside their players and motivate them.
—Vince Lombardi

LES . . . ON SEEING THE PRACTICE IN ACTION

When communicators speak to audiences, a funny thing often occurs. You have a clear purpose in mind, prepare your message carefully, and deliver it. But when people come up to you to talk about what you said—each person seems to have heard a different message. It never fails.

I asked John if he had experienced the same phenomenon. "Absolutely," he answered. "When I first started preaching, I was surprised. I used to wonder if everybody had heard the same sermon. In a way, they hadn't. The words I say may be the same for everyone, but the members of the audience listen differently because they all have different keys to their hearts. That's not only a great lesson for a speaker, but it's also important to remember anytime you work with people."

Whenever I spend time with John, I see him connect with people at the heart level immediately. For example, the other day while I was with him, John met with Kirk Nowery, the president of one of John's companies, ISS. Many times when a leader meets with someone who works for him, he or she immediately gets down to business. But the first thing John did was talk to Kirk about his family. He wanted to know how his wife was doing. He asked about their grown children. John seemed to know all about Kirk's family. And once they had caught up, then they talked business.

John does this intuitively with everyone he knows. He asks about many people's spouses and children by name. He inquires about what's happening at a person's church or business. And he seems to remember the details. Why? Because he makes it his goal to know what's important to the people who are important to him. And by the way, he is able to know these things because he listens with his heart, as we explained in the previous chapter.

JOHN . . . WITH A MAXWELL MENTORING MOMENT

In the 1980s, I had the privilege, along with about thirty other leaders, to spend two days with the father of modern management, Peter Drucker. One of the things he said was,

"Leading people is like conducting an orchestra. There are many different players and instruments that the conductor must know thoroughly." Drucker challenged us to *really* know the key players on our team.

For the last twenty years, I have purposefully tried to discover the keys to the hearts of the people in my life, starting with the people in my family and my inner circle. Here's what I've learned along the way:

Accept the Fact That People Are Different

I've written in previous books about how, when I was young, I used to believe that everyone ought to be like me in order to be successful. I've matured quite a bit since then. Some of my growth has come as a result of traveling and meeting many kinds of people. Books such as Florence Littauer's *Personality Plus* (Revel, 1992) have also helped me. I've come to realize with time that I've got major gaps in my skills and abilities, as everyone does, and if people with different talents and temperaments work together, we all win and get a lot more done. We also enjoy the journey of life much more.

If you have a healthy self-image, you may fall into the same trap I did. However, you cannot win with people if you secretly harbor the belief that everyone ought to be more like you. Accept that people are different, and celebrate that God made us that way.

Find the Keys to Their Hearts by Asking Questions

It may seem fundamental, but asking a good question is essential to discovering the keys to a person's heart. Through the years, I have developed a list of questions that have helped me in this endeavor time and time again. You may want to use them too:

> "What do you dream about?" You can learn about people's minds by looking at what they have already achieved, but to understand their hearts, look at what they dream of becoming.
>
> "What do you cry about?" When you understand people's pain, you can't help but understand their hearts.
>
> "What do you sing about?" What brings people joy is often a source of their strength.
>
> "What are your values?" When people give you access to their values, know that you have entered the most sacred chambers of their hearts.
>
> "What are your strengths?" Whatever people perceive as their strengths makes their hearts proud.
>
> "What is your temperament?" Learn that, and you often discover the way to their hearts.

Obviously, you don't want your questions to feel like an interview, and you don't need to find out all of the answers in one sitting. The process can be natural while being intentional.

Establish Common Ground

Our English word *communication* comes from the Latin word *communis*, which means "common." Effective leaders, communicators, and people persons always find something they have in common with the people they are speaking to. It is on common ground that they connect with others. If you've asked questions and listened, then you will have discovered common ground.

Sometimes in meetings, hidden agendas can make communication ineffective because they make it difficult for people to meet on common ground. When that happens, try suggesting that all parties agree to a simple little ground rule. When one person disagrees with another, before he's allowed to make his own point, he has to understand and be able to articulate his opponent's point. You would be amazed at how quickly this practice puts people on common ground.

Realize That with Time, People Change

It is a major leap for some people to tune into others' dreams and desires and to discover the keys to their hearts. But it's not enough to do that once with a person and then think you've "got it" forever. Time changes all things, including the human heart.

Fred Bucy, former president of Texas Instruments, observed, "It is much easier to assume that what worked yesterday will work today, and this is simply not true." What's effective in motivating people at one point in their careers will not necessarily be effective in motivating them later. What touches their hearts at one stage of life may not be the same as they grow older. Successes and failures, tragedies and triumphs, goals achieved and dreams laid to rest all make an impact on a person's values and desires.

So what does that mean to someone who wants to win with others by finding the keys to their hearts? It means you should . . .

STAY IN CONTINUAL CONVERSATION WITH OTHERS. Keep connecting on the heart level. Ask about what has touched their hearts up to now; if their responses are different, then you know they are changing, and you have a new opportunity to learn about what matters to them now.

LOOK FOR THE "CHANGE INDICATORS" OF A PERSON'S LIFE. There are certain times in people's lives when they are most likely to change: (1) when they *hurt* enough that they *have to*, (2) when they *learn* enough that they *want to*, and (3) when they *receive* enough that they are *able to*.

If you practice these two disciplines, especially with your family and the key players in your organization, you'll be able to stay connected with them.

I need to tell you one more thing about finding the keys to people's hearts, and this is the most important point: Once you have found a key to a person's heart, you must act with integrity, because you have been entrusted with something of great value. Never use it to manipulate someone. "Turn" the key only when you can add value to that person.

LES . . . ON BRINGING IT HOME

Genuine concern for others is a lifestyle more than a technique. Sure, you can practice the tips John suggests and find immediate benefit, but they will never really pay off in your relationships until you practice them consistently. In fact, research shows that

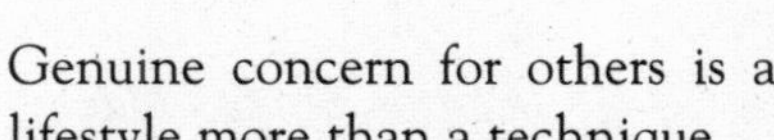

Genuine concern for others is a lifestyle more than a technique.

in learning to develop this quality, you are far more likely to see it become a part of your personality if you work at it on a daily basis, if you make it a reflexive habit with the people around you.[1] In other words, this needs to be something you *are* more than something you *do*.

To apply John's teaching to your own life . . .

Forget about:

Your inclination to believe that everyone is (or should be) just like you.

Ask:

What "change indicators" have I seen in the person whose heart I'd like to understand?

Do it:

Purposefully try to discover the keys to the hearts of your inner circle.

Remember:

Leaders who succeed are those who understand the hearts of their team.

17

Be the First to Help

After the verb "to love," "to help" is the most beautiful verb in the world.
—Berth von Suttner

LES . . . ON SEEING THE PRACTICE IN ACTION

"Les, where are you?"

"I just passed the Hotel del Coronado, and I'm pulling into the complex," I said.

"What color is your rental car?"

"It's silver," I told John over my cell phone.

"Okay, I can see you coming up right now," John said. "Take an immediate right and you'll see a parking space that is just now opening up."

"Where are you?" I asked.

"Look up." John was standing on a balcony of the high-rise building on Coronado island in San Diego. He had rented a condo, and I had just flown in for a day of meetings with him.

"Oh, there you are!" I started to laugh as I saw him waving at me from the balcony. Only John would think of actually scouting out parking spaces from a bird's-eye view so that he could make it easier for me to find a space.

I've long known that offering help to others is a key to winning with people. It's one of the first lessons you'll pick up in any social psychology class. But John puts a new twist on it. He goes out of his way to be helpful, and when someone's in need, he's often the first on the scene.

"Sometimes it's the little things with John," said employee Ken Coleman. "When I'm traveling with him, I've often seen John help someone struggling to get his or her suitcases into the airplane compartment while most other passengers are oblivious and trying to maneuver around the person. John makes a conscious effort to help in the moment. It seems to be an almost reflexive action with him."

John's twenty-six-year career in ministry probably has made a great impact on him in this area. Good pastors seem able to tune in to people's needs. But you don't have to be a professional shepherd to see people's needs and be the first to help. It's the kind of thing that anyone can do—regardless of age, talent, or socioeconomic status.

JOHN . . . WITH A MAXWELL MENTORING MOMENT

My friend Zig Ziglar said, "You can get everything in life you want if you will just help enough other people get what they want." Zig is certainly living proof of that. He has helped so many people, and he has been a success as a result.

> "You can get everything in life you want if you will just help enough other people get what they want."
>
> —ZIG ZIGLAR

I like helping people. I think it's one of the reasons God put us here on earth. But helping others does more than benefit others. It also helps you win with them. I say that because whenever you are quick to help others, it makes a statement. It's like leaving a calling card they will never forget.

So how do you become someone who is the first to help? Follow these guidelines:

MAKE HELPING OTHERS A PRIORITY

We are often so consumed with our own agendas that helping others never becomes important to us. The solution is to make helping others part of your agenda—a top priority. I read recently about something Academy Award–winner Tom Hanks did years ago on the set of *The Green Mile* that shows how helping others is a priority for him. Frank Darabont, director of the film, reflected on Hanks's commitment to helping rising actor Michael Duncan achieve his best, and the impression it had on him. Darabont said:

> Fifteen, twenty years from now, what will I remember [about filming *The Green Mile*]? There was one thing—and I'll never forget this: As we're shooting, [the camera] is on Michael Duncan first, and I'm realizing that I'm getting distracted by Hanks. Hanks is delivering an Academy Award–winning performance, off-camera, for Michael Duncan—to give him every possible thing he needs or can

> use to deliver the best possible performance. He wanted Michael to do so well. He wanted him to look so good. I'll never forget that.[1]

Tom Hanks, like some other Hollywood actors, could have been the first to bail out on Duncan. Instead he was the first to help. It obviously paid off. In 1999, Michael Clarke Duncan was nominated for an Academy Award in the Best Actor in a Supporting Role category. And Duncan's career has since taken off.

Make Yourself Aware of People's Needs

This may sound obvious, but you can't meet a need that you don't know exists. Each of us must begin by caring about the people around us and looking for their needs. Sometimes that knowledge can come from listening with your heart. Sometimes it comes from just paying attention to what's going on around you. Other times it comes from mentally putting yourself in another person's place.

There is a Jewish legend that says two brothers once shared a field and a mill, each night dividing the grain they had ground together during the day. One brother lived alone; the other was married with a large family.

One day the single brother thought to himself, *It isn't fair that we divide the grain evenly. I have only myself to care for, but my brother has children to feed.* So each night he secretly took some of his flour to his brother's storehouse.

But the married brother considered his brother's situation, and said to himself, *It isn't right that we divide the grain evenly, because I have children to provide for me in my old age, but my brother has no one. What will he do when he's old?* So every night he secretly took some of his flour and put it in his brother's stores. As a result, both of the brothers found their supply of grain mysteriously replenished each morning.

Then one night they met each other halfway between their two houses. They suddenly realized what the other was doing, and they embraced each other in love. The legend is that God witnessed their meeting and proclaimed, "This is a holy place—a place of love—and here it is that my temple shall be built." The first temple is said to have been constructed on that very site.[2]

Be Willing to Take a Risk

Sometimes helping another person can be a risky proposition, yet that should not keep us from lending a hand. There's a story Ken Sutterfield tells from the 1936 Olympic Games in Berlin, Germany, that illustrates the impact that can be made by taking such a risk. Coming into the games, American sprinter Jesse Owens had set three world records in one day, including a leap of 26 feet 8 1/4 inches in the running broad jump—a record that would stand for twenty-five years. However, Owens faced great pressure during the games. Hitler and his fellow Nazis wanted to use the competition to establish Aryan superiority, and Owens, a black man, could sense the hostility toward him.

As Owens tried to qualify for the finals during the games, he became rattled as he saw a tall, blue-eyed, blond German taking practice jumps in the 26-foot range. On his first jump, Owens leaped from several inches beyond the takeoff board. Then he fouled on the second attempt. He was allowed only one more attempt. If he missed it, he would be eliminated.

The tall German approached Owens and introduced himself. His name was Luz Long. As the Nazis watched, Long encouraged Owens and offered him some advice: since the qualifying distance was only 23 feet 5 1/2 inches, Long suggested that Owens make a mark several inches before the takeoff board to make sure he didn't foul. Owens qualified on his third jump. In the finals, he set an Olympic record and earned one of his four gold medals. And who was the first person to congratulate Owens? Luz Long!

Owens never forgot the help Long had given him, though he never saw Long again. "You could melt down all the medals and cups I have," Owens wrote, "and they wouldn't be plating on the 24-carat friendship I felt for Luz Long."[3]

Follow Through Once You Begin to Help

Philanthropist Andrew Carnegie was approached by members of the New York Philharmonic Society, one of Carnegie's favorite charities, for financial support. He was about to write a check to wipe out the Society's entire deficit when suddenly he stopped. "Surely there must be other rich, generous music lovers in this town who could help out," he said. "Why don't you raise half this amount, and come back to me for the other half," said the great philanthropist.

The next day, the treasurer came back and told Carnegie that he had raised $30,000 and would like now to get Carnegie's check. The patron of the arts was immensely pleased at this show of enterprise and immediately handed it over. But he was curious. "Who, may I ask, contributed the other half?"

"Mrs. Carnegie," came the reply.

Sometimes when we are the first to offer help, we discover that the person to whom we made the offer isn't in as great a need as we first expected. Follow through anyway. Being the first to help is a great way to win with people. Offering to help and then not following through is a sure way to lose.

LES . . . ON BRINGING IT HOME

Studies on altruism fill volume after volume of academic journals. If there is one thing the professional community of psychologists knows, it's that being helpful is one of the shortest distances between two people—especially when you are the *first* to help. And like John says, helping others speaks volumes about you.[4]

To apply John's teaching to your own life . . .

Forget about:

Thinking only about what's in it for you and think about how you can offer a hand.

Ask:

How can I help you?

Do it:

Be the first to volunteer your services, offer assistance, or lend a hand.

Remember:

If you help enough people get what they want, you'll get what you want too.

18

ADD VALUE TO PEOPLE

Try not to become a man of success,
but rather try to become a man of value.
—ALBERT EINSTEIN

LES . . . ON SEEING THE PRACTICE IN ACTION

I've heard John speak to all kinds of audiences all over the globe, and a theme that runs like a ribbon through many of his talks has to do with adding value to people. Whatever the conference or topic, he often weaves the importance of "adding value" into it. I've also been in meetings around a conference table where John focuses on value added—to him from others and by him to others. It's a John Maxwell trademark.

So when I started researching the subject for this book, I went to Dan Reiland, a friend and colleague of John's for more than twenty years.

"John has desired to add value to people for as long as I've known him," said Dan, "but in recent years he has identified that as his primary purpose in life. And he does it in so many ways. He takes members of his staff to conferences and training events to make them better. He sets aside time for individuals to personally mentor and coach them. He gives the people he leads freedom to risk and succeed and a safe place to fail and learn. He even adds value by paying his people well."

"But how has he added value to you personally?" I asked Dan.

"Where do I start?" exclaimed Dan. "I could give you a list." And he did:

Believing in me.
Speaking the truth in love to me.
Stretching me—way beyond my comfort zone but not outside of my gift zone.
Opening the world to me through foreign travel.
Modeling leadership in both the tough times and the fun times.
Speaking to others more highly of me than I deserve.
Opening doors in life that I could never have opened myself.
Consistently having my best interest at heart.
Allowing me into his inner circle.
Treating me like a younger brother—a gift of immeasurable value.

"If I had never met John, my whole life would be different—my career, my skills, my relationships," Dan explained. "He has added value to me every step of the way for two decades. How do you measure that?"

John never seems to miss an opportunity to add value to people. And that priority, as much as anything else, has made him a winner with people.

JOHN . . . WITH A MAXWELL MENTORING MOMENT

At the core of my being, I believe that there is nothing in this life more important than people. Having embraced that truth, I try to live it out with integrity. To me that means doing everything in my power to add value to people.

If you desire to become a value adder, then take these things to heart:

Value People

It all starts with your attitude toward people. Human relations expert Les Giblin remarked, "You can't make the other fellow feel important in your presence if you secretly feel that he is a nobody." Isn't that true? Don't you find it difficult to do something kind for people when you dislike them?

> "You can't make the other fellow feel important in your presence if you secretly feel that he is a nobody."
>
> —Les Giblin

The way we see people is often the difference between manipulating and motivating them. If we don't want to help people, yet we want them to help us, then we get in trouble. We manipulate people when we move them for our *personal* advantage. However, we motivate people when we move them for *mutual* advantage. Adding value to others is often a win-win proposition.

How do you see people? Are they potential recipients of value you can give, or do they tend to be nuisances along your path to success? Author Sydney J. Harris said, "People want to be appreciated, not impressed. They want to be regarded as human beings, not as sounding boards for other people's egos. They want to be treated as an end in themselves, not as a means towards the gratification of another's vanity." If you want to add value to people, you have to value them first.

Make Yourself More Valuable

We've talked about the phrase "you cannot give what you do not have." There are people who possess good hearts and the desire to give, yet they have very little to offer. Why? Because they have not first added value to themselves. Making yourself more valuable is not an entirely selfish act. When you acquire knowledge, learn a new skill, or gain experience, you not only improve yourself, but you also increase your ability to help others.

In 1974 I committed myself to the pursuit of personal growth. I knew that it would help me to be a better minister, so I began to continually read books, listen to tapes, attend conferences, and learn from better leaders. At the time, I had no idea that this commitment would be the most important thing I would ever do to help others. But that has turned out to be the case. As I improve myself, I am better able to help others improve. The more I grow, the more I can help others grow. The same will be true for you. If you want to add value to people, you must make yourself more valuable.

Know What People Value

Since you have read the chapters "Listen with Your Heart" and "Find the Keys to Their Hearts," you have a good grasp on the principle behind this practice. If you've already begun to practice it, then you know that it can be very time-consuming. But you also know it can be the most important step in adding value to others. Once we know what people value, with some effort we can add value to them.

I make it standard practice to note what the people in my life value from me, and you should too. Here are some examples from my own life:

Margaret, my wife, values my time with her, and my attention.

My children, Elizabeth and Joel Porter, value the legacy Margaret and I are leaving them.

Larry, my brother, values my prayers and our time together.

Eric and Troy, my nephews, value the fatherly advice and unconditional love I give them.

Linda, my assistant, values my time and effectiveness, because she is an integral part of it.

John, the president of my nonprofit organization, EQUIP, values the leadership and opportunities I give him.

Kirk, the president of my company ISS, values my friendship and partnership.

Tom values my friendship and mentoring.

Rick values my "big brother" relationship with him.

Joel values the networking opportunities I can give him.

I could go on, but I don't want to bore you. The point is that we must take the time to know what our most valuable people value.

By the way, adding value to others is not only a gift to them; it is a gift to you. The people I have just listed continually add value to my life. Some have given so much to me that no matter how much I do for them, I will never even the score.

LES . . . ON BRINGING IT HOME

Adding value to people is one of the reasons God put us here on earth. You cannot go wrong by helping others to live a better life or to reach their potential.

To apply John's teaching to your own life . . .

Forget about:

Trying to become a person of success, and instead become a person of value.

Ask:

Who adds value to my life, and to whom would I most like to add value?

Do it:

Make a list of the people in your life and note exactly what they value most from you.

Remember:

If you don't truly value the person, he or she will never feel important in your presence.

19

Remember a Person's Story

Many a man would rather you heard his story than granted his request.
—Phillip Stanhope, Earl of Chesterfield

LES . . . ON SEEING THE PRACTICE IN ACTION

"Les," John will say, "tell me about your dad. How are he and your mom doing since they moved to Phoenix?"

It's just like John to recall that my parents recently moved.

"And tell me about your brothers," he'll continue. "What's the latest with them?"

John always seems to remember my story—just as he does with so many people. He does it well, often, and consistently. When he has met people, I've heard him flat-out ask them to tell him their stories. So I asked him how he learned to be a collector of people's stories.

"To begin with, I love a good story—whether I'm learning about someone I've just met or hearing about an adventure from someone I've known my whole life. In fact, when I spend time with my dad, who is now eighty-two, our time is always filled with storytelling. We talk about the new things that are happening in our lives, but often the stories are ones I have heard dozens of times. Some Dad loves to tell over and over. Others I ask him to tell. Some I love retelling."

"But you seem to go out of your way to get the story of someone you just met," I commented.

"That's true. Whenever I have a few minutes with someone," John said, "I ask him to tell me his story, because I know that time in the conversation will focus entirely on him, his interests, dreams, uniqueness, disappointments, questions, hopes—his journey. While that person enjoys the personal attention, I gain insight into the keys to his life. Learning a person's story is a great way to connect with him. Remembering his journey and building on it is the greatest way to develop a strong relationship.

"Just the other day I took a taxi from the San Diego airport over to Coronado. And I talked to the cab driver," said John. "His name was Raphael. I asked him his story, and he told me that he had lived on Coronado thirty-five years, and there he had found something he'd not found anywhere else in his life: community. Every afternoon he meets his friends at a local market, where they talk and play games. He was so pleased that I asked and he was so delighted to tell his story that he invited me to the market."

That shows how great a connection you can make in a

short time by simply asking people to tell you their stories. And just imagine the impression it will make when you remember each story: it will help you to reconnect with people very quickly.

JOHN . . . WITH A MAXWELL MENTORING MOMENT

There are so many good reasons to learn a person's story. Here are just a few that keep motivating me to continue this practice with others:

Requesting a person's story says, "You could be special."
Remembering a person's story says, "You are special."
Reminding a person of his or her story says, "You are special to me."
Repeating a person's story to others says, "You should be special to them."

The result? You become special to the person who shared a story with you.

There are really just three small steps when it comes to embracing this practice in order to win with people. The key is to cultivate the habit of actually taking these steps with the people in your life.

1. Ask

When you meet someone new, after the introductions and initial pleasantries, don't hesitate. Dive in and ask to hear the person's story. You can do it any number of ways: you can flat-out ask, "What's your story?" You can request that he tell you about himself. You can ask where he is from or how he got into the field he's in. Use your own style.

If you've never tried this kind of thing before and you worry that it might be awkward the first few times you do it, then practice with people you are unlikely to see again—the driver in a cab, a passenger on a plane, a waitress in a restaurant. Once you become comfortable asking questions of total strangers, the rest will be easy.

2. LISTEN

Years ago I came across a list of suggestions for good listening. (I think I clipped it from *Bits and Pieces*.) Here were some of the tips:

Look the speaker in the eye.

Be attentive—don't roll your eyes or grimace when you hear something you don't agree with.

Don't interrupt—try phrases like "Go on" or "I see" instead of "Now, that reminds me . . ."

Tell the speaker what you think you heard; begin by saying, "Let me see if I understand . . ."

The main idea is to really focus on the other person. The problem many people have is that while the other person speaks, they are thinking more about what they want to say when it's their turn instead of focusing on listening. When you give people your undivided attention, then you are in a better position to achieve the next step.

3. REMEMBER

Some people have a knack for numbers, others for names or faces. But just about everyone has the capacity to remember stories. Small children remember them. And stories have been recited and sung from memory for thousands of years. Even long stories, such as the Iliad and the Odyssey—believed to have been created nearly three thousand years ago—were sung for three centuries before being written down. Stories stay with us.

A couple of years ago, the conference department at Injoy received a letter from Ellis Brust, formerly of St. Michael and All Angels Episcopal Church, that tells the power of remembering a person's story. Here's what it said:

> One of my leaders in the church has just opened a franchise fast-food place in the small East Texas town of Gilmer. He is in business with two other men in the church and they are committed to running the business with sound Christian principles. I took him to hear John three or four years ago and he recalled John's Nordstrom's stories [about how their employees go the extra mile]. He has tried to train his employees using these principles.
>
> On the first week of operation, he overheard two little old ladies talking about the soft drink selection and one of them was disappointed that there was no Diet Dr. Pepper offered. He spoke with the woman who was diabetic and preferred Diet Dr. Pepper to other diet drinks. He got in his car, drove to the 7-11, purchased a six-pack of Diet Dr. Pepper, took the woman a cup of ice and a can of the drink. He told her that there would always be a case

of Diet Dr. Pepper in the refrigerator with her name on it, and she just needed to tell the person at the counter who she was and what her beverage preference was and she would get it.

The shocked woman said, "Young man, I have been in this town my whole life. I have many influential friends and they will all hear what you just did for me. Thank you, and we will be regular customers."

I thought you would want to know one small way your work is changing lives. Keep up the good work.

Was what the restaurant owner did a big deal? Did it change the lady's life? No. In fact, we don't know if he ever talked to her again or learned anything else about her story. But he made her feel special, and it served her well. If we care about people, really listen to them, and try to remember their stories, we can make an impact on them. And we can make them feel like a million bucks.

LES . . . ON BRINGING IT HOME

Researchers call it a "commitment script." It's part of a person's life narrative that is particularly meaningful and personal. From my own experience and from numerous studies, I can attest to the fact that when you tap into it with another person, when you take the time to explore it and remember it, you will make an extremely valuable connection.[1]

To apply John's teaching to your own life . . .

Forget about:

Telling your own story and listen to the story of others.

Ask:

What's your story?

Do it:

Bring up some aspect of a person's story the next time you see him or her.

Remember:

Everyone loves to tell his story.

20

TELL A GOOD STORY

The universe is made of stories, not atoms.
—MURIEL RUKEYSER

LES . . . ON SEEING THE PRACTICE IN ACTION

I spotted John on the curb at the Seattle airport and pulled up to get him. After tossing his bag into the back of my Jeep, I slid in behind the wheel. Then off we went to dinner at a hotel before a speaking engagement.

After a few minutes of catching up, we arrived at the hotel. As we walked through the lobby, John said, "Hold on a second. I want to tell you a story." He took me down a hallway, and we ducked into a meeting room.

"This place is very special to me," John explained. He pointed to a chair at the end of a conference table. "I was sitting in this chair right here when ISS evolved into the company it is today," John began, referencing one of his organizations. He pointed to each chair and explained who had been seated in it. Then he laid out the entire process of what happened that day: how he had flown to Seattle to get advice from a business executive; how his dream to help pastors raise money to expand their churches crossed over from vision to reality that day; how he recruited that business leader to assist churches on a national level.

The way John told it, I could easily visualize the whole thing and feel his enthusiasm. "I tell you, Les, coming back to a place where something good happened always renews my gratitude."

The lesson of this story stuck. John told me that story eight years ago, and I still remember it vividly. In fact, I can't help but think of it every time I drive by that hotel. It was an important point of connection to John for me at the time. He included me in a private part of his life—sharing his heart, his dreams, and his personal history. It made me feel good—and still does.

As a communicator, I'm always watching to see how people speak to an audience. John always tells a good story—in front of an audience as well as one-on-one. And he uses lots of stories when he communicates. So I asked him why.

"That's easy: stories stick; principles fade," said John. "If you want people to remember what you said, tell a story.

"Let me tell you something else," he continued. "It took a while for me to learn the lesson about stories in my writing. I'm so bottom-line that I used to just teach principles without many stories. But a friend convinced me to change my style. And it's made a big difference for my readers. As a writer, you've got to ask yourself, 'Will the reader turn the page?' The person most likely will if I am telling a good story."

I haven't met a person yet who doesn't love a good story. That's one of the reasons storytellers are so magnetic!

JOHN . . . WITH A MAXWELL MENTORING MOMENT

In the fall of 1999, Margaret, some friends, and I visited the small town of Jonesborough, Tennessee. More than seven thousand people from all over the country, many at considerable expense, came there to sit for hours on end on blankets, on folding chairs, sometimes even in the rain. Why? They wanted to attend the annual National Storytelling Festival.

We watched one storyteller after another captivate listeners. The stories were diverse—sad, happy, funny, sentimental, historical, fictitious, mythical. Some had a great message; others simply entertained. But all the stories and storytellers had one thing in common: they had the power to captivate their listeners.

At the end of the conference, my friends and I discussed why these storytellers were so effective. "What traits did they have that made them so successful?" we asked. Here's the list we came up with:

Enthusiasm—They enjoyed what they were doing and expressed themselves with joy and vitality.

Animation—The presentations were marked by lively facial expressions and gestures.

Audience participation—Nearly every storyteller involved the audience in some way, asking listeners to sing, clap, repeat phrases, or do sign language.

Spontaneity—The storytellers responded freely to their listeners.

Memorization—Telling their stories without notes allowed for eye contact.

Humor—Humor was interjected in both serious and sad stories.

Creativity—Classic themes were told from a fresh perspective.

Personal—Most stories were told in the first person.

Heartwarming—Their stories made people feel good for having heard them.

Storytelling is very effective one-on-one, in small group conversation, and in front of large audiences. Invariably, the person who tells the best stories becomes the one to whom others turn their attention.

Storytelling is a skill that comes with practice, and anyone can learn to develop it. If you don't have much experience with it, or you would like to improve, then allow me to give you a few tips:

Share Something You've Experienced

The stories we tell the best are the ones we've lived. We care about them, we know the material, and we know how they have affected us. And we can shape and embellish them any way we want. Everybody has had experiences that others would be interested in.

> The stories we tell the best are the ones we've lived.

Tell It with the Goal of Connecting

The people who have the toughest time telling stories are the ones who try to impress others with them. If that describes you, then change your goal. Tell stories with the purpose of connecting with others. Put the focus on the listener, and your storytelling skills will improve overnight.

Put Your Heart into It

People love humor, but not everyone can tell a funny story. If you can, go with it. But never underestimate the power of a story from the heart. (If you want evidence, look at the sales figures of the *Chicken Soup for the Soul* books!) If you want to tell a connecting story, make it warm. Put your heart into it. And don't be afraid to show people that you care about what you're talking about.

Assume That Others Want to Hear It

One of the biggest mistakes novice storytellers make is being tentative. Nothing makes a story go flat more quickly than a timid delivery. If you're going to tell a story, be bold. Be energetic. Be engaging. Go for it, or don't go at all.

I've read that the "elite" often criticized President Lincoln for telling too many stories. But he didn't let it stop him, because he knew what worked with people. He remarked, "They say I tell a great many stories; I reckon I do, but I have found in the course of a long experience that common people, take them as they run, are more easily informed through the medium of a broad illustration than in any other way, and as to what the hypercritical few may think, I don't care."

Follow the lead of Lincoln and other great leaders who knew how to win with people. Tell a good story, engage them at the heart level, and win them over.

LES . . . ON BRINGING IT HOME

Research supports the value of being able to relate your thoughts and ideas through stories. In fact, one recent study revealed that those who use storytelling as a means of relating to others engender greater authenticity and self-esteem. It turns out their self-expression makes others feel good, and they feel better about themselves in the process.[1]

To apply John's teaching to your own life . . .

Forget about:
Being a professional storyteller.

Ask:
How can I make my point come through stronger with a story?

Do it:
Tell a story instead of relaying only facts.

Remember:
Stories stick—principles fade.

21

Give with No Strings Attached

Life's most persistent and urgent question is:
What are you doing for others?
—Martin Luther King, Jr.

LES . . . ON SEEING THE PRACTICE IN ACTION

Whenever I visit John at his office in Atlanta, one of the people I always see is Linda Eggers, John's assistant. On a recent trip as I chatted with her, I began querying her for stories to illustrate the idea of giving with no strings attached.

"Who's got a good story?" I asked. "Who should I go talk to?"

"How about me?" Linda responded. She began telling me one story after another, but one in particular seemed to mean the most to her. It occurred when her youngest daughter, Kim, was getting ready to graduate from high school. It was an especially hectic time at the office too. And Linda's middle child, Jennie, who was living in California, had recently given birth under difficult circumstances.

The day before Kim's graduation, Linda got word that Jenny was having serious complications that would require surgery.

"I'm a very steady person," said Linda. "There aren't too many things that can get to me. But I was totally overwhelmed by the situation."

Linda said that when she sat down and told John about all that was happening, after some kind words and prayer, John offered to step in and help her. The first thing he did was buy her a ticket so that she could be with Jennie that day for the surgery—a ticket with a return flight on the red-eye so that Linda could get back for Kim's graduation. And he bought her another ticket so that Linda could go back out again to be with Jennie during her recovery.

"How many employers do you know who would do something like that?" said Linda. "Because of his busy schedule, it was a real inconvenience for John to lose me during that time. But he just said, 'You take whatever time you need and do what needs to be done,' and he really meant it. I was gone for another whole week."

Linda's wasn't the only story I heard. Charlie Wetzel, John's writer for more than a decade, told me about the time John offered to send him to a weeklong writer's conference after he had worked for John only a year. When Charlie explained that he couldn't go because it was his first wedding anniversary, John offered to send Charlie and his wife. And more than one person told about a time when they were barely making it financially and John slipped them money so that they could go out for a nice dinner with their spouse.

Generosity is an extremely appealing quality. When someone gives to others—with no strings attached—it really makes them feel special.

JOHN . . . WITH A MAXWELL MENTORING MOMENT

Jesuit theologian Pierre Teilhard de Chardin said, "The most satisfying thing in life is to have been able to give a large part of one's self to others." Anyone who has unselfishly helped another person knows this to be true. Yet not everyone is able to adopt an ongoing mind-set of giving toward others. Why is that? First of all, I believe it has nothing to do with circumstances. I've met generous people with almost nothing who were willing to share what little they possessed. And I've met well-off people who were stingy with their time, money, and talents.

The issue is really attitude. I've found that people who enjoy giving with no strings attached usually exhibit two characteristics that anyone can embrace:

1. They Have an Abundance Mentality

If you've read Stephen Covey's book *The Seven Habits of Highly Effective People* (Free Press, 1989), then you are familiar with the concepts related to scarcity and abundance mind-sets. In a nutshell, people with a scarcity mind-set believe that in life, there's only a limited supply of anything to go around, whether it's money, resources, opportunity, and so forth. They see the world as a pie with a limited number of slices. Once they're gone, they're gone. As a result, they fight to get their piece—and once they have it, they protect it.

People possessing an abundance mind-set believe that there is plenty of everything to go around. If life is a pie, and others are helping themselves to pieces, the solution of the person with the abundance mind-set is to bake another pie. There is always more money to be made, more (or different) resources to be discovered, additional opportunities to be pursued. An old solution isn't working anymore? Don't worry: someone will find a new one. The inventors, entrepreneurs, and explorers of the world are continually creating new "pies" so that everyone can get a slice.

My own take on this is that people tend to fall into one of two categories: they are either takers or makers. Takers are people who take, grab, and consume whatever they can to meet their own needs. They see life as a rat race. Of course, the main problem with that is that even if you win, you're still a rat. Makers, on the other hand, are people who give, create, and make things happen. They create progress and foster success for others. They are just as likely to give as to take because they are continually helping to create more for everyone.

> "When we refrain from giving, with a scarcity mentality, the little we have will become less. When we give generously, with an abundance mentality, what we give away will multiply."
>
> —Henri Nouwen

People who habitually give with no strings attached almost always have an abundance mentality. They are generous because they believe that if they give, they will not run out of resources. Pastor and former college professor Henri Nouwen states, "When we refrain from giving, with a scarcity mentality, the little we have will become less. When we give generously, with an abundance mentality, what we give away will multiply."

I have found this to be true. Someone once asked me why he should adopt an abundance mentality, and he was surprised by my answer. I told him that if you believe in abundance, that's what life gives you. If you believe in scarcity, then that's what you get. I don't know why that is, but after fifty years of paying attention to people's attitudes and watching how life unfolded for them, I know it to be true. So if you desire to be more generous, change your thinking and your attitude when it comes to abundance. Not only will it allow you to be more generous, but also it will change your life.

2. They See the Big Picture

People who give with no strings attached are usually aware of the help *they* have received along the way. They recognize that they are standing on the shoulders of previous generations. The progress they make is due, at least in part, to the work and sacrifice of those who have gone before them. Because of this, they are determined to do for the next generation what was done for them.

I came across a poem by W. A. Dromgoale called "The Bridge Builder." It beautifully illustrates this desire to give to others:

> An old man walking a lonesome road,
> Came at the evening, cold and gray,
> To a chasm vast and wide and deep.

The old man crossed in the twilight dim,
The rolling stream had no fears for him;
But he turned when safe on the other side,
And built a bridge to span the tide.

"Old man," said a fellow traveler near,
"You are wasting your strength with building here,
Your journey will end with the passing day,
You never again will pass this way.
You've crossed the chasm, deep and wide,
Why build you this bridge at eventide?"

The builder lifted his old gray head,
"Good friend, in the path I have come," he said,
"There followeth after me today,
A youth whose feet must pass this way.
The chasm that was nought to me,
To the fair headed youth may a pitfall be.
He too must cross in the twilight dim—
Good friend, I am building this bridge for him."[1]

To become better givers, we need greater perspective. When we realize how much we have benefited from the kindness of others, it becomes much easier for us to be generous. And one of the best things is that giving is so rewarding. College president and educational reformer Horace Mann commented, "We must be purposely kind and generous or we miss the best part of existence. The heart that goes out of itself gets large and full of joy. This is the great secret of the inner life. We do ourselves the most good doing something for others." When we give unselfishly, we will gain something in return.

LES . . . ON BRINGING IT HOME

This lesson certainly rings true in my therapy sessions with clients. And it's backed up by plenty of research. Studies have shown that the higher one's level of helpfulness to others, the greater well-being one will experience. Researchers call it "generativity," and it is consistently linked to greater personal growth and even physical health.[2]

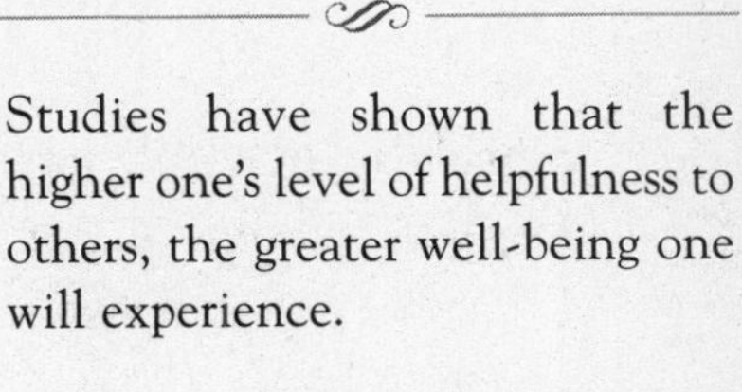

Studies have shown that the higher one's level of helpfulness to others, the greater well-being one will experience.

To apply John's teaching to your own life . . .

Forget about:

Scarcity; instead, focus on abundance.

Ask:

Whom can I help that will give nothing in return?

Do it:

Be purposely kind and generous to a specific person.

Remember:

You do yourself the most good when you are doing something good for others.

22

Learn Your Mailman's Name

Remember that a person's name is to that person the sweetest and most important sound in any language.

—Dale Carnegie

LES . . . ON SEEING THE PRACTICE IN ACTION

John tells the story about how he used to memorize the names of people who attended his church when he was the senior pastor of Skyline Wesleyan Church in San Diego, California. He used to make an offer to visitors: if they would allow someone to take their pictures on Sunday after the service, John promised to learn their names by the following Sunday. John did that until he finished his tenure at the church in 1995. Fulfilling that promise, John was able to memorize the names of more than twenty-two hundred people and greet them by name.

In the summer of 2004, Skyline Church celebrated its fiftieth anniversary, and John and Margaret were delighted to return and be a part of the celebration. John told me that thousands of people attended, many of whom he had not seen in nine years. He was thankful that each person had a name tag. "But as I approached one couple," John told me, "the husband covered his name tag. When I called him by name he laughed and said, 'I was just checking to see if you could still remember names.'"

"That doesn't surprise me," I said, "but it still impresses me."

"You know," John replied, "at fifty-seven, it's not as easy as it once was, but I still work at remembering names."

I've long admired this skill and personal approach of John's. In fact, it inspired me in my work as a professor to learn the names of several hundred students in my classes each semester at the university. Why do we do it? Because we know that a person's name is his personal signboard to the world, his most intimate, distinctive possession. And when you remember a person's name, it can make him or her feel like a million bucks.

A person's name is his personal signboard to the world, his most intimate, distinctive possession.

JOHN . . . WITH A MAXWELL MENTORING MOMENT

In 1937 the granddaddy of all people-skills books was published. It was an overnight hit, eventually selling more than fifteen million copies. That book was *How to Win Friends and*

Influence People (Simon & Schuster, 1981), by Dale Carnegie. What made that book so valuable was Carnegie's understanding of human nature. I love his simple words of wisdom. Something that I learned early from Carnegie was this: remember and use a person's name. "We should be aware of the *magic* contained in a name . . . The name sets the individual apart; it makes him or her unique among all others. The information we are imparting or the request we are making takes on a special importance when we approach the situation with the name of the individual. From the waitress to the senior executive, the name will work magic as we deal with others."

What was true in 1937 is even more applicable in our fast-paced world. These days an account number or a title too often replaces a person's name. Remembering names can help enhance your personal image, improve your style, and, most importantly, increase your impact on others. And when you take the time to learn the names of not only your clients and important acquaintances, but also the everyday people you interact with—such as your postal worker or neighborhood store owner—you go to another level of relational connectivity.

If you desire to improve your skill with names, here are a few suggestions:

Recognize the Value of a Name

How do you feel when someone calls you by the wrong name? How about when you kindly correct the person and spend time with him, and he still gets your name wrong? How about when people haven't seen you for a long time, and they still remember your name? Doesn't it make you feel good? (And doesn't it also impress you?) When people care enough to know your name, they make you feel valued.

Playwright William Shakespeare wrote, "Good name, in man or woman, is the immediate jewel of their souls.—Who steals my purse steals trash; but he that filches from me my good name, robs me of that which not enriches him, and makes me poor indeed."[1]

Use the SAVE Method

My friend Jerry Lucas is known as "Dr. Memory." He has spent the years following his hugely successful run in the NBA helping schoolchildren and adults improve their memories through a variety of innovative techniques. One of the things he teaches is called the SAVE Method. Here's how it works:

S—Say the name three times in conversation.

A—Ask a question about the name (for example, how it is spelled) or about the person.

V—Visualize the person's prominent physical or personality feature.

E—End the conversation with the name.

Years ago Jerry showed how useful his method could be by remembering the names of every guest in the audience at the *Tonight Show*. I believe it can also help you remember the first and last names of the people you meet.

In Case of Memory Failure . . .

Almost everyone has trouble recalling names on some occasions. When this happens, try to recall the situation in which you met the person or last saw him or her. If you can't recall even that, then ask, "How long has it been?" Perhaps that will jog your memory.

If you're meeting people along with a friend or colleague, sometimes you can help each other out. Introduce the person whose name you do remember to the person whose name you don't, and perhaps the individual will volunteer his name. Or you can agree with your friend ahead of time to come to each other's aid. My wife and I do this. When we make introductions, Margaret knows that if I don't introduce someone by name, I'm not sure I remember it correctly. And she will quickly introduce herself and get the other person's name in return.

When all else fails, just say, "I'm so sorry; I remember you well, but I'm afraid your name has slipped my mind." Then after the individual reminds you, use the SAVE method so that you are less likely to forget it again in the future.

Go Easy on Yourself If You Forget

If you work at it, you *will* become better at remembering people's names. Don't be too hard on yourself, however, when you blow it. That's what I did recently when meeting a couple whose last name was Lake. One of the things I do when learning a name is to link the name to a mental image. When I was introduced to the Lakes, I immediately placed a mental image of a lake on their heads and thought of Hargus Lake where I grew up. A few days later when I saw them again, I mistakenly asked, "How are you doing tonight, Mr. and Mrs. Hargus?" Sometimes even our best practices fail us!

LES . . . ON BRINGING IT HOME

One hardly needs a research study to validate the points John is making about the value of remembering people's names. However, if you want to know whether it is substantiated by studies, I could point you to a mountain of research that shows exactly how a person's mood and self-evaluation are consistently improved when another person remembers him or her personally.[2] There is simply no question of the value of remembering people's names.

To apply John's teaching to your own life . . .

Forget about:

Blaming your "bad" memory and exert some effort to remember people's names.

Ask:

What can you tell me about the origin of your name or how it's spelled?

Do it:

Use the SAVE Method with each new person you meet this week.

Remember:

A person's name is one of his or her most valuable possessions.

23

Point Out People's Strengths

The praises of others may be of use in teaching us, not what we are, but what we ought to be.

—August W. Hare

LES . . . ON SEEING THE PRACTICE IN ACTION

I am constantly amazed by the number of high-caliber people John has on his staff. He seems to be surrounded by all-stars. When asked about his secret, he responded, "Two things. First, I try to hire the best leaders I can find. If I can hire a few '9s' and '10s,' then they will attract and hire '8s' and '9s.' Second, I always try to put people in their areas of strength."

"Okay," I said, "let me quiz you on some of the people in your circle. I'll give you a name, and you tell me their strength."

"Okay, shoot," John answered.

"Tim Elmore."

"There's nobody better than Tim at examining a passage of Scripture, searching it thoroughly, and pulling out teaching points from it."

"Linda Eggers."

"Linda's attention to detail is off the charts; she runs my whole life. But I'd have to say that her greatest strength is the confidence she instills in others. When someone talks to Linda, they feel that they've talked to me."

"Dan Reiland."

"Dan's greatest skill is leading and developing leaders on his staff. You know, back at Skyline he was my executive pastor; he led the staff and ran the church day to day while I traveled nationally."

"Did Dan come to you with experience as an executive pastor?" I asked.

"No, no, when I met Dan, he was an intern," John explained. "He had worked briefly as a youth pastor, and when he started working for me as a regular employee after seminary, I put him in charge of children's education. But over the years, he did a lot of different things. Anytime I wanted to start a new ministry, Dan was my man.

"As we worked together, a pattern of strength emerged. Dan always had the big picture, championed the vision, and possessed influence with his peers and volunteers. And he had a particular knack for developing people. As those strengths emerged, it became obvious that he was the right person to become my executive pastor."

Jim Collins, in his book *Good to Great* (Harperbusiness,

2001), writes about the concept of getting the right people on the bus and then making sure each is in the right seat. That's essentially what John was saying. When you look for and point out people's strengths, then you are able to help people take the place that's best for them and the organization. And that helps everyone win!

JOHN . . . WITH A MAXWELL MENTORING MOMENT

People often make a mistake in their personal development when they focus too much on their weaknesses. As a result, they spend all their time trying to shore up those weaknesses instead of maximizing the strengths they possess. Similarly, it's a mistake to focus on the weaknesses of others. The self-proclaimed "experts" who spend their time telling others what's wrong with them *never* win with people. Most people simply avoid them.

Instead, we need to focus on finding people's strengths and pointing them out. Here's why:

POINTING OUT STRENGTHS UNDERLINES PEOPLE'S UNIQUENESS

Most people have strengths that they rarely get to use. Those strengths may be job skills, knowledge, general abilities, personality characteristics, or other attributes. I once read an interesting fact based on research, saying that every person can do at least one thing better than ten thousand other people. Think about that! You possess an ability that can't be matched by anyone in your town or neighborhood . . . or in your college or university . . . or in your company or maybe even in your industry.

Have you discovered that ability? If so, you are probably well on your way to pursuing your life's purpose. If you haven't, wouldn't you love it if someone came alongside you and pointed it out? How would you feel about that person? I bet you'd be pretty grateful.

Why not try to become that kind of person in someone else's life? When you do, you just might be helping others to discover the thing God created them to do.

People Are Motivated in Their Areas of Strength

I once read that a survey was taken of workers across the United States in which it was found that nearly 85 percent of those interviewed said that they could work harder on the job. More than half of them claimed they could double their effectiveness if they wanted to. Why would that be? It is because so few people are working in their areas of strength. Do you get excited when asked to work in an area of weakness? I certainly don't.

Marcus Buckingham and Donald O. Clifton have done tremendous research in this area. If you want to learn more, I suggest you read their book: *Now, Discover Your Strengths* (Free Press, 2001). But know this: when you work in your areas of strength, you don't need much external motivation. If people have been grinding away at tasks in their weak areas, and they are reassigned to work in areas of strength, watch their motivation, enthusiasm, and productivity skyrocket.

People Add the Most Value in Their Strength Zones

People often ask me what the key to my success is. And I tell them that I think it can be attributed to three things:

(1) the goodness of God; (2) the excellent people around me; and (3) my ability to stay in my strength zone. It took the first five years of my professional life to figure out what my strengths were. But with the passing of years since then, I've narrowed my focus down to fewer and fewer things.

The Law of the Niche in my book *The 17 Indisputable Laws for Teamwork* states, "All players have a place where they add the most value." That place is their "strength zone." I'm worthless at most things. But I do four things really well: lead, create, communicate, and network. And as much as possible, I stick to those things.

As a leader and employer, I try to help others do the same. I help them find their strength zones, and I try to position them there as much as possible. You see, a successful person finds the right place for himself. But a successful leader finds the right place for others. How do I do that?

A successful person finds the right place for himself. But a successful leader finds the right place for others.

First, I look for the best in others. Anybody can see weaknesses, mistakes, and shortcomings in others. That's no unique skill. Seeing only the good things is harder. Hall of Fame baseball player Reggie Jackson said that the best major-league baseball leaders possess that ability. He observed, "A great manager has a knack for making ballplayers think they are better than they think they are. He forces you to have a good opinion of yourself. He lets you know he believes in you. He makes you get more out of yourself. And once you learn how good you really are, you never settle for playing anything less than your very best." That's true in any area of life: business, parenting, marriage, ministry, and so forth. Don't look for the flaws, warts, and blemishes in others. Look for their best.

Second, I speak up. You can think the world of others, but if you never actually tell them, then you don't really help them. I have always believed that all people have a "success seed" within them. Most never find it and therefore fail to reach their potential. I often look at other people and ask, "What are their success seeds?" When I discover them, I point them out to those individuals. Then I fertilize those seeds with encouragement and water them with opportunity.

LES . . . ON BRINGING IT HOME

One of the most cutting-edge aspects of contemporary research in psychology has to do with what are termed "signature strengths." Everyone has a number of positive qualities that represent his or her strengths, but some of those are more important and more central to a person's identity. When you can point them out to others, research shows, a person is far more likely to use them, to put them on display, and to embrace them as a key component of his or her identity.

To apply John's teaching to your own life . . .

Forget about:

The weaknesses of others.

Ask:

What does this individual do exceptionally well?

Do it:

Every day this week, tell at least one person what strength you see in him or her.

Remember:

Every person in the world possesses the seeds for success.

24

WRITE NOTES OF ENCOURAGEMENT

The power of words is immense. A well-chosen word has often sufficed to stop a flying army, to change defeat into victory, and to save an empire.

—EMILE DE GIRARDIN

LES . . . ON SEEING THE PRACTICE IN ACTION

I always love to see the inner sanctums of great leaders. You can learn much about people when you see where they work. Recently I was in John's home office, where he does most of his thinking, dreaming, writing, and creating. Among the memorabilia that is important to him, one cannot help but notice an impressive collection of John Wesley's works. In fact, it may be one of the most extensive privately held historical collections of its kind. And as a student of Wesley myself, I was intrigued.

"What's your most prized piece in this collection, John?" I asked, pointing to a shelf of antique books.

"It would have to be a letter I have that was signed by John Wesley and postscripted by his brother Charles," John said as he took me around the corner to see it hanging in a frame on the wall.

"Is it an important letter?" I asked, trying to decipher Wesley's spidery handwriting.

"It's a letter to a friend, giving him parenting advice. I prize it because it is written in Wesley's hand and signed by him," John said. "But if you want to talk about *important* letters by Wesley, then you have to consider the letter he wrote to William Wilberforce.

"In 1791, William Wilberforce was facing one more discouraging defeat in his attempt to abolish Britain's slave trade," explained John. "Then he received a letter from John Wesley. That now-famous letter would prove to be a continuing source of strength for the rest of his life."

John went quickly into his files under the topic of "encouragement" and found the text of that Wesley letter and read it aloud to me:

> London, February 26, 1791
>
> Dear Sir:
> Unless the divine power has raised you up . . . I see not how you can go through your glorious enterprise, in opposing that execrable villainy, which is the scandal of religion, of England, and of human nature. Unless God has raised you up for this very thing, you will be worn out

> by the opposition of men and devils. But, "if God be for you, who can be against you?" Are all of them stronger than God? O "be not weary in well doing!" Go on, in the name of God and in the power of His might, till even American slavery (the vilest that ever saw the sun) shall vanish away before it.
>
> . . . That He who has guided you from your youth up, may continue to strengthen you in this and all things, is the prayer of,
>
> Your affectionate servant,
> J. Wesley

"Four days after writing that letter," John recounted, "Wesley was dead. And once again Wilberforce was defeated when the vote was taken in Parliament. Ultimately Wilberforce prevailed, but in the intervening years, he was vilified and faced so many disappointments. His opponents even arranged for him to be challenged to a duel and made an attempt to kill him."

John continued, "He was tempted to give up the fight more than once. But every time he became discouraged, he returned to Wesley's letter. Each time he read it, it was like the first time. It never failed to encourage and strengthen him.

"If you don't believe in the encouraging power of the written note after hearing about that," John said, "you probably never will."

I can attest to the fact that John believes in that power. I've received several notes of encouragement from him over the years, and I still have many of them. They may not hold the historical value of Wesley's note to Wilberforce, but their value to me is priceless.

JOHN . . . WITH A MAXWELL MENTORING MOMENT

If you haven't already guessed it, I'm a real history buff. Let me tell you the rest of the story: in 1806, after working tirelessly for twenty years, Wilberforce finally succeeded in getting a bill passed that abolished the slave trade. Twenty-eight years later, on July 31, 1834, slavery itself was outlawed throughout the British Empire, freeing approximately 800,000 slaves. Although he did not live to see the realization of his dream, having died on August 5, 1833, no one was more responsible than William Wilberforce for the demise of slavery in the British Empire.

Wilberforce died one of the most esteemed men of his day and was buried in Westminster Abbey. His epitaph reads in part:

> Eminent as he was in every department of public labour,
> And a leader in every work of charity,
> Whether to relieve the temporal or the spiritual wants
> of his fellow men
> His name will ever be specially identified
> With those exertions
> Which, by the blessing of God, removed from England
> The guilt of the African slave trade,
> And prepared the way for the abolition of slavery
> in every colony of the Empire.

Wilberforce had devoted his entire life and political career to a great cause: ending slavery. Yet he might not have prevailed had it not been for the encouraging note of John Wesley.

I have believed in the power of written notes of encouragement for many years—beginning before I received the Wesley letter as a gift from the people of Skyline Church after serving as their pastor. In fact, it was while leading Skyline that I asked my staff members to devote time every Monday to handwriting notes to people.

Written notes don't have to come from someone famous to be encouraging. A kind word given from the heart is always well received. If you've never mastered the practice of sending handwritten notes to people, then I want to encourage you to try this often neglected way of winning with people. Here's why:

Encouraging Notes Have a Personal Touch

Today we communicate by telephone, digital pager, cell phone, fax machine, e-mail, and the Internet. In the hectic pace of our busy lives, who has time to correspond the old-fashioned way? Yet the more convenient our communication becomes, the more temporary it is. We forget how meaningful that personal touch can be. Few things beat opening a mailbox and pulling out a real note written by a real person. When you see the thoughts of someone you respect written in his or her own hand, it really means something.

Six days a week, regular mail service is provided by the United States Postal Service. Annually postal workers handle 170 billion pieces of mail. Yet, in this huge sea of mail, officials say personal letters account for less than 4 percent of the total. So on average, you will have to wade through twenty-five pieces of mail before you put your hands on one that contains a personal word. More than ever in this day and age, a handwritten note communicates that you care.

Notes Represent an Investment by the Writer

In his book *The Power of Encouragement* (Multnomah, 1997), my friend David Jeremiah says, "Written encouragement comes directly from the heart, uninterrupted and uninhibited. That's why it's so powerful." Haven't you known that to be true?

"Written encouragement comes directly from the heart, uninterrupted and uninhibited. That's why it's so powerful."

—David Jeremiah

Nineteenth-century writer Walt Whitman struggled for years to get anyone interested in his poetry. He became very discouraged. Then he received a note that read: "Dear sir, I am not blind to the worth of the wonderful gift of *Leaves of Grass*. I find it the most extraordinary piece of wit and wisdom that America has yet contributed. I greet you at the beginning of a great career." It was signed by Ralph Waldo Emerson.

I can't help but wonder what might have happened to Whitman had Emerson not invested in him by writing those kind words. That note was like fresh air to Whitman, who breathed in that encouragement and was inspired to keep writing. But you don't have to be a professional writer to make a difference in someone's life. Just taking the time to write is evidence of your willingness to invest in that person.

Notes Are Remembered Long After the Writer Has Forgotten Them

For years I have made it a practice to write personal notes to others. I often forget what I have written, but occasionally someone who has received a note from me will show it to me and tell me what an encouragement it was. It is in those moments that I am reminded of the sustained and repeated encouragement people receive from the written word.

You never can tell when something you write to others will light them up in down times or sustain them when life gets difficult. In the first *Chicken Soup for the Soul* (Health Communications, 1993) book, teacher Sister Helen Mrosla recounted how a spur-of-the-moment assignment in class became a source of encouragement for her students. On a day when her junior high math students were especially ornery, she asked them to write down what they liked about each of their fellow students. She then compiled the results over the weekend and handed out the lists on the following Monday.

Years later when one of those students, Mark, was killed in Vietnam, she and some of those former students got together for the funeral. Afterward, Mark's father told the group, "They found this on Mark when he was killed," and he showed them a folded, refolded, and taped paper—the one he had received years before from his teacher. Right after that, Charlie, one of Mark's classmates, said, "I keep my list in my desk drawer." Chuck's wife said, "Chuck put his in our wedding album." "I have mine, too," Marilyn said, "in my diary."

Standing there, Vicky reached into her pocketbook and brought out her frazzled list, showing it to her teacher and former classmates. Each person cherished the kind words of encouragement they had received. That's the power of a few kind words.

LES . . . ON BRINGING IT HOME

You may be reluctant to take time writing notes to others because you believe that complimenting people verbally is enough. If so, you may be surprised by recent research into the topic of authenticity, which found that when a word of encouragement is written down for another person, it is often perceived to be more genuine than when it is spoken.[1] That leaves little doubt about the value of writing notes of encouragement to others.

When a word of encouragement is written down for another person, it is often perceived to be more genuine than when it is spoken.

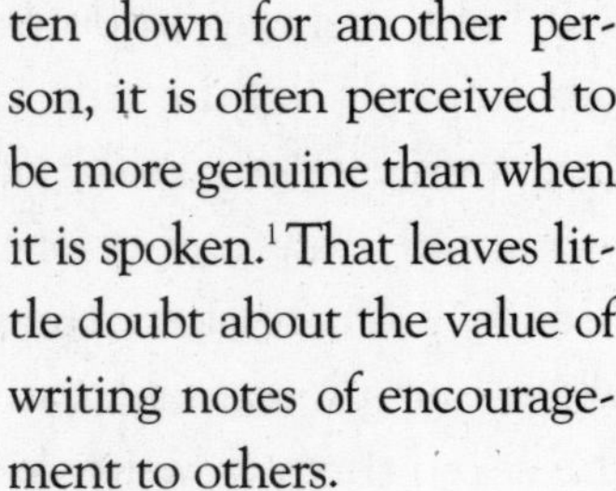

To apply John's teaching to your own life . . .

Forget about:

Being a perfect writer and focus on writing from the heart.

Ask:

What can I say that will be an encouragement now, as well as someday in the future?

Do it:

Take one hour today to write several notes to people for the sole purpose of encouraging them.

Remember:

Words have the power to give encouragement long after the writer has forgotten them.

25

Help People Win

The most important measure of how good
a game I played was how much better
I'd make my teammates play.

—Bill Russell, winner of more NBA championships than any other player

LES . . . ON SEEING THE PRACTICE IN ACTION

If I've ever met anyone who loves to see people win, it's John Maxwell. That's the reason he writes books and leads seminars and conferences. He believes he has something to offer to others to help them succeed. But John also helps people win on a smaller scale, whether it's teaching his daughter how to sell candy door-to-door for school when she was little, taking time to give a struggling pastor advice to help him through a tough time, or giving a young person with potential tremendous responsibility. John loves to win, and he enjoys seeing others win even more.

For many years, John did a one-day seminar that taught pastors and their church members how to partner in volunteer ministry. At the end of the session, he used to tell one of my favorite stories. It really typifies John's attitude toward helping others.

When John's nephew, Eric, was seven years old, he got ready to play his first game in his first season of Little League baseball. John and Margaret went to see the game, and of course, John wanted to help Eric win. Here's the story as John often tells it:

> You've got to understand, Eric had never played baseball before. He's intimidated, he's scared, he's fearful, he's frightened. And his coach thinks it's the World Series! So Eric walks up to the plate. His helmet is way down over his ears, his uniform is way too big for him, and he can hardly hold the bat. He's petrified. So there he stands, facing the other team's pitcher, who is always the biggest kid. His name is Butch; he's got a big wad of bubble gum in his jaw, and peach fuzz all over his face.
>
> Eric just kind of hugged the bat and closed his eyes and prayed. And that ball went whoosh! Strike one. Whoosh! Strike two. Whoosh! Strike three. I mean, just like that; and when the umpire said, "You're out," Eric just looked glad to be alive.
>
> As he walked back to the dugout, parents started yelling at him and the coach was hollering at him. And I'm sitting there thinking, *This is my nephew, and he's scared.* So I went down to that little fence where Eric was, and I said, "Sweetheart, I don't know what they've told

you about baseball, but let your Uncle John teach you something. Baseball is a very simple game."

He said, "What do you mean?"

I said, "You only have to do one thing. The next time you go up to bat, every time Butch throws the ball, you just swing the bat. That's all you have to do. Butch throws the ball; you swing the bat. Butch throws the ball; you swing the bat."

He looked at me and said, "That's all I gotta do?"

I said, "That's all. Don't worry about hitting that ball; just swing the bat." And all of a sudden a smile broke out on his face, and he said, "I can do that."

I said, "Sure you can do that! Go get 'em, boy."

The next time Eric got up to bat, Butch threw the ball and Eric swung the bat. He missed it by a mile. In fact, he swung so late the ball was already in the catcher's glove. I am now beginning to clap my hands. I am saying, "Wonderful swing, Eric, wonderful swing. That-a-boy! Every time Butch throws the ball, you swing the bat."

Butch throws the ball; Eric swings the bat. Butch throws the ball; he's missing it by about three feet. Finally, he strikes out on the third strike. I'm on my feet shouting, "Eric McCullogh, that is the finest strikeout I have ever seen in my life. Way to go!"

At that point, the coach looks up into the bleachers and gives me a dirty look. And the parents aren't too happy either. Margaret says, "Sweetheart, I'm gonna go to the car and read a book." But I don't care, because after this at bat, Eric is smiling.

Now, to be honest, I didn't think Eric was going to get

a hit that day. Besides, in Little League baseball, there's no such thing as a hit. If there's any kind of contact, it's not the bat hitting the ball; it's the ball hitting the bat. And if there's one thing I know, it's this: if the ball hits the bat, it doesn't have to go far; it just has to go fair. And in Little League baseball, if the ball goes anywhere in fair territory, you never stop running.

Well, I didn't think it was gonna happen, but it did. The third time up, Butch threw the ball; Eric swings; the ball hits the bat. It wasn't a crack out into center field; it was a thud. As soon as I saw the ball was fair, I'm out of the bleachers and I'm running down the first base line, saying, "Eric, keep on running, keep on running!"

As Eric goes around first base, I cut across the infield as fast as I can. I'm now at third base and I'm saying, "Come on, Eric! Come on, Eric!" Eric rounds third base, and together we slide safe into home. Eric gets up and brushes off his uniform, I get up and brush off my suit; and as we walked off the field, I just looked at the coach and gave him a smile.

We went home that day to Eric's house. His parents had to work and didn't get to see the game; but we replayed it for them. I stood in the middle of the living room and I pretended to be Butch, and Eric stood by the piano bench, which was home plate. I threw that pitch; he hit that ball. He went around the bases and Eric slid safe under the piano bench. We all stood up and gave him a standing ovation, and that day we launched Eric into his Little League baseball career.

Eric is all grown up now. But at about the time he was

> ready to graduate from high school, Eric came out to visit me. And he said, "Uncle John, I've got something exciting to tell you. You remember my first Little League baseball game?"
>
> "Of course I do," I said, and we reminisced about it.
>
> "I've never forgotten it," Eric said. "And I just wanted to tell you, this year I'm going to college on a baseball scholarship."

You don't have to be rich, famous, or talented to help others win. You just need to care and do your best to help them. And know this: when you have the ability to help someone win, you will be that person's friend for life.

JOHN . . . WITH A MAXWELL MENTORING MOMENT

Helping another person to win is one of the greatest feelings in the world. I haven't met a person yet who doesn't like to win. And everyone I know who's made the effort to help others has said that it is the most rewarding part of life. As poet Ralph Waldo Emerson said, "It is one of the most beautiful compensations of life that no man can sincerely try to help another without helping himself."

"It is one of the most beautiful compensations of life that no man can sincerely try to help another without helping himself."

—RALPH WALDO EMERSON

If you want to help people win, then take the following steps:

Believe in People

After a conference in Toledo, a man came up to me and asked a pointed question: "How do I get unbelievable results from a person?"

"Have unbelievable expectations about that person," was my answer.

If you don't believe in people, then you are unlikely to do everything you can to help them win. People know when someone doesn't believe in them. They see right through pretense and insincere backslapping. But when they know you believe in them, magic begins to happen. What writer John Spalding said is true: "Those who believe in our ability do more than stimulate us, they create for us an atmosphere in which it becomes easier to succeed."

Give People Hope

A reporter asked Prime Minister Winston Churchill, who led Britain during the dark moments of the Second World War, what was the greatest weapon his country possessed against the Nazi regime of Hitler. Without pausing for even a moment, Churchill said, "It was what England's greatest weapon has always been—hope."

Hope is one of the most powerful and energizing words in the English language. It is something that gives us power to keep going in the toughest of times. And its power energizes us with excitement and anticipation as we look toward the future.

It's been said that a person can live forty days without food, four days without water, four minutes without air, but only four seconds without hope. If you want to help people win, then become a purveyor of hope.

Focus on the Process, Not Just the Win

Many of us desire the win so much that we forget what it takes to get there. We're like the kid who plays chess with his grandfather. When he loses, he says, "Oh no! Not again! Grampa, you always win!"

"What do you want me to do, lose on purpose?" the old man replies. "You won't learn anything if I do that!"

"I don't wanna learn anything," the boy says. "I just wanna win!"

That's the way we often feel, but let's be honest. Which wins are the most satisfying: the easy ones or the ones we really have to work for? When you help somebody win, don't just hand it to him, even if it's in your power to do so. Help *him* win. If you assist him in the process, then you're not just giving him the victory; you're giving him the means for additional future victories. He can win and win again. And the only thing sweeter than a win is a whole bunch of wins.

Understand That When You Help Others Win, You Also Win

In 1984, Lou Whittaker led the first all-American team to the summit of Mt. Everest. After months of grueling effort, five members of the team reached the final campsite at twenty-seven thousand feet. With two thousand feet to go, they met in a crowded tent. Whittaker had a tough decision to make: he knew how highly motivated all five climbers were to stand on the highest point on earth. But two would have to go back to the previous camp, load up food, water, and oxygen, then return to the camp where they now met. After completing this support assignment, these two climbers would be in no condition to make a try for the summit. The others would stay in the tent that day to drink water, breathe oxygen, and rest, preparing them for the summit attempt the next day.

The first decision Whittaker made was to stay at the twenty-seven-thousand-foot camp to coordinate the team's activities. The next was to send the two strongest climbers down the mountain to get the supplies; it was the tougher job. The two weaker climbers would rest, renew their strength, and receive the glory of the summit.

When asked why he didn't assign himself the summit run, his answer showed his understanding of people and the strength of his leadership. He said, "My job was to put other people on top."

Whittaker understood that when people make the right decisions that help the team to achieve its goal, everybody wins. You can't help winning when you help others win.

LES . . . ON BRINGING IT HOME

When I think back, I can remember many people in my life who have helped me to win. The chair of the psychology department at the college I went to honed my vision for graduate school. He showed me what steps to take and how to succeed. George, a friend of mine, helped me win by showing me how to land and host a radio show. Janice, my publicist, helps me win every time she gets me on a national television show to talk about one of my books. Kevin, another friend, helped me win by showing me how to craft a meaningful mission statement for my life. Of course, John has helped me win in my career on several fronts. Everyone likes to win. And nobody wins without help.

More than three decades ago, a research study examined the kinds of people who relate well to others. It looked at 268 Harvard sophomore men, considered to be "the best and the brightest," and followed them for forty years. Among the findings was the fact that men who were emotionally healthiest recognized that a good life was not about the absence of problems, but about how one chooses to react to problems. In other words, these men perceived themselves as winners and helped others to win in spite of their circumstances. Not surprisingly, they also had far more meaningful relationships with others.[1]

To apply John's teaching to your own life . . .

Forget about:

Approaching life as a competition where you have to beat everyone else in order to win.

Ask:

Whom would I most like to help win and how can I do it?

Do it:

Make a game plan. Chart the road you will travel together on your way to victory.

Remember:

Once you help someone win, you will have a friend for life.

A CLOSING WORD FROM JOHN

All my life, I've believed that anyone can learn to win with people. All it takes is a belief in people and a sincere desire to help them. I hope that after reading this book, you believe that too.

We also hope that you will embrace the practices Les and I have endeavored to teach. If you have already tried some of them out, then you've probably already discovered that they really do work. If you want to learn to master all of them, then here's how I suggest you proceed: put yourself on a twelve-week program for winning with people. After starting with you, select two of the practices and do them every day for an entire week. If you do that, you will go through a process where you will . . .

1. Become conscious of how that winning way works,
2. Learn the basics of how to do it,
3. Practice it until you master it, and
4. Begin to make it a habit.

You may not feel instantly comfortable doing some of them, but there isn't a single one you can't master. And of course, keep adding other practices that you learn on your own or from others. You can never learn too many ways to win with people.

Here's to your success: may you keep winning by helping others win.

NOTES

CHAPTER 1

1. James Patterson and Peter Kim, *The Day America Told the Truth* (East Rutherford, NJ: Prentice Hall Press, 1991).

CHAPTER 2

1. Wes Smith, *Hope Meadows: Real-Life Stories of Healing and Caring from an Inspiring Community* (New York: Berkley, 2001).

CHAPTER 3

1. J. G. Nicholls, "Creativity in the person who will never produce anything original and useful: The concept of creativity as a normally distributed trait," *American Psychologist*, 27 (8) (1972), 717–27.

CHAPTER 6

1. James C. Humes, *The Wit and Wisdom of Winston Churchill* (New York: Harper Perennial, 1994), 119–20.
2. Genesis 17:5.
3. Genesis 32:28.
4. Howard Gardner, *Creating Minds: An Anatomy of Creativity Seen Through the Lives of Freud, Einstein, Picasso, Stravinsky, Eliot, Graham, and Gandhi* (New York: Basic Books, 1993).

CHAPTER 7

1. Proverbs 25:11.
2. James Kouzes and Barry Posner, *Encouraging the Heart: A Leader's Guide to Rewarding and Recognizing Others* (San Francisco: Jossey-Bass Publishers, 1999).
3. H. S. Leonard, "The many faces of character," *Consulting Psychology Journal*, 49 (4) (1997), 235–45.

CHAPTER 10

1. M. E. McCullough and C. R. Snyder, "Classical source of human strength: Revisiting an old home and building a new one." *Journal of Social and Clinical Psychology*, 19 (1) (2000), 1–10.

Chapter 11

1. G. E. Vaillant, "Adaptive mental mechanisms: Their role in a positive psychology," *American Psychologist*, 55 (1) (2000), 89–98.

Chapter 12

1. John 8.
2. E. E. Werner, "Resilience in development," *Current Directions in Psychological Science*, 4 (3) (1995), 81–85.

Chapter 13

1. D. A. Kramer, "Wisdom as a classical source of human strength: Conceptualization and empirical inquiry," *Journal of Social and Clinical Psychology*, 19 (1) (2000), 83–101.

Chapter 14

1. R. M. Ryan and E. L. Deci, "Self-determination theory and the facilitation of intrinsic motivation, social development, and well-being," *American Psychologist*, 55 (1) (2000), 68–78.

Chapter 15

1. J. W. MacDevitt, "Therapist's personal therapy and professional self-awareness," *Psychotherapy*, 24 (1987), 693–703.

Chapter 16

1. Les Parrott, *Counseling and Psychotherapy*, 2nd ed. (Pacific Grove, CA: Brooks/Cole/Thomson Learning, 2003).

Chapter 17

1. "Walking the Mile: A Behind-the-Scenes Documentary" (Warner Home Video, 1999).
2. Belden Lane, "Rabbinical Stories," *Christian Century*, 98:41 (16 December 1981).
3. Ken Sutterfield, *The Power of an Encouraging Word* (Green Forest, AR: New Leaf, 1997).
4. J. J. Campos and K. C. Barrett, "Toward a new understanding of emotions and their development," *Emotions Cognition, and Behavior*, eds. C. Izard, J. Kagan, and R. Zajonc (New York: Cambridge University Press, 1988).

CHAPTER 19

1. D. P. McAdams, A. Diamond, E. de St. Aubin, and E. Mansfield, "Stories of commitment: The psychosocial construction of generative lives," *Journal of Personality and Social Psychology*, 72 (3) (1997), 678–94.

CHAPTER 20

1. I. K. M. Sheldon, R. M. Ryan, L. J. Rawsthorne, and B. Ilardi, "Trait self and true self: Cross-role variation in the big-five personality traits and its relations with psychological authenticity and subjective well-being," *Journal of Personality and Social Psychology*, 73 (1997), 1380–93.

CHAPTER 21

1. Source Unknown.
2. D. P. McAdams and Ed de St. Aubin (ed.), *Generativity and Adult Development: How and Why We Care for the Next Generation* (Washington, DC: APA Books, 1998).

CHAPTER 22

1. Othello, Act III, Scene 3.
2. J. D. Brown and T. A. Mankowski, "Self-esteem, mood and self-evaluation: Changes in mood and the way you see you," *Journal of Personality and Social Psychology*, 64 (1993), 421.

CHAPTER 23

1. M. E. P. Seligman and M. Csikszentmihalyi, "Positive psychology: An introduction," *American Psychologist*, 55 (1) (2000), 5–14.

CHAPTER 24

1. S. Harter, "Authenticity," C. R. Snyder and S. J. Lopez, eds., *Handbook of Positive Psychology* (New York: Oxford University Press, 2002), 382–94.

CHAPTER 25

1. Vaillant, *Adaptation to Life* (Boston: Little Brown, 1977).

ABOUT THE AUTHORS

John C. Maxwell, known as America's expert on leadership, speaks in person to hundreds of thousands of people each year. He has communicated his principles to Fortune 500 companies, the United States Military Academy at West Point, international marketing organizations, the NCAA, and professional sports groups such as the NFL. Maxwell is the founder of several leadership organizations dedicated to helping people reach their personal and leadership potential, such as Injoy Stewardship Services. He dedicates much of his time to training leaders worldwide through EQUIP, a non-profit organization. A *New York Times* bestselling author with more than 8 million books in print, Dr. Maxwell has written more than thirty books, including *Developing the Leader Within You*, *Today Matters*, and *The 21 Irrefutable Laws of Leadership*, which has sold more than one million copies.

Les Parrott, Ph.D., is founder of the Center for Relationship Development on the campus of Seattle Pacific University and the best-selling author of *High-Maintenance Relationships*, *The Control Freak*, *Shoulda Coulda Woulda*, and *Love Talk*. Dr. Parrott is a sought after speaker to Fortune 500 companies and holds relationship seminars across North America. He communicates annually to a wide variety of audiences, including professional athletes, government agencies, military personnel, and business leaders. He also hosts the national radio broadcast "Love Talk." Dr Parrott has been featured in *USA Today*, the *Wall Street Journal*, and the *New York Times*. His television appearances include *The View*, *The O'Reilly Factor*, CNN, *Good Morning America*, and *Oprah*.

To learn about his speaking availability and seminar schedules, as well as all of Dr. Parrott's resources, contact: www.RealRelationships.com.

Books by Dr. John C. Maxwell Can Teach You How to Be A REAL Success

Relationships

Everyone Communicates, Few Connect

Encouragement Changes Everything

25 Ways to Win With People

Winning With People

Relationships 101

The Treasure of a Friend

The Power of Partnership in the Church

Becoming a Person of Influence

Be A People Person

The Power of Influence

Ethics 101

Attitude

Self-Improvement 101

Success 101

The Difference Maker

How Successful People Think

The Journey From Success to Significance

Attitude 101

Failing Forward

Your Bridge to a Better Future

Living at the Next Level

The Winning Attitude

Be All You Can Be

The Power of Thinking Big

Think on These Things

The Power of Attitude

Thinking for a Change

Equipping

Teamwork 101

My Dream Map

Put Your Dream to the Test

Make Today Count

The Choice Is Yours

Mentoring 101

Talent is Never Enough

Equipping 101

Developing the Leaders Around You

The 17 Essential Qualities of a Team Player

Success One Day at a Time

The 17 Indisputable Laws of Teamwork

Your Road Map for Success

Today Matters

Partners in Prayer

Leadership

Leadership Promises For Your Work Week

Leadership Gold

Go for Gold

The 21 Most Powerful Minutes in a Leader's Day

Revised & Updated 10th Anniversary Edition of *The 21 Irrefutable Laws of Leadership*

The 360 Degree Leader

Leadership Promises for Every Day

Leadership 101

The Right to Lead

The 21 Indispensable Qualities of a Leader

Developing the Leader Within You

The Power of Leadership